THE OFFICIAL
SLOANE RANGER
H·A·N·D·B·O·O·K
THE FIRST GUIDE TO WHAT REALLY MATTERS IN LIFE

ANN BARR & PETER YORK

FI

If you can keep your seat when all about you
Are losing theirs and blaming it on you,
If you can trust your shoes when all men doubt you,
But make allowance for their background too;
If you can hail (and tip) a railway porter,
Or read a person's nature in his ties,
Or being outmanoeuvred, don't manoeuvre,
But win, by honest means and *small* white lies.
If you can choose a house just for its cellars
To gut your pheasant in and keep your wine,
Or fill a Volvo full of dogs and wellies
And park it on a double yellow line . . .
If you can fill the unforgiving minute
With sixty seconds' worth of jolly fun,
Yours is this book and everything that's in it,
And—which is more—you'll be a Sloane, my son!
(or daughter, depending on which way the genes jumped)

EBURY PRESS
LONDON

Published by Ebury Press
National Magazine House
72 Broadwick Street
London W1V 2BP

First impression 1982
Second impression 1982
Third impression 1982
Fourth impression 1982
Fifth impression 1982

ISBN 0 85223 236 5 (Paper)
ISBN 0 85223 248 9 (Cased)

Design by Harry Green

Artists Merrily Harpur
        Natacha Ledwidge
        Mike Davidson
        Susanne Lihou

The authors would like to note that the prices
and addresses quoted were correct at time
of going to press. They cannot accept
responsibility for changes which may
subsequently have occurred.

Filmset in Great Britain by
Advanced Filmsetters (Glasgow) Ltd.
Printed and bound in Great Britain by
The University Press, Cambridge

Contributors

Many writers provided words, observations and facts for this book,
some from inside the Sloane Ranger stable, others from outside the
fence. The book owes an enormous amount to:
SARAH DRUMMOND, SUE CARPENTER and SUSIE WARD

and also to:
Jane Abdy, Olinda Adeane, Peter Astaire, Amanda Atha, Diana
Avebury, Andrew Barrow, Mary Bass, Richard Bassett, Diana
Berry, Lucy Bett, Robin Brackenbury, Philippa Braidwood, Patricia
Braithwaite, Robin Bryer, George Cardona, Mirabel Cecil, Nicholas
Coleridge, Amanda Craig, Simon Crutchley, Tim de Lisle, Andrew
Edmunds, Bryony Edmunds, Kathy Elliot, Henrietta Elwell, Henry
Elwell, Paolo Filo della Torre, Michael Fish, Sophy Fisher, David
Galloway, Victoria Hugill, Timothy Jonathon, Fiona King, Gill
Lund, John Lund, Patrea More Nisbett, Fiona Macpherson, David
Mann, Victoria Mather, Jonathan Meades, Mary Muir, Alexander
Mulloy, Deirdre Mulloy, Michael Mulloy, Caroline Phillips, Julie
Ronald, Carey Schofield, Alistair Scott, Caroline Silver, Francis
Sitwell, Simon Taylor, Katie Tute, Anabel Veale, Arthur Ward,
Nick Warwick-Baily, Susan Watts, Claire Wickham, Vicki Woods,
James Zeitlinger.

CONTENTS

4   Contents

First Commandments for Sloane Scholars

You round a corner, enter a room, pick up a telephone—and there are *that* voice, *those* mannerisms, *those* clothes, that *style*, THOSE PEOPLE. It all comes back. It never went away. It's all going on now, *still*.

Sloane Rangerhood is a state of mind that's eternal. You might believe it's all different now, that nobody's like that anymore. You'd be wrong.

In 1982, after you've been in shock, in dialysis, into and out of all kinds of foreign rubbish from modern design to Earth Shoes, the disciplined commonsensical Sloane Life looks comfortable and reassuring. Good manners, nursery food, the same shirts for five years: it *must* be right, mustn't it?

This is the handbook of the Sloane's style, the eternal stream of English Life, an invaluable reference for a lifetime of decisions about What Really Matters in Life. You can't go wrong.

The Look
The look is eternal. Those pink cheeks; the way Tory hair rises in wings above the ears; those curious dental configurations. There are some looks only Sloanes have. The Face of the Sixties—an attractive monkey of either sex with a furry nose and huge sexy mouth—was very unSloane. Sloanes tend to have longer noses and more discreet mouths altogether. And there are certain grooming rules that remain eternally Sloane.

Don't Interfere with Nature
Unlike aristos, foreigners, film stars and most other sorts nowadays Sloanes tend to look more the way they are. The scrubbed look (fresh as the day) reasserts itself generation after generation. Elaborate diets, retextured hair, toupees for men and really fanciful dentistry are not Sloane.

Keep Hair Under Control
Mainstream Sloanes of both sexes do not have agitated (*mouvementé*) hair styles. The hair is a garden to be controlled. Sloane women do not wear freak-outs. Sloanes follow the no-facial-hair rule—no moustaches, side whiskers, above all no hair over or forward from the ears. Ears should show.

Don't Look Sexy
Your clothes shouldn't suggest what's underneath them. Except for the generous *official* Sloane bosom at parties. Guernseys for both sexes disguise a lot. Trousers are cut well clear of anything tedious. AVOID TIGHT CLOTHING.

Keep It Clean
The Sloane look is fresh, effortless. Never mistake the dressed-down look for full-tilt Bohemianism. Sloanes do not have nails in mourning. They may not like chemical deodorants, but they do bathe and change. You don't turn up unshaven.

AND REMEMBER, IT'S YOU THEY WANT TO SEE, NOT YOUR CLOTHES
Elaborate get-ups or toilettes are *distracting*. They break the fundamental Sloane rule: one shouldn't spend too much time thinking about these things. Effortless rightness is the watchword. *Simple, practical* are the words for the look that's taken five generations to perfect.

TO BE
A
SLOANE

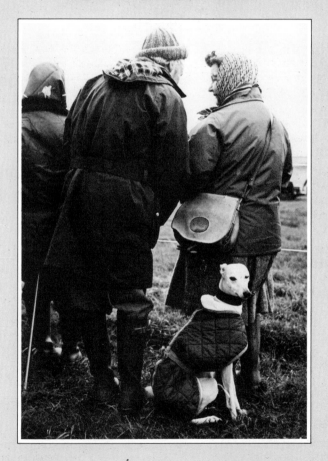

Rangerland—Sloane Is Where You Find It

Known London is basically the route between the great Institutions, and they haven't really changed since the eighteenth century. Well, not much. It's the City, the West End and SW1 (3, 5, 7, 10 and 11), which is where 'everyone' tends to live. Lots of later Victorian and Edwardian London doesn't really exist.

Sloane gentrification isn't the same as trendy intelligentsia gentrification. The problem areas are in the North. You have friends there, but you don't really *understand* The North (the *established* arty intelligentsia areas—Islington, Highgate and Hampstead). Those nice old houses can have such terrible lefties like Michael Foot—as well as media types—within. St John's Wood too is a problem.

But you feel totally at home in Holland Park, because it's a logical westward move from Kensington, as Battersea is a logical move from Chelsea.

There are outposts of Empire in Kew, Barnes, Clapham, Kilburn and Kennington (furious young political swot Tory wet Sloanes live there. They're almost off the rails; their wives have degrees and do Major Jobs).

Sloane Britain is so heavily weighted towards the South and the West it's not true. In England, Gloucestershire, Wiltshire, Hampshire and Sussex are the Sloane First Division. Certain parts of Kent and Berkshire are next. East Anglia has lovely light, and Suffolk and Norfolk echo to the squelch of green wellies (a true Sloane knows how to pronounce Heveningham).

The West Country has its enclaves, but for Sloanes to the acre in rectories, mill houses and manor houses, there's nowhere like the first division. As for the Cotswolds and the Shires, Sloanes go anywhere where there is good air, big houses and fast trains to London.

Sloanes understand Scotland too, after a fashion. They know that Edinburgh, parts of it, are very Sloane . . .

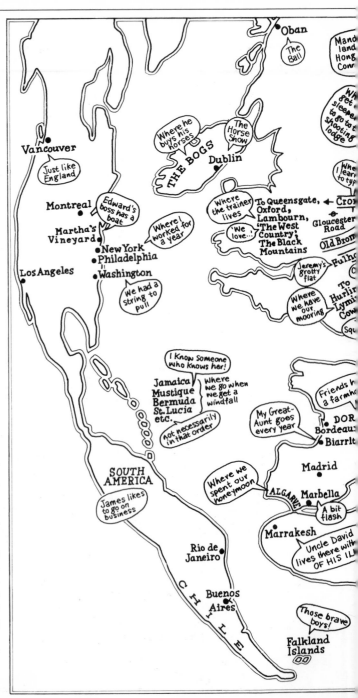

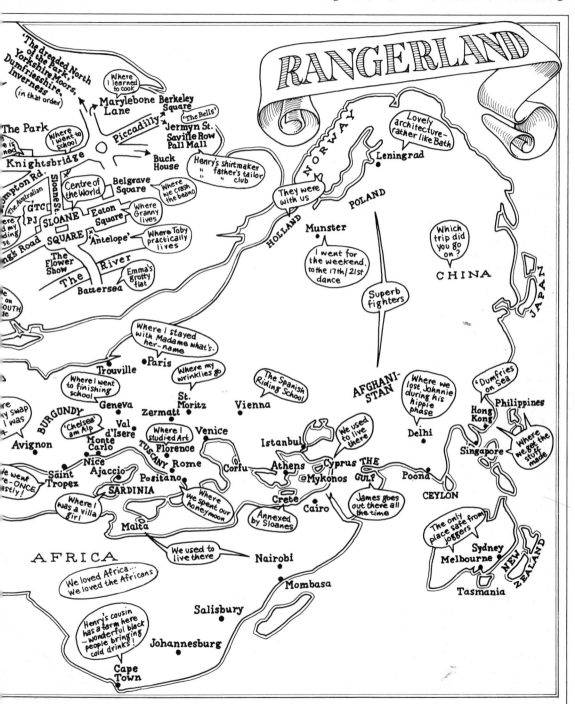

What Really Matters (in life)

The world according to Sloane

Being a Ranger One Just Knows. What Really Matters (WRM) is solidly codified in language and conduct. They're buried underground now, these codes, so the pundits say it's all over—outdated in the Modern World. Nobody who knows the code believes that.

What Really Matters is usually left unsaid. It comes across in a gesture, in the odd phrase. These are the things that Really Matter:

1) Background

Rangers are 'we' people, not 'me' people. Background means a lot to a Ranger. They want to establish it—name, rank and number—when they meet someone. Family/school/university/job/connections should all be made clear; ambiguities are worrying to the highly tuned. Hence the eternal Ranger queries: 'You live in Shropshire . . . do you know the Sloane-Rangers?' or more politely 'You live in Shropshire . . . you must know the Sloane-Rangers.'

Sloane Rangers hesitate to use the term 'breeding' now (of people, not animals) but that's what background means. *Family* is a magic word (as in Royal): it means more than the sum of individuals. Rangers think 'blood' and 'bloodstock' in a romantic way. It's ancestor worship. They enjoy references to grand roguish great-grandparents: 'It's her bad Percy blood coming out'.

2) The Past

Sloane Rangers love the past. You can't have background without lashings of The Past. All the good things have been going for ages. In The Past it was clear who were life's officers.

It means old houses, old furniture, old clothes, old wine, old families, old money —everything lovely and faded and *patinated* and always-been-there. The Rangers' favourite bit of the past is the English eighteenth century. Then everything was right: Hepplewhite, Sheraton, Chippendale, Adam, Chatsworth, Syon, Coutts and Hoare. (They put everything they like into the eighteenth century, even if it was really in the seventeenth or nineteenth. And they ruthlessly remake fine 1680 cottages and 1880 flats into 1780 manor-houses.)

The nineteenth century is when the Bad Things came in: industry, towns, new money and the wrong kind of legs on furniture.

3) Aristocracy

Rangers love aristocrats (pronounced with the stress on 'Arry—nothing wristy). Aristocrats prove it's all worth while. The senile Earls and dowdy Viscountesses and naughty rogue Hons all have What Really Matters in buckets—old houses and certainty.

All Rangers see themselves as *connected* to aristocrats; a younger son, a lesser branch, a marriage at least. Non-aristo Rangers want to marry The Real Thing—hand-carved solid wood aristocrat.

Rangers love the Simplicity of Great Men, things that illustrate the inimitable unfathomable wonderfulness of aristocrats. And of course, the royal family are pretty good here with their understated asides about 'living above the shop' and 'family business'. Royalty holds the whole thing together.

4) The Country

A Sloane Ranger's heart is in the country. 'Will you be in London this weekend?' they ask, on the off-chance. Rangers always assume you've access to somewhere in the country. The country means land and land is grand—even if it's only three acres, because there isn't much to go round in Britain. The country doesn't mean cottages or Arts and Crafts or any of that to Rangers: it's simply a matter of land-owning; every rectory a miniature stately, every real (ie non-commuter) village a Social Order.

Rangers *hate* the New Country People —the commuters and people who buy into the country after they've made it in the town. Rangers know that these people don't shoot and can't stand the sight of blood.

Just saying you were brought up in the country stands for so many things: having the old stuff, handling village people, understanding animals, riding well. That's why Rangers look for country symbols in everything.

5) The City

The City is magic money—the only kind Rangers like. Brass without muck. You never have to see the industry ('widget factories') and commerce ('selling brushes') that make the money. There's something about the way the City works—the old-ness, the public-schoolness, the merchant bank 'word-is-my-bond' code of honour —that makes it all seem like an ancient profession, not business at all. Even the dodgy side is a bit dashing and roguish, like eighteenth-century gambling.

And the City is the last Empire, still controlling things everywhere, linked up with marvellous places like Hong Kong (you love dropping the names Keswick and Jardine Matheson). You love the architecture, the banks, the old City Halls, the institutions like the Honourable Artillery Company.

In the City, you could make that couple of million through a wonderful *fluke* overnight (not by building up messy supermarkets or electronics firms), and buy back the estate and retire and raise your own pheasants.

Sloanes at Wylye Horse Trials. *Left to right:* Puffa, Husky, Barbour, Barbour, Barbour.

6) The Army

Lots of Ranger families are 'Army families'. You're officer class, warrior caste. The rest are 'other ranks'. The army is brave, hierarchical, dashing. The army has a form and you *have* to know it: not like the softness of civilian life. *'That's not officer-like'*, you're told at Sandhurst. The army is the other great source of Ranger symbols: flags and crossed lances and swords and glorious uniforms. The army may be high-tech now but the officers' mess—the regimental plate and the portraits—is pure Light Brigade.

7) The Status Quo (*not* the pop group)

As a Ranger you honour What's Already There; you secretly want a better share of it (City fluke, marrying heir/heiress), but you really don't believe there's any more where it came from. You don't believe in The Future in the way other types do. Not because you're pessimistic but because you don't see the point. The Good Stuff is here already and always has been. It *is* nice that now one can buy BMWs, powerboats and new garden machinery, and where would the City be without telex, but you certainly don't want to *live* in the Video Age. So you like the idea of Parliament, the Law (and the law's lovely buildings and chambers), Oxbridge, public school and anything with a certain amount of pomp and historic circumstance attached, however you may play it down.

All these concepts merge together in your mind, creating a Sloane heaven. They're interconnected and reinforcing.

The Sloane conversational gambit

You bring the sacred, reliable things into conversation to establish where you are and who. On first meeting, all Sloane Ranger conversations cover the main aspects of What Really Matters. A points system operates: for people known, where one lives, family background, school, job etc. The more of WRM you put across, the better you score. Viz:

'Are you involved in this horse game?'
– 'Not personally (*0 points*), but my children insist on keeping a selection of greedy brutes (*5 points × whatever number 'a selection' means*) that eat their heads off and never seem to win anything' (forget the 5 points, it's *10 points* for every competing horse).

'So you're a prisoner of the Pony Club?'
– 'With the two younger ones, in the holidays (*10 points × 2* for boarding-school), but my elder daughter's graduated to the grown-ups. She's entered for Burleigh (*100 points*), if her horse stays sound.'

'How old is she?'
– 'She'll be twenty in March.'

'The dangerous age'
– 'We haven't had much trouble, touch wood. She's got an awfully nice boyfriend, Nick Baring (*100 points*) who she's announced her intention of marrying (make that *500 points*) when he's done his law finals (*15 points*).'

'Are those the Barings over at Ashtead?'
(*25 points*)
– 'No, Nick lives near York with his
mother, who married old Wartshire
(*1000 points*) the second time around.'

*'Does the riding leave your daughter any
time for gainful employment?'* (Rangers like
these Victorian clichés.)
– 'Yes, she designs jewellery.' (*0 points*)

'A talented girl! Does she manage to sell it?'
– 'Some shop called Jones (*25 points*)
and Harrods (*15 points*) have taken pieces
off her.'

By this time, the interlocutor is thinking the scorer a great show-off, notching
up 1695 points so quickly—but she's impressed, enormously. Two hundred points
would have been enough to establish
Ranger credentials.

The enemy

Sloane Rangers are tolerant and for-
bearing. They take criticism with grace,
aiming to sail above it with a little joke.
But in their secret hearts they recognise
there is an Enemy, a type of person who
doesn't think We're All In It Together.
These carping critics don't really believe
in What Really Matters and ask the questions you don't ask. Intellectuals and
politicians, trade unionists, the new kind
of academic with facial hair; these people
are all 'chippy', 'bolshie' or 'stroppy'. It
reflects, no doubt, personal misfortune—
over-education or a poor deal physically
—that has turned the balance of the
mind, but nonetheless, the enemy need
watching. Rangers do not like Tony Benn
(a class-traitor Ranger), Arthur Scargill or
anyone who's a thinker not a doer.

Selective perceptions

Sloane training helps you keep your mind
uncluttered. Knowing WRM means you
needn't worry about what doesn't. What
doesn't matter isn't *real*, it's either a
giggle (TV soap opera) or bor-ing political
critiques from Ken Livingstone types. You
like the one, detest the other, but you
don't feel involved in either.

Sloanes aren't embarrassed by ignorance of things that aren't WRM, they're
proud of it. (As an Edwardian hostess
might say—'do we *know* him?')

Things outside the Known World *don't
really exist*, so Sloanes talk about them in
invisible inverted commas, as if there was
something wildly humorous and *unlikely*
about:

Constructivism
Romford
Computer graphics
Social work departments
Bolton
Anyone called Wayne or Gary.

The range of what Sloanes don't know,
don't acknowledge as real, is enormous.
Great chunks of the world, whole TV
regions of Britain, teeming boroughs of
London. Has anyone ever *been* to Croydon?
Well, exactly . . . .

Sloane Language

By their speech shall ye know them

A Sloane's feelings about things is shown in conversation and letters. It's a *verbal* culture, extremely subtle and secret. After the U/non-U debate and that long list of words which allegedly distinguished the upper-class U from the middle-class non-U, all *aspiring* to the fold learned the words by heart; they still almost die when they hear someone say something 'wrong'. These oh-to-be-top people have adopted the Sloane idea of monumental invisible gaffes but they don't understand how the Sloane *ethos* dictates Sloane speech. These same people, after carefully enunciating N-velope, will describe someone as 'a gutsy lady', and any Sloane who hears it decides she can't ever have them to dinner. 'Lady' is a sacred Sloane word, not used for the kind of 1968 New Woman these people mean. And 'gutsy' is an *unadopted* New York Jewishism. Sloane speech is British nationalist. Sloane speech is codified, archaic and a trap to the unwary. Certain principles are paramount:

1 *Do not disturb*. Don't think too hard.
2 *Exaggeration*. One must amuse.
3 *Understatement*. One must not bore or whine.
4 *Nationalism*. One is British, in fact the British Speech Museum.
5 *The voice*. The right words in the right voice.
6 *Elitism*. They shall not pass.

Do not disturb

Sloane minds are undeveloped but intuitive, wild places where they go out to bag an idea or see how things are going. They do *not* like theory, unless it produces a joke. Their values—and God and the Queen—are all suspended in the mystic moors of their heads. They do not welcome the space invaders of question or analysis. One does not discuss certain things (eg one's claims to be a gentleman, or one's money) and one is safe from anyone else bringing up the subject. It's Not Done to be personal. And one doesn't *go on* about things. Obsessions are boring.

Sloanes don't like or understand psychoanalysis—or in fact any urge to be personal or analytical. They just think it's bad manners. ('The loony bin' is somewhere you may have been briefly, however, suffering from, say, post-natal depression or 'the baby blues'. There are favourite Sloane 'bins' where one's uncle goes to dry out: the Crichton in Dumfries, the Priory in Roehampton, St Andrew's in Northampton—'a luxury liner going nowhere'). You may adopt bits of jargon however: 'the top-hat syndrome', 'it's *Freudian* the way he knows when I get the cheap stuff', 'I was hysTERical'—but you don't want anyone picking at what's in your head. You would be a behaviourist—if you knew what it meant.

Exaggeration

One must exaggerate. Wildly. Little things mean a lot in Sloane. The dinner party is *fabulous*, brilliant, riveting, the most. The fridge breaking down is *ghastly*, a '*major disaster*', 'I don't *believe* it', 'God has struck'.

One must amuse. To a Sloane, talking is *the* art. Music and architecture might be there too—a long way behind it. You have all been taught to speak elegantly, and you are punctilious about it, listening keenly to other people, scorning the second-rate, coming in on the beat, trying to be 'on form' for the evening like a great jazz musician. You dislike and distrust people who keep their vivacity for the boardroom or the printed page. You Sing For Your Supper. What thrills a Sloane? Two things. A great horse on top of his form. An amusing Sloane on top of his form. It's a pity the art is ephemeral.

Understatement

Conversely, one can amuse by understating really major things. And one must be stiff-upper-lip. 'I've got this stupid arm' means broken in three places. Disaster and tragedy, wholesale mutilation are

How fascinating, absolutely riveting, and rather fun!...

'boring', a motorway crash is 'a spot of bother on the way', war is 'a little local difficulty'. It's a consciously cod version of stiff-upper-lip-ism, but it sometimes leaves outsiders thinking Sloanes are extraordinarily callous.

Nationalism

Sloane is *the* national speech, 'BBC English' as it used to be known before regional accents were let in. But the way Sloanes use it is richer than radio writers write it. Sloanes have been brought up to despise fussy things, from furniture to pâtisseries. Twiddles are for people with pretensions—the despised middle classes. So Sloanes despise French and Latin derivations, and American conceptualisations, as an attempt to make simple things sound grand. They mock 'toilet' and 'serviette' (lavatory and napkin), 'an ongoing open-ended relationship' (they're living together). They are particularly against Americanisms for which there is a Sloane word (eg *joky*, for Sloane 'amusing'). They say they like *simple English words* (Anglo-Saxon derivation).

At the same time, they have assimilated many French and Latin words (amusing itself; infra dig), and they like to preserve Victorian circumlocutions in their speech as a reminder of solid background. The more stodgy and provincial the Sloane, the more Victorianisms, legalisms and pompousisms he will come out with.

Henry and Caroline, not being intellectual, like to be physical in conversation. At least it's something they know about, and it's amusing, they feel. 'He's a turd and I'm a fart—shouldn't we be next to each other?'

Nothing is funnier than a funny voice, particularly an Indian voice. Look what it's done for the Prince of Wales. All the dear dead heroes are lettered in gold: Peter Sellers, Tony Hancock. Bluebottle will buzz in the brains of Sloane Ranger men over 35 until they die. And the reason they preferred the Beatles to the Rolling Stones was the Liverpool accent.

One of the things Sloanes have against both television and state education are the flattened As, the North Circular vowels. They love using non-U words in common accents: 'Come into the Leeownge'. This amuses them like anything.

The voice

Even when not doing imitations, Sloanes play with their sentences. As their vocabulary is limited (intentionally—they believe in the rhythmic use of set words), emphasis and repetition are important. Henry punctuates his stories (or fills in the silences—Sloanes have been taught that socially, silence must never fall) with sporting sounds: the hunting horn, gunfire, motor-cars, horse, hound, motorbike on the TT course, bomb falling, or just metal—neewow, peeeeow, chunggg. Hunting women have voices as loud as Henry's, pitched to be heard across two wind-swept fields. There are quiet Sloanes, but the others are the typical ones.

Words are emphasised, and bits of words are emphasised. 'AbsolOOtly', 'He's complEEEtlimad', 'He's TOTEallyover the top', 'She's rair-ly, rair-ly nice'.

Elitism

One-up/put-down. Most Sloanes are put-down merchants to some extent. They like heavy-duty sarcasm. That favourite word 'really' can be transformed by an inflection into 'That's the most unutterably banal thing I've ever heard'. Sloanes say the enthusiastic exaggerated things—marvellous, terrific, amazing—in a different tone. Most Sloane put-downs are attempts to *keep* down aspirant non-Sloanes, a tradesman who is 'far too grand for us now' because he's bought a new 'Bent-li', the swot who is almost a professor' ('I wish he'd learn to *shave!*'), the 'terribly trendy exquisite' and his '*lovely* white suit'.

A consequence of Nationalism is that foreigners are funny. Sloanes *adore* Franglais. Henry's French is terrible, but he speaks it loudly abroad, then breaks into English to discuss the 'bloody wops', 'frogs', 'eyeties' and 'krauts', forgetting that most foreigners speak and understand English. At home he and Caroline love to say things like 'Mercy buckets' and 'Où est le tombola?' They also have fun with Italian, and Os on words: vino, pronto, successo.

Money Talks (Quietly)

The Sloane Ranger faces finances

Sloanes learn double-think and double-talk about money from birth. They have amnesia about their own money—about where it comes from and how much there is. They talk *income*. This allows them to plead poverty compared with the scrap-metal dealer up the road earning £50,000 pa in used notes. They forget capital and *things* in the calculation.

There are two reasons for this vagueness. It implies—to those who know the code—that you don't have to worry. It implies—to outsiders—that money isn't what it's all about. People like to believe that the upper classes are down on their uppers. Rangers like this view themselves —it's romantic.

Unlike crass New Boys and foreigners (awash in minks and Rollses), Rangers believe in Extravagant Display only when it serves a greater purpose—an SR (sanctioned ritual) that you *have* to splash out for. A proper wedding with a marquee and Juliana's is a *duty*. And if one's candlesticks are stolen one must buy new ones. At the same time, Rangers are capable of diluting scrambled eggs and serving them as 'eggy bread'. Such privation is an important lesson for the children to swallow. It's easier to crash 'Society' with big money than Rangerland, which takes an abnormal amount of self-discipline in the tiny things that *really* matter.

But, in the long term, Rangerdom does require a bit of money. The 'gent's res' instinct makes Rangers always want a bigger house than they need; school fees have to be afforded; certain things are hard to give up—like club subscriptions. So the poverty is self-imposed, all about *priorities*. If you want to live like a miniature eighteenth-century gentleman in the 1980s, it costs something like:

> £8,000 pa at 20
> £18,000 pa at 30
> £35,000 pa at 40.

INVISIBLE ASSETS

Something better for Sloanes than loans

'Poor' Sloanes get the benefit of a level of hospitality and other help from the Sloane network which would cost a heap if they were buying their way into it. Take the case of Caroline X, tragically widowed at 34. She describes herself as '*literally* a poor widow woman'. She is reckoned to be plucky. She has to work, as a secretary in a charity, for which she gets £6,000

However,

Two flats in the Fulham house are let, bringing in a useful extra £4,000

She's got the use of a third of a house in Suffolk at the weekend, which if she had to pay for it would cost at least £3,000

She's got Henry's 'tiny' capital of £30,000, badly invested but bringing in £2,000

Henry's father has fixed both grandchildren's school fees with one of those insurance schemes £6,000

A friend with children just older often passes on their clothes and uniforms and skis and saddles £1,000

Which means she lives on a gross annual income of £22,000 not counting owning her house, and the inherited silver and furniture which bring the dinner parties up to scratch ('They'll have to have chicken à la lunatic and lump it'). She's thus got the equivalent of an earned income of about £25,000—like the people with whom she compares herself when she's explaining what she can't afford.

Deprivation is very relative, though Caroline doesn't see it that way.

Sloanes love talking about *other people's* money: 'He's a Bloggs of Bloggs mustard', 'She was the soapflakes heiress'. Henry finds big round figures macho and sexy. 'He's got two or three hundred thou' (£150,000), 'She's a millionairess' (£500,000), 'He's got a bob or two' (£1,000,000), 'He's one of the richest men in the world' (£10,000,000).

The Sloane Ranger's problem frequently is that while brought up with enough, they are later expected to live on what they earn. It's always assumed in Rangerland that you've got some money 'of your own'—ie 'the trust'—a little slug of family capital from which one receives an allowance; though in many cases, inflation and incompetence have made it almost worthless. There is still that proprietorial attitude affected towards those concerned with your money: '*my* bank manager', '*my* stockbroker'. You put yourself out to find a 'really sharp accountant'—without a Sloane bone in his body—who can cut your tax bill and bump up your tax claims. You need all the money you can get to subsidise badly-paid Ranger jobs. All along you continue to rue your lack of cash, 'I'm a bit skint this month.' *Pleading poverty* is not special pleading among Rangers: they have been brought up to expect something better.

Sloane Danger

Putting a foot wrong

Despite your eighteenth-century sympathies, you're a nineteenth-century person at heart. Your emotional axis is indignation/embarrassment; so says Christopher Ricks in his seminal work on nineteenth-century mores, *Keats and Embarrassment*—which you haven't read.

You are constantly being *plunged* into a state of shock by someone breaking a rule that is CRASHINGLY obvious to you but invisible to most other people. Its invisibility is its power. Not for nothing were you brought up on A. A. Milne and the cracks taboo:

Whenever I walk in a London street,
I'm ever so careful to watch my feet;
And I keep to the squares,
And the masses of bears
Who wait at the corners all ready
    to eat
The sillies who tread on the lines of
    the street
Go back to their lairs
And I say to them, 'Bears,
Just look how I'm walking in all
    the squares!'

To the Sloane Ranger, crossing the invisible line is like stumbling into a yawning pit. In fact, it's a CRIME. (It's been drilled into them that it's wrong to use such and such a word, as wrong as to *do* bad things. And Sloane men go in for fraud and adultery in later life with far fewer qualms than into a frilled nylon evening shirt.) To transgress the invisible taboo is so terrible it's funny. Sloanes love telling each other about gaffes they have witnessed or committed.

Bateman understood the horror of seeing somebody do something one *doesn't* do. Henry Mayo Bateman, 1887 to 1970, that greatest of humorists, had the gift of the gaffe. The fat little berk of his cartoons is a walking *faux pas*, 'The man who threw a snowball at St Moritz', 'The man who asked for a second helping at the Lord Mayor's Banquet', 'The man who coughed at the first night'. Sloanes wish Bateman were still quivering with them, since the targets for his wit now flourish unabashed.

Like the new colonel who arrived to command the 5th Royal Inniskilling Dragoon Guards and mentioned *horse riding* in the mess!! Twenty cavalry officers felt a cannonball hit them in the midriff. Riding is RIDING and only people who don't know or care about it would put any word of explanation before it (and apart from this deeper significance, the term horse riding or horseback riding is ferociously non-U). Bateman, thou shouldst have been living at this hour.

To you, the wrong clothes aren't just a matter of 'bad taste'—marking the obvious difference between being a gentleman or not—they breach SACRED TABOOS.

Meanwhile, of course, you are merrily committing what Other People think of as taboo actions (wearing shiny disco trousers and a Hawaiian shirt to the ball, or putting the claret on the Aga and remembering it only as it almost boils, or absent-mindedly addressing the boss as Stinker). Subconsciously you know that the uncertain social climber wouldn't dare: which adds to your pleasure in these 'gaffes' which are not *real* gaffes, but jokes. Not gaffes because nothing *sacred* has been violated (unless the Queen was at the ball).

John Wells understands these class skirmishes. What a funny little weasely face he has! You *adore* embarrassment comics like Wells, Rowan Atkinson and John Cleese. They're terribly amusing. *Fawlty Towers* was a PALACE of embarrassment.

Royal Rangers

Sloanes and the royal family

Royalty is crucial to Sloanehood. It is the fount of all honours—literally—and everything else that matters. Sloanes would rather be introduced to a member of the royal family than win the pools.

They worship Queen and country and, a long way after that, the Government (Sloanes often cheat on their income tax and always commit traffic offences). Their ancestors (they like to think/say) came over with William the Conqueror, and so it is part of their tradition to be on the side of the Establishment against the hairy Celts. The only underdog a Sloane automatically sides with *is* a dog.

If you are an archetypal Sloane, you are an officer in the Ruling Class. Though usually not an ardent churchgoer, you support the Church Militant (in England, the orthodox Church of England; in Scotland, orthodox Church of Scotland; in Wales, orthodox Church of Wales; in America, orthodox Episcopalian; in Japan, orthodox Zen; in France, orthodox Roman Catholic; in Greece, Greek Orthodox). Similarly, you do not hold peaceable views on things ideological. Nukes are nasty, but then so are the Reds. The warrior mentality lives on—Knights Templarmental.

The Sloane character of our present Queen—married to the fact that she's on top of the hierarchy—makes you love her the other side idolatry. The rest of her family is judged by how it supports her.

THE PANTHEON
The Queen
HM. Almost divine. You love her for her self-control and, paradoxically, for her inability to pretend (unless good manners

Left to right, standing: arty, blossoming, hunky, roguish, game, promising, foggy. *Seated:* wayward, simply marvellous, treasured, brisk.

are pretence). The way she obviously only enjoys herself when she's with her family or at a racecourse. You would think her clothes a bit middle-aged and middle-class if you allowed yourself to judge them. But instead she is vociferously admired for wearing striking all-one-colour outfits so that she stands out, and for the fact that her hair is scraped back so that people can see her face—even though it doesn't suit her. She has the ability—only indifferently achieved by lesser beings, despite Nanny—to Sit Still. She doesn't move an inch when she's on her horse at Trooping the Colour.

The Duke of Edinburgh
Prince Philip. Speaks his mind and is the most attractive man in the family. Jolly good he does so well with the carriage-driving. Hope he's nice to her in private.

Princess Margaret
PM. Not a Sloane—a 'me' person and too social. But you must admit she gave up a lot for duty. What a pity she went for such pipsqueaky men after that. Let's hope she'll find some nice widower and boo snubs to the weeds.

The Queen Mother

The Queen Mum (though you hate it when the *popular* papers call her that!). Wonderful, super. A pretty, comfy, walking sofa. Her clothes are all wrong, but they suit her. And her charm is natural (the rest of Sloanedom find being charming hard work).

Princess Alexandra

One of us to Sloanes. And, with a husband in the City, you feel that the Ogilvys are *almost* friends (though Alexandra *did* tell one cavalry wife 'I'd hate to be an Army wife!'). She is completely unforced and attractive, with that slightly lop-sided smile and Sloany clothes.

Prince Charles

PC. He's nice, generally kind to horses, quite good-looking, too (in Sloane terms). He made a miracle marriage in the end, clever old thing, and he's a super father. Pity him his Burden, but be pleased he carries it so well. Good luck, Sir!

Princess Anne

A Sloane sans charm. In fact, to be fair, Sloanes are seldom *really* charming, but one *must* smile and be gracious. (Another view, held by riders, says that Princess Anne has done extremely well to excel in a demanding profession and do her royal job on top.)

Mark Phillips

A Sloane called Fog. We all know that this means 'Thick and wet'. But since we haven't any A-levels ourselves, Sloanes squeak 'I don't know why everyone is so mean about him. He's jolly good-looking and he's a top eventer.'

Prince Andrew

Very brave. Can he *really* be so sexy? What does the Queen think of it? Hope he settles down before she gets embarrassed.

Prince Edward

A nice boy, the best-looking of the lot. But only time will tell if he is the right husband for Henrietta or Sophie.

★OTHER★HEROES★AND★HEROINES★

BOADICEA (*not* Joan of Arc)

KING ARTHUR (*not* Lancelot—adultery)

FRANCIS DRAKE (*not* Nelson—too open with Lady Hamilton)

THE DUKE OF WELLINGTON (*not* Cardigan—he let the army, history and 600 Sloanes and honorary Sloanes down)

LORD CARRINGTON

CHURCHILL

LADY CHURCHILL

MOUNTBATTEN

THE SAS

THE GURKHAS

SIMON WARD (because he appears to be a gent)

DAVID NIVEN (because he conquered Hollywood and stayed a gent. And he's such a good worker)

ANTHONY ANDREWS (after *Brideshead*)

MRS THATCHER (not an uncontroversial choice, 'but at least she's tough')

HAROLD MACMILLAN (Grand Old Boy, so Edwardian and so funny)

REGGIE BOSANQUET (everyone's favourite black sheep)

ROBERT REDFORD (he's been a generation's hero—but he's beautiful, sexy and skis)

PAUL NEWMAN (the same. *Amazing* blue eyes. People who say he puts coloured drops in them are just jealous)

PRINCESS GRACE (*not* Jackie O)

J. P. R. WILLIAMS (playing rugger)

NIGEL STARMER-SMITH (talking rugger)

BARBARA WOODHOUSE (so funny and direct— an amazing woman)

JOYCE GRENFELL ('George, don't DO that,' they bellow)

RICHARD MEADE (Oh, why didn't Princess Anne marry *him*?)

LADY YOUNG (*not* Lady Diana Cooper. Philip Ziegler's biography showed her to be a bit of a tease)

NANCY MITFORD (in fact, all the Mitford girls except Unity)

THE DUCHESS OF WESTMINSTER (for her youth and shyness)

LADY LONGFORD (*not* Lady Antonia Pinter. She *was* a heroine, despite all the gossip, until she married THAT man who all Sloanes fear will one day win the Nobel Prize)

THE DUCHESS OF KENT (the English Rose)

LADY ELIZABETH SHAKERLEY (a DOER. So capable. *Not* Lady Rothermere—wasn't she a starlet?)

JIMMY GOLDSMITH (The Man They Love to Hate. And there's an element of admiration—although SRs tend *not* to admire people with names like Goldschmidt or Greenbaum)

ROWAN ATKINSON (ha! ha!)

JILLY COOPER (however hard she tries to look blowsy)

BETTY KENWARD

BETTY PARSONS (she got me through it)

LUCINDA PRIOR-PALMER GREEN

TINY ROWLAND (capitalism *has* to have a face)

TINY MICHAEL EDWARDES (somebody had to stand up to those Unions—even if he is only 5 foot 3)

TINY LESTER PIGGOTT

TINY LORD OAKSEY

TINY WAYNE SLEEP

IF YOU THINK SOMEONE'S MISSING, TURN THE PAGE....

Supersloane

The Princess of Wales is the 1980s Supersloane. When Diana Spencer began to appear in newspapers in the summer of 1980, the Sloane Ranger style started its gallop down the high streets. What the papers called the 'Lady Di look' (very un-Sloane and a contraction she hated) was actually pure SR—a walking lesson in Mark II Sloane style at its best.

Lady Diana—even when she was still a semi-private person and not Royal—showed that the hard-edged Mark I style could evolve. Like many of her contemporaries—flat-sharing SW7 and SW10 girls under 20—she did the old things, but with a new flair.

New Look, new feel
BC—Before Charles—she wore the *Young* Sloane wardrobe: ruffled shirts with ribbons at the neck; baggy jumpers with straight skirts or jeans; a touch of ethnic. When she wore it, it turned overnight into the major rag trade look of 1981/82.

Clothes apart, she showed that a 1980s Sloane was allowed to be more in touch with her emotions. She cried, she blushed, she *swore* when her starter jammed on her new Metro. She kissed people. Suddenly it was no longer COOL to be cool.

Old mores
But, underneath it all, were the Old Guard instincts; the tenets of noblesse oblige: virginity, marriage—and the wedding list; love of the country, animals; lack of formal education—in short, everything that Really Matters.

She did all the right jobs—part-time cooking, nannying, teaching kindergarten (at a *nice* Sloaneshire school, the Young England in Pimlico). And, like a properly brought-up girl, she knew better than to ever mention the Queen or Prince Charles. They were both 'the Palace'.

'Romantic' revival
When she won her Prince, she blossomed into an English Romantic: bare shoulders

---

THE QUALITIES THAT WON THE PRINCE

(S-L-O-A-N-E spells loyalty)

Sexual ignorance
Love of jokes
Only tells teddy
Ambles like a
　thoroughbred
No long words
Eager to please

in black taffeta; knee breeches and flat shoes—the Prince*ling* look. Both visions stepped, fully fashioned, from out of the frames of nineteenth-century upper-class paintings by Lawrence and Winterhalter. And having the baby in short order confirmed that she was a thorough professional and would Fit In.

What we owe the PoWess
(*pronounced Powys*)

★ Those flat shoes (though we know *why* she wore them). Now even shorties wear the eternal Sloane page-boy footwear for tall girls.

★ She brought back the shoulders and bosom, and the lush taffeta rustle of big skirts after eight. Her Sloane chest is generous, somewhat low-slung and thoroughly Windsor.

★ Granny's multi-strand pearl choker. Triple rows—and more—are favoured for the first time since Queen Mary.

★ Salute the leader of the bocker brigade. Sloanes took to breeches the moment they became fashionable.

★ That hair broke the old rules. Before, it was long and straight, or upswept—but always 'out of the eyes, Caroline'. Today, bobs, fringes and highlights are all OK.

★ She has freed Sloanes from the tyranny of the horse.

★ Like many true Sloanes, Diana Spencer didn't come out. (Stay in, be in.) She was never café society and never appeared in a gossip column until 1980. Moral: Keep out of Dempster; save yourself for the front page.

★ Mrs Average she may not be—but her lack of O-levels made her one of the crowd—and the crowd loved her for it.

★ Be loyal to your friends and your friends will be loyal to you. Look who got three front row seats at That Wedding.

★ And she knows that Mummie is her *best* friend. All Sloanes do.

Sloane Senses

Smell—a Sloane is a dog in disguise

Smell is beautiful. Sloanes, not normally sensitive, have noses as keen as bloodhounds. They know that people aren't the same in the dark with no clothes on. They could tell you by your smell. Some blends are acceptable, but not one smell trying to conceal another. A *clean* smell is, however, a good thing. Soap is at the top of the Sloane shopping list, followed closely by Badedas chestnut bath essence. Overscented things are upsetting (like too much fuss). Scented products like lavender polish, shop pot-pourri and air fresheners (aerosol gas smells frightful) do not litter the Sloane household.

Foreigners are too smelly, except for the Dutch and Scandinavians; Americans don't smell *enough*.

Sloanes sort the school trunk, select melons, know when a room needs cleaning, choose their pubs and their friends by smells. You automatically sniff knickers, socks, armpits, hair and drains, and you believe in washing or airing clothes rather than sending them to the cleaners. Caroline loves the sink/washing line/linen cupboard circuit of smells (she uses Dreft and Fairy Snow).

Sloane mothers diag*nose* babies' and animals' health from the look and smell of their droppings, and *all* Sloanes continually test the air itself ('It smells like snow') ('God, don't these diesels pong'). It's one reason they love the weekend and want to live in the country: they are homesick for the air. You are what you breathe.

Stephanotis, followed by Ormonde (sandalwoody) are the smell favourites of British Sloanes, sandalwood for Italian and French Sloanes, Jasmine and Red Rose for Arab Sloanes. Floris stopped making Violet three or four years ago—the supply of high-grade oils failed—and it was the end of an epoch. Caroline's great-grandmother smelt of violets (no lady wore anything else), her grandmother of Chanel No 5 (breakthrough!), her mother of Balmain's Jolie Madame (the New Look), and she wears Diorissimo (The Princess of Wales's favourite) and Hermès Calèche. As we all know, Sloanes call it scent, not perfume.

The other Sloane-scented soaps (Pears has a non-scent smell) are made by Roger et Gallet, honorary British in Sloane eyes. Liberty's and Culpeper have a share of the Sloane scent market: Sloanes like Culpeper's little scented pillows.

Caroline loves Henry's smell and probably chose him for it. She has a theory that if you make a list of the best-smelling men you will find that the better the smell the better the husband. Active men smell better: horsemen, rugger players, sailors, skiers and racing drivers, none of whom wear aftershave. (The only exceptions are made for Eau Sauvage, Trumper's Lime and now Polo, by American Ralph Lauren.) These sportsmen have a pure smell. The unfit smell slightly acrid (constipated). It's the difference between horse manure and sheep droppings.

Smell is the key to good hay, bread, fish, wool, leather, soap, paper, soil, chips, fruit, veg, dung, temper (Sloanes are embarrassed when they smell fear on someone they are having a row with).

THE GOOD SMELL GUIDE

Nice everyday smells

Sunburnt arms; Rémy Martin; Leather riding boots; The sea
Composting vegetables; Manure; Old macintoshes and wellington
boots; Boats; Gunpowder; Old houses and barns; Dubbin;
Mould; Creosote; Furniture wax; Dettol; Babies; Sweat;
Inside of drawers, cedar pencils; Lawn clippings; Bonfires;
Porridge; Horse-chestnut buds; High-octane petrol; Kippers;
The Daily Telegraph; *Country Life*; Rosemary (and all herbs)

Bad smells (pongs)

Bad breath. *The slightest would mean death, even to Robert Redford*;
Dirty hair. *But red usually smells foxy even when clean*; Imitation
leather; Aeroplanes (*air freshener on top of sick on top of imitation
leather*); Sour baby milk (*sour babies*); Old vase-water;
Mouse decaying under the floorboards; Most other nationalities

Sight—long-distance spectacles

A Sloane can tell a rabbit from a hare at a hundred yards; but art's a fart, you suspect in your heart: avoid Artiness.

Does art exist? Daddy says it's all a conspiracy to fool the public and that Picasso was a genius conman and good luck to him but don't you fall into the trap. You have your own criteria for judgment:

1) *Things that Matter* The pictures you

3) *Sex* Henry loves coy frou-frou'd Frenchies, gleaming naked Indonesians, even, heaven forbid, Russell Flints.

4) *Most old is good* Henry and Caroline both like Olde English oils of five-year-olds with big eyes and lots of fair hair; and lambs; and foals; and kittens. Within these criteria, many Sloanes have good pictures or reproductions of them. Sloanes know that Gainsborough and Stubbs were the greatest artists in the history of the universe, including as they do the Persons of Quality and HORSES. They

The Horse Motif

The Horse is the Sloane's sacred animal. That's why we don't eat it here. All Europe eats horse, but the Sloane gorge rises. 'How *could* you?' Horses are everything that was ever romantic or WRM about Sloanery: knights in armour, *Came a Horseman*, the hunt, the Sport of Kings, polo, Caroline's own pre-pubescent Horse Period. Everything to do with horses: stables, grooms, jockeys, harness, stirrups and spurs, snaffles, *takes on a symbolic life of its own*. That's why you like pictures of horses or equine things wherever you can put them. No matter that aesthetes hate hunting-print table mats and the whole horsy style, you love to see it.

The classic Gucci loafer, beloved of Sloanes from the mid Sixties on and still worn, appealed because it had that smart but military equine look, like a good piece of uniform with regimental brass. The marvellous Hermès scarves, staples of Sloane kit for the last twenty years and more, have wonder-

ful military, royal and equine symbols—tassels, harness, drums, printed in lovely bright clear colours on beautiful silk. They're a kind of montage of *everything that's good*. The Hermès scarf is as good as wearing a Stubbs round your chin. Rangers, of course, like pictures by John King. They also like Herriot and Landseer and anyone else who showed dogs and horses at their best.

There's no limit to the things you can put a horse on. The *whole* horse can be sculpted, painted, engraved; it can go on scarves, curtains, table-mats, wastepaper baskets. It can be bronze or silver and, of course, it's wonderful if it's old statuary.

And there's literally no limit to the application of the horse *symbols*: You can have snaffles all over your Gucci shirt or your Marks & Spencer one. You can have it jacquard, woven into your luggage. Gucci is fine as long as you anglicise it. You don't want to look like one of those sunstreaked Pignatelli types. There are those who say the Sloane Ranger man's fondness for leather-looped braces has something to do with harness, but this may be taking things too far....

approve of relate to history (the eighteenth century), field sports, family history, places you know. That's what beauty means, so you look for hay and cows, the ancestor of a Derby winner, a British king or one of his relations or mistresses, a still-life with pheasants, a plenteous bosom. You try to detect social standing. Is that house a gentleman's house? Is the coach a grandee coming to call, or the local doctor?

2) *Triggers to the subconscious* Waves of the sea, white horses galloping, geese against the sunset—they please you under category (1), but they also seem to understand how you feel.

love eighteenth and nineteenth-century pictures from category (1). Sloanes ruled the world then and the painters were jolly good, too. Mediaeval and Renaissance pictures are boring (all those Marys and babies). Seventeenth-century pictures are boring—people are boring unless it's Someone One Knows. Pre-Raphaelites are terrible—sickly colour—and that beetle-browed woman who's in them all (was she Jewish?). Impressionist women or racehorses are lovely (though Cézannes are awful). Hockney seems Perfectly All Right as long as he keeps off bottoms. Lovely colour—all that Marina blue.

A true Sloane finds the kind of picture

sold on the pavements around the Royal Parks strangely pleasing under category 2, 3 or 4—but you don't buy them from railings, you go to the auction rooms, country galleries or ('Shhh, don't tell') to Harrods.

The fact is you find all this talk of 'visual sense' quite mystifying. In dress, one wants to look tidy, reassuring and appropriate (Sloane), not visual and arty-farty. People want to see you, not your clothes, as Nanny said. And just look at how these arty people dress—the old ones like Michael Foot, the younger ones like David Hockney, or Helen Mirren in gymshoes, or the Woody Allen Type of Person.

Hearing—that Glyndebourne to which every traveller returns

The country and the military develop a special kind of hearing tuned to individual noises rather than the metropolitan overall buzz. So Sloane hearing is acute in youth, especially for car noises. Henry likes to imitate the different makes of car and motorbike, specially when he's pissed. Vroom vroom. Neeeeeowwwww. Caroline can hear a taxi drawing up outside and panting while it's paid off: so sexy, like a motor boat. In old age, Henry goes deaf, one ear at a time.

Predictably, you thrill to the hunting horn (about the only French you can quote is 'Dieu, que le son du cor est triste au fond des bois'), dog sounds, horse sounds.

Your musical ear is based on church and later, military music. The 'Last Post' kills you. In church, the organ gives a muted call to holy war: 'The Church's one foundation is Jesus Christ our Lord ... and to one end she pres-ses with every grace endued.' Sloanes pressed in a car start off by singing songs from musicals ... but not everybody knows the words, so they then move on to national songs like 'John Peel', 'Greensleeves', the 'Eton Boating Song', 'The Road to the Isles', 'The Ash Grove', 'Danny Boy', and 'The British Grenadiers' ... but not everybody knows the words, so then it's on to hymns and carols, and 'God Save the King' and 'Land of Hope and Glory' and *everybody* knows most of the words.

Carols are a Sloane thing. A good Sloane likes to be reminded of the Latin. You spend a working day at least on carols at Christmas—singing them yourself, or suffering the village children to sing unto you—flat—for 10p, or attending your children's school carols (so *dreary* —all this modern bleak mid-winter stuff —what's wrong with 'God Rest Ye Merry Gentlemen'?), or listening to King's College Cambridge and wondering if they really do sound more homosexual this year. Your favourite carol is 'The Holly and the Ivy' because of the mysterious tune and the running of the deah.

You like classical music to be tuneful and juicy: Purcell, Vivaldi, Chopin, Bizet, Ravel, Schubert, *The Tales of Hoffmann, The Beggar's Opera,* Strauss, Mozart, Beethoven (he is an honorary Sloane. The Ninth's a Sloane signature tune), Tchaikovsky (1812), Borodin, Benjamin Britten. You like listening for things in the music—the trout, the storm, the cannon. Handel's *Water Music* is another Sloane favourite.

You like opera: glamour and story plus music. Glyndebourne is part of the season, ie a duty. *Carmen* is best, but you like Wagner—he has a heroic vision, swelling with a patriotism like your own. You are a musicals nut—particularly *old* musicals —and know the tunes: 'Just the Way you Look Tonight'; though you have the Lloyd Webber soundtracks like *Jesus Christ Superstar, Cats* and *Evita.* You *love* jazz and ragtime—Louis Armstrong and Scott Joplin, and you can sing Fats songs ... 'My very good Friend the Milkman . . . .'. Young Sloanes love everything they can bop to—'Rock Around the Clock'.

You like pop music to be *popular*, tuneful and juicy: big sellers like *Tubular Bells* and *Dark Side of the Moon*, soundtracks of your favourite films—*Grease, Saturday Night Fever, Tess, Chariots of Fire*. William Bartholemew of Juliana's Discotheque knows you like middle-of-the-road songs with melodies, something you know and can hum to. His dance tapes for Sloanes of 35 to 50 include Neil Diamond, Manhattan Transfer, Frank Sinatra, Herb Alpert, Bee Gees, Abba, Stevie Wonder, Barbra Streisand, and all the Sixties and rock 'n roll golden oldies.

Probably the most moving song known to Sloane is 'Auld Lang Syne', despite its slip into Andy Stewart television clichédom. On New Year's Eve when massed Sloanes cross arms and sing it the Sloane heart is full. It is your excuse to fall into a neighbouring Sloane's arms most unSloanely, kiss them and chirp 'Happy New Year'. But any song which smacks of power and majesty—God's, man's or nature's—rends the old Sloane heartstrings. 'For Those in Peril on the Sea', an awesome whinge to the Almighty, not only reminds you of your ancestors on the wreck of the *Birkenhead*, your great-great-aunt on the *Titanic* and Daddy in a hair-raising moment on the Atlantic convoy, but also conjures up the embattled Raj, embattled Dunkirk, embattled Cambridge nearly winning the Boat Race. Sloanes rule the waves.

Touch—this'll texture knowledge of the breed

Sloanes operate on two principles when it comes to touch:

1 Hard 'n' soft

The Sloane feel is for hard and soft mixed, A Sloane room, outfit, garden, sponge-bag is never a cosmopolitan cashmere world of soft things, never pure Puritan designer 'hard-edge', but both at once. You like covers to things (cupboards), preferably hard covers to soft things (like yourself): choc ices, patent shoes over

A TOUCH OF THE SLOANES

Bulbs, corms and garlic (*Woods, spring, magical properties—a whiff of the unknown*)
Conkers (*There be none of beauty's daughters with a magic like these*)
Cotton (*Oh yes. Last days of the Raj*)
Silk (*Mad about it. Silk is always 'pure silk'*)
Sponge (*Every Sloane has one and you have to be loyal even after it gets slimy*)
Loofah (*Nothing Pooftah about a Loofah*)
Plastic loo seats (*Yes. Warm and clean. Sloanes are nothing if not practical. So no lovely wooden loo seats, draining boards etc.*)

UNTOUCHABLES

Celanese, Tricel and all the other man-mades (*Under suspicion unless Marks & Spencer have brought them into the fold*)
Crimplene (*Top hate and source of mockery*)
Nylon (*Sheets and shirts make your teeth go on edge*)
Organdie, piqué (*Nice 'feel' not worth the ironing*)
Rayon (*Ugh, ugh*)

silk socks, soft walls above bare floorboards (see Home truths).

2 Butter fingers

Sloanes don't like anything spindly, over-delicate, poncy, Viennesey. Anything that feels *breakable*. Sloanes think of themselves as clumsy, and delicate people as potentially unBritish sodomites.

Anyway, Sloanes always have mental override, on top of the vaguely sensual criteria of what they like to touch (eg ivory chess-men)—about what is class acceptable (eg no mink please, we're *old money*) and what is practical (plastic washing-up bowls feel greasy to you, but they're useful and so you have one). Sloanes' choice of china and glass is a result of practicality plus butter fingers. The fragility of 'antique' china would put them off even though they'd recognise it. It's the same with glasses. The typical Sloane glass is as heavy and strong as a miniature tank (it does see a lot of service).

The touch you like is fur and feathers —on a live body and a *big* body (pheasants, not canaries). You like the skin of big

muscly animals (like Henry!). With horses, you like the velvety noses. But Sloanes aren't really fur *coat* people. Sloanes also like the feel of wool: the Sloane population supports the sheep population. You love Winceyette and flannel nighties.

Sloanes hate anything really fussed up that a dog's nails will catch in: lace, intricate knits, cross-stitch embroidery. They also hate anything hard and shiny: satin bedspreads, satin dressing-gowns, polythene bags.

Actually, Sloanes don't talk about touch —they find phrases like Rupert Brooke's 'the rough male kiss of blankets' vaguely obscene.

Which brings us to sexual touching... well, Sloanes are similar to other men and women when warmed up, but can be inhibited. An experienced lover pompously applying carefully studied caresses to special Sloane places is liable to hear a sudden giggle.

Taste—you've got a lot on your plate

Sloane food should be simple and old-fashioned. You feel safest with the food of your childhood, bland and overcooked, but as you are grown-up now you have to have it in grown-up guises. A typical Sloane dinner-party menu could be jellied consommé and mock-caviar with *scrambled eggs*, followed by a roast, with *mange-tout*, followed by a *mousse*.

Sloanes as a species distrust sauces and variety. But Sloane girls have been expensively trained to pour out sauces and variety like a cuisine machine. This impasse is got past by dinner parties. Sloanes give or go to dinner parties at least three times a week, and drink so much they would even eat brains, a natural Sloane hate.

Fourteen simple principles will keep a Sloane from leaving home:

1 A Sloane loves nursery food: bangers and mash, cauliflower cheese, soup, gooseberry fool, ice cream, steamed pud-

dings, tapioca. When one hears a plaintive request for that almost extinct commodity tapioca in a shop it's always a Caroline trying to humour a Henry.

2 A Sloane is either for or against school food: rice pudding, luncheon meat and beetroots; but never forgets his/her gratitude to the *study-made* food that came to the rescue: beans on toast, cinnamon toast, Marmite toast, Gentleman's Relish toast, bananas and butter and brown sugar on bread, crumpets, Ambrosia creamed rice and tinned cherries, tinned tuna (Sloanes say tunny-fish).

3 Male Sloanes like pub food. Olives, pickled onions, crisps, gherkins ('like a spare prick at a wedding', as the Sloane joke goes).

4 Sloanes like food to wear a hat. Shepherd's pie, soufflé (Sloanes adore all forms of soufflé), crême brulée, any meat en croûte, vol au vent, apple pie, apple crumble. Sloanes also like rack of lamb for the row of little paper hats (non-U but who cares?).

5 Sloanes like archaic breakfast food. Porridge, kedgeree, kippers, eggs, kidneys, which all suggest the spirit-burner sideboards of Edwardian house-parties.

6 Sloanes like game (of course). They struggle with the little bones with their big knives and forks. Game-eating is not a meal, it's a *ritual*, with the lambs' lettuce salad, matchstick potatoes, etc. Out comes the silver on game nights.

7 Sloanes like Indian food. Grandfather ate it in the Punjab; Henry ate at Indian restaurants (cheap) when he was a student, and he still loves curry and pappadums and chutney and the rest. His macho-masochisms decree that he must order the hottest—Vindaloo, Madras or even Bangalore Phal—and he gets a ring burner next day.

8 Sloanes like pasta. They moved from Indian restaurants to Italian restaurants before they locked into the dinner-party circuit. Pasta is the mainstay of the Sloane army. 'Spag bog' (spaghetti bolognese) is the best. Eat lots of spag bog and you won't get the bog sag.

9 Sloanes say Save the Spud, threatened with extinction by pasta and weight-watching. They like them every possible way and have just discovered potatoes boulangère.

10 Sloanes play safe with cheese. Their choice is limited by the smell. 'God what a pong. Has someone dropped a beast?' Ripe Stilton is often as far as they'll go—drinking lots of port to counteract.

11 Sloanes do not like crustaceans in the shell or fish on the bone. They pretend to share their rich friends' praise of lobster and crab but actually they loathe poking and prying into small recalcitrant legs and getting one mouthful for ten minutes' work.

12 Ditto artichokes vinaigrette.

13 Sloanes dislike salad, fruit, spinach and even Christmas pudding (they keep the last a secret).

14 Sloanes could live on avocados. The hard-over-soft principle again.

Turn down an empty glass. Wine is a nice idea. Selling it's a nice job—but don't get boring about it, just get *drunk*. Sloanes should be drunk. The Sloane does not have a great palate. You drink any kind of beer. The favourite white wine (called 'wait wain' when offering it) is *Muscadet*, followed by Blanc de Blancs (plonk de plonks). Champagne is the superwine, but Sainsbury's sparkling Saumur and Blanquette de Limeaux are useful for celebratory Buck's Fizzes. Sloanes would prefer to drink claret and burgundy, of course, but... the move is toward Spanish Rioja; for the money it's grander than plonk. Not that there is any objection to plonk. So much wine is drunk it is necessary to get two kinds, one from Oddbins, Waitrose or Sainsbury's, and grander wine from the Wine Society, Berry Bros, your Sloane brother-in-law's wine firm or a local wine merchant you found through the *Which Wine Guide*.

The talk all through dinner is about lavatories and adventures which involved being sick.

Caroline's Clothes

Wearing the uniform

Sloane Ranger clothes exactly reflect regimental values and solid background—conservative and reassuring. They are made to last, both in style (never high fashion, thus never out of fashion) and in material—tweeds, wools, silks, cottons; natural and dateless fibres. (An exception is made for the dreaded nylon when it comes to the Husky.) Caroline is a walking example of what any Frenchwoman knows: one can't afford cheap clothes if one's not rich. Quality counts, but Sloane clothes also show the way the wind is blowing—literally. There is always a pennant substitute or an erstwhile wind-sock fluttering at Caroline's neck, bag, bodice or arms. The Sloane is the upper middle class on parade.

Glossy magazines, from time to time, make much of le Style Anglais or the Rich Girl Look, but to Caroline her sort of clothes are not a 'look'. They express her real values and her solid country roots. Rangers don't aim to look sexy, nor do they have to dress in an exotic Original to get attention.

The old Ranger Brigade (Knightsbridge Knotted era) looked like an endangered species at the end of the Seventies. But when Diana Spencer hit the lenses she pepped up the Ranger wardrobe and boosted morale, reaffirming the Sloanes' looks and qualities but reinterpreting them for the Eighties, encouraging Sloanes everywhere to be a touch dressier, a little more dashing. Caroline, of course, looked natural in frilled high necks, not mutton dressed as lamb cutlets like many Princess-followers. Trad Romance has never been far beneath the Sloane surface: it appears again and again in the Victorian heroine evening dresses that epitomise Caroline's deepest feelings towards a ball (Ranger-speak: a bollock).

The principles underlying Caroline's dress code are: Quality, Conservatism, Classicism.

Range Roverette

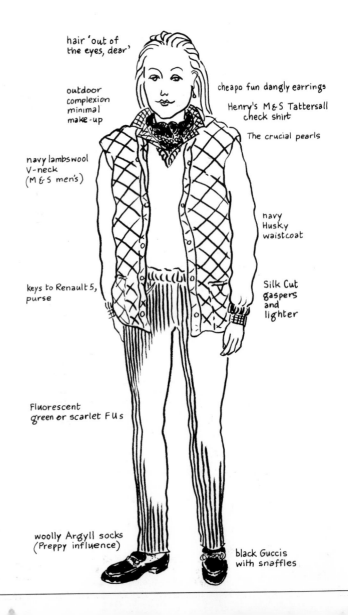

hair 'out of the eyes, dear'

outdoor complexion minimal make-up

cheapo fun dangly earrings

Henry's M&S Tattersall check shirt

The crucial pearls

navy lambswool V-neck (M&S men's)

navy Husky waistcoat

keys to Renault 5, purse

Silk Cut gaspers and lighter

Fluorescent green or scarlet FUs

woolly Argyll socks (Preppy influence)

black Guccis with snaffles

Pearly Princess

Baby Legs

Pearly Princess labels:

Princess Di-style by Kevin Shanley at Headlines

pearl studs

the crucial pearls

Laura Ashley white ruffles

burgundy cashmere (Harrods sale)

good black leather belt (Harvey Nichols)

Hong Kong copy of tapestry bag Contents: bulging leather purse (receipts pound notes and bus tickets), Williams & Glyn's cheque book and Cashline card, H & Q diary and address book (stuffed with SR men's cards), bus and tube map, Diorissimo, blunt eye pencil, empty lipstick, dried-up mascara, Optrex eye-drops, lip salve, emery board, Tampax, letters, match books, sugar cubes, flat and bike keys, photo of Labby

Laura Ashley spriggy cotton skirt

pale Dior tights

Bally low-heeled black patent pumps

Baby Legs labels:

spiky post-punk cut by Sissors or Smile

same pinko white skin - no punk make-up

one diamanté earring

pout

well-worn denim jacket

not much of a chest (country girls are better endowed)

in pocket: Marlboro fags, cash (in grotty little purse), matches from Parsons

Mulberry belt

chunky bangle

King's Road ra ra

black opaque tights

good legs (all that bopping)

suede pixie boots

Rustic roots

Breeches, sporting styles in town, flower prints, Huskys, sensible shoes.

Romance

The Victorian heroine, the governess, touches of lace, soft frills, high necks. The choker.

Signal colours

Sloane regimental colours are navy blue, Husky green and burgundy. The importance of navy blue goes right through the wardrobe. It always looks right (unlike black, which is heavy, Urban Smart and ageing). It is discreet, safe, grown-up. It looks good with white, and with pink and red and emerald green, other Sloane favourites. When not in regimental colours, Sloanes dare much more brilliant shades than other people—because the Queen does and so do smart drawing-room curtains.

Coats

Caroline still believes in the Good Coat.

The loden: a must. An excellent traveller, first sighted on foreign Rangers. Lodens sail through Customs unchallenged because only decent people wear them. Caroline's comes from Gordon Lowe or Born & Bred. Green is classic, but navy blue is a good alternative.

A belted wool wrap coat: this can be tweedy, checked, or camel. It is heavy and warm.

An A-line coat, carefully tailored and shaped, rather dated now in this unstructured era, but Caroline bought it when it was fashionable. It's a Good Coat by a well-known designer, expensive—and it looks smart for weddings and christenings.

A good mac. Probably a Burberry. Also black, yellow or green oilskins. In foul-weather country gear, all attempts at glamour go out of the window.

Jackets

Caroline is very fond of her jackets, an important part of her practical look.

The Husky: green. She has a navy blue

waistcoat too, and wears her Husky with trousers, skirts, bicycling, to work. When she moves to the country, Caroline wears her Husky over her evening dress with wellies, going out to dinner. She carries her shoes.

The velvet blazer in navy blue or burgundy is a classic, so is her long navy blue wool jacket, for everyday uniform.

The quilted floral/Paisley cotton Indian jacket (in lovely washed-out summer pudding colours) is the lightweight alternative to the above.

Country jackets include old tweeds and reefers, a vintage sheepskin, and a Barbour coat (just like Henry's), big and baggy, dirty green colour, that goes to Scotland and Ireland and away at weekends.

Jerseys

At least one guernsey (navy blue of course). An *Aran* sweater. *Fair Isle* jerseys and cardigans are fashionable with women Sloanes (grown-up versions of the clothes Caroline wore as a child).

Cashmere is bought in the sales from Harrods (or from M & S).

Lots and lots of lambswool jerseys, plain not patterned, that are worn with a whole variety of skirts, over a shirt, with a row of pearls; or a little scarf knotted at the neck; or over the shirt that goes over those silky-acrylic body-hugging polo-necks. 'Super and warm, I first wore them skiing.' Caroline has lots in different colours.

Polo-necks and big baggy sweaters in lambswool for sloppy wear.

Peruvian knits from Inca—a V-neck sweater and a little waistcoat. Older Rangers recall the twinsets of the Fifties with reverence, and even now Caroline has a penchant for *cardigans*, especially in lambswool with a grosgrain band backing the buttons.

Skirts

These are basic to Caroline's wardrobe. The most worn, most loved and most

That jacket, that skirt: Sloane classics on parade.

classic of all is the *navy blue pleated skirt*. Caroline has several variations on this theme: fine pleats, box pleats, hip pleated, gathered (sitting in an office, Caroline is self-conscious of the possibility of a baggy bum. And at 35, the centaur-like bottom appears on a Sloane Ranger and the bouncy hair flattens a bit...like hay). Her best—newest—navy blue pleated skirt can be worn out to dins with a boyfriend, dressed up with a ruffled white shirt and a good belt, gold rings and ropes of pearls.

Other skirts in Caroline's wardrobe are in *tweed*; *a Liberty print* (one or two of these, some made by herself): *corduroy*; *flannel*. She has, naturally, *a kilt*, which she wears with toning tights. The tweed suit (many older Sloanes still call it a coat and skirt) is no longer essential, but smart country Sloanes have one, made to measure by Moto.

She also has, and occasionally wears, a long *wool* or *velvet skirt* for the evening.

Shirts
Lots, 'You can't have enough.'

Caroline loves stripes, checks, spriggy prints in Viyella, cotton, silk, cotton jersey. She gets French labels (Cacherel, for instance), haunts Laura Ashley, wears Henry's old ones when they have frayed beyond hope for him, gets her best ones from James Drew. Simple fresh unsexy shirts just like her man's are Caroline's thing. She always looks nice that way, never threatening.

As well as crisp and classically tailored shirts, Caroline loves the Edwardian and Victorian softness of ruffles and frills, high necks, big sleeves. She has at least one shirt with a stock, and likes to tie big pussy-cat bows at the neck, or adds a velvet ribbon.

Trousers

are straight-legged: they suit her pear-shaped bottom better. Caroline wears trousers a lot at weekends; rarely to work in London; often in the evenings for supper with a girlfriend (pre-marriage Caroline). Her trouser wardrobe includes:

Jeans. Worn with Gucci-type brogues, a Husky, a whole variety of shirts, ruffled blouses, or thick sweaters. Many Sloanes with small babies live in jeans.

Velvet trousers, in bright colours; figure-hugging, for evenings at home. Useful après-ski wear.

Grey flannels. To wear with a silk shirt, good jewellery and a blazer.

or nylons, always with loafers or her Gucci-look brogues.

Dressing up

Caroline puts on her Good Clothes for Special Occasions.

Thus, she has a suit: probably navy blue wool and very discreet. Out comes the good jewellery, the brooch, the silk shirt with a stock, or the pussy-cat bow. This is classic wedding kit.

So is her velvet suit (which may have frogging), in bottle green or burgundy, worn with shiny Guccis or plain court shoes. The velvet suit is very useful for the theatre too, and drinks parties.

☆ RANGERETTES ☆
ROGUE DEBS AND BABY LEGS

Rebecca Baby-legs has a mini-dress with a pie-crust frill on the thigh, black stockings, suede pixie boots and short tousled, blonded hair cut like a boy's.

She wears her father's coat, oversized. Covert coats especially. She sometimes reads *The Face* or *The New Musical Express.*

Outrageous, contagious, you wouldn't believe the new girls at Queen's College now—Baby Legs has spread like wildfire. Their mothers think they're punks.

Baby Legs is about 25% of teen Sloanes—usually smarter London ones. But below the crop there's that pink and white skin and after the club they're

still away for the weekends. They smoke of course, they sometimes talk about drugs, but in the same Sloane voice full of little strangulated 'yas'. She has more advanced taste than mainstream Sloanes. She goes slumming, to events at the Hammersmith Odeon, to discos that aren't on The List and to parties in Ladbroke Grove. Sometimes. With her friends.

At nineteen or twenty she appears to go back On The Rails and rediscover What Really Matters. She finds a Nice Boy with whom she's got a lot in common. Her wardrobe straightens up. She feels she's got out of a pretty heav-y scene. It all became a bit much.

Corduroy trousers, cut like jeans, in regimental colours—Husky green, navy blue, burgundy. Plus one fun pair of FUs in scarlet or bright green, like the Princess of Wales's, from the Jean Machine in the King's Road.

Knickerbockers. Rangers took to the bocker and breeches fashion of late 1980 like ducks to water, removing the unhealthy New Romantic element (paint, posing), substituting the Sensible Look. Caroline wears hers with all the separates in her wardrobe, and thick textured tights

The little black dress—this is discreet, not a slinky sexy affair. Pretty, safe, silk jersey, it goes out to dinner and to the theatre.

Caroline has a collection of little dresses in silk and wool and Viyella. They are mostly variations on the shirt shape, buttoned, usually belted, often with big sleeves. Sloanes are almost the only people who wear these sorts of dresses now.

Indian dresses and skirts plus waistcoats plus blouses have become a necessity to

Caroline's wardrobe too, and make great sense to Rangers at night because they are pretty, slightly frivolous (being so flimsy and sometimes embroidered), and ethnic, thus a bit exotic, but in the Right Way.

For hunt balls, coming-out dances, charity bollocks and a gala night at the opera, Caroline wears her *evening dress*. It is long. She is a Victorian heroine. It is high-necked and prim with big sleeves and lacy edgings, or it has a low scoop neck, revealing her generous bust. Her wedding dress (from Bellville Sassoon) may have been cut down, the neck plunged. Caroline likes silk and cotton and taffeta, floozy materials printed or plain.

Underwear and nightclothes

Invariably pretty but not sexy. Janet Reger is for honeymoons and rocky marriages only. A good line in slips (all called petticoats). Gossard Wonderbra/Triumph, bought in John Lewis. Underwear from Fenwicks, Marks & Spencer and Harrods. Dressing-gown is towelling, or Indian from Monsoon; nighties are Victorian-esque by Laura Ashley. Lots of textured tights: navy blue and very pale ivory for good, plus lime and other sickly colours matching a colour in the skirt or dress—but the black shoes spoil the effect.

Shoes

Vital, as with Henry. A lady has to be known by her shoes alone now that gloves have dropped out. 'Like a bed, you spend half your life in them' quotes Caroline, who has just given the price of a chair for a pair. The pop group who called themselves The Sloane Ranger and the Guccis (1982) weren't just fantasising. Caroline has:

Guccis (the real things) and *lookalikes* (Russell & Bromley, Susan). These are smart tough slip-ons, in black or dark blue patent or leather, with a chunky heel and gilt snaffle or chain across the top, possibly another twinge of gilt at the heel: worn with everything from jeans to the little dress. The next few years, the 'best' Guccis slip down the ladder to become everyday shoes and a new pair takes their place.

Slingbacks, in two colours, for the summer; and a lighter pair for evening.

Satin shoes dyed to go with her evening dress (the wedding shoes, possibly).

Idlers/loafers in brown or navy or black leather, the same that Caroline wore on Sundays at school. They suit her sporty legs, and now that the fashion is for flat shoes they look just right.

Court shoes, high heels, plain, probably patent leather.

Flat patent pumps, black with a black petersham bow.

Green wellingtons, and possibly Lady Northampton boots—clever old her!

Moon boots for skiers (and what Sloanes aren't?).

THE **HUSKY**: A WAY OF LIFE

The Husky has become a symbol of Sloane-ness, the way the Lacoste alligator is to Preppies (save an alligator—kill a Preppy; save a Husky—kill a Sloane). Colonel and Mrs Guylas, the perpetrators of this multi-purpose Ranger robe (worn indoors, outdoors, in the country, in the City, under topcoats, over evening dresses), are themselves non-Sloanes. They settled in Tostock, Suffolk, in the early Sixties, when Col Stephen Guylas retired from the US Air Force, in which he worked at research and development of specialist clothing. He is an American citizen, though his parents had come to the United States from Hungary. Edna Guylas's family come from Sunderland.

A keen sportsman and a very fine shot (he won the British Open in 1963), Col Guylas designed a padded waterproof waistcoat, and next a jacket, to wear shooting. At once the shooting fraternity of Suffolk wanted one too, and soon, by word of mouth and next by mail-order catalogue, Huskys were out on the grouse moors, up on the hills, on the river banks, on the hunting field. The Guylases knew they were into a good thing the day the Duchess of Roxburghe sent back her quilted waistcoat heavily pinned with an accompanying note explaining her need for this garment to be both roomy and close-fitting enough to wear under her hunting coat. The public seal of approval came at the Game Fair at Burghley in 1963. Nowadays they sell (annual turnover around £1,000,000) through 50 stockists throughout the country, at game fairs and agricul-tural shows, through the catalogue and direct from the showroom below the offices in Stowmarket. 'Royalty come here, and they never seem to mind it being scruffy. Of course we never forewarn the staff or make a fuss.' Mrs Guylas remembers receiving an order from Prince Charles for a girlfriend just as he was going up to Cambridge. The Guylases' daughter Fern is now an eventer following in Princess Anne/Mark Phillips' hoofprints.

The jacket and waistcoat—green, followed by navy blue—remain best-sellers and styles never alter. The Husky has imitators, 'but people in the end still want the Husky label,' says Mrs Guylas. 'We had a letter from a woman once saying "Please never change the poppers on your jackets, because I know just who I can talk to on trains."'

Never happier: Sloanes modelling a Barbour and a Husky.

Tennis shoes. For playing tennis in, and for wearing with jeans.

Leather boots, with a squarish toe, almost knee-length. Mark I pair must be black.

Trellis gold evening sandals. A classic.

Espadrilles for the summer.

Accessories

Hats. For winter weddings, the large velvet beret (can be pinned with a brooch). Smarties have them in several colours, each with its own brooch sewn in, for race-meetings.

Brimmy felts (the governess trying to express herself).

Big brims with flowers and grosgrain bands, and in summer, straw hats with flowers to wear with those pretty flowery cotton dresses: Caroline knows she looks good in a hat.

Umbrella. Sloanes hear the weather forecast, and might respond with: a see-through, popularised by Princess Margaret. An Italian flowered. Always cane or wooden handle. Perhaps a goffing (some Sloanes pronounce it golfing. *Never* goalfing).

Bags. Often called 'handbag' (sorry, Nancy Mitford), though it may well be a shoulder bag. Any 30-plus Caroline still tends to think, as she was taught to, in terms of matching bags and shoes. She has an Hermès (or lookalike); a little bag with a long gilt chain (for Dressed Up occasions); a fishing bag, in canvas and leather. Bags are a good item to buy from friends' sales. Evening bag for the long dress is a gold encrusted pochette (Henry bought it in Hong Kong) or a little petit-point embroidered bag. A good wallet or purse is also a must. Vuitton, Dior or Gucci—instantly recognisable and long-lasting.

Belts. Black, navy blue, brown, maroon. Leather. Gucci and Hermès; Fenwick's is an excellent source for cheap lookalikes. Slim belts preferred.

Scarves. Hermès. Knightsbridge Knots

(the knot on the point of the chin) are a rare sight in the Eighties; but grey days, damp weather and rain itself bring Rangers out in this important item of uniform. The headscarf is patterned with horse insignia and enough whips and straps to excite memories of prep school in Henry. Interestingly, two-thirds of Hermès business is in sales of their famous silk scarves. No Sloane would touch a lookalike: but she does of course have drawers full of silk scarves and squares, years of pressies from boyfriends (wrinkled and weighted by numerous empty bottles of Calèche, also aged love-tokens). The scarf may be tied around the strap of Caroline's bag or loosely knotted at her neck, if not on her head. Caroline's other scarves have famous labels—Jacqmar, Jaeger, Dior, YSL, Liberty—or they bear the insignia of the Country Landowners' Association, CLA, on plush white, wine or green silk (£10 on production of a CLA member's card).

A PASSION FOR INDIA

All Sloane Rangers suffer from nostalgie d'India, even if their grandfather *wasn't* in the Indian Army or the Indian Civil Service. It's a deep and quite unconscious feeling. The tribes of the north-west frontier are the Sloanes' spiritual ideal, Kipling the Sloane tribal poet. The Middle East and Far East, seen by modern people as a collection of different countries, Sloanes know to be a homogeneous culture, beads on the Silk Route, of which the central jewel is India. It must be said for the Sloanes' approach that they *love* the *whole* East, unlike the less romantic, more specialist student of culture.

Henry as a young man lived on curries from Indian restaurants. After they get married, Caroline furnishes the house with that little wormy print that Colefax & Fowler and Designers Guild sell, and dhurries and Mogul hangings and Indian bedspreads.

The Sloanes' best amusements—polo, gymkhanas—come from India. The Sloanes' tea is Indian. At a tea-party, when the hostess offers 'China or Indian?', aesthetes and social climbers answer 'China, if I might', Sloanes say, 'Indian, *please*.'

But most of all, Sloane clothes salaam India. When 'we' were still in India, Paisleys and cashmeres were Sloane staples, but it wasn't done to dress ethnically. But since 1967, Silk Route has been a main Sloane style. In 1967, Thea Porter set up her couture business in Soho, selling rich Middle Eastern fabrics made into giant cushions and Silk Route clothes. British couturiers and decorators were shocked by the coarse gold and silver threads and the slippery satins, but the Sloanes recognised their rightness immediately. Here were clothes in the spirit of the hippies, but Thea Porter was doing the East *for us*. Here were luxurious old *natural* materials. Sloanes have never liked man-made fibres and jumped on the first signs of their retreat. Shops in Oxford Street soon copied the look, and in 1972, Peter Simon started Monsoon in Beauchamp Place, with Janet Wood from Thea Porter as the designer. He put Sloanes into kaftans, but his great innovation, though it seems obvious now, was having western clothes made in India in Indian silks and cottons. Monsoon provided dresses and matching padded jackets for all the young Sloanes' needs. The Monsoon padded jacket became the warm-weather Husky. Monsoon now has twelve branches, seven in London and others in Oxford, Cambridge, Guildford, Salisbury and Perth in Australia. They stopped the padded jacket in 1976. But Sloanes can get their own particular 'ethnic' style privately, from entrepreneurial friends. Having one's designs made up in India-and-points-East has become the big Sloane game. Let's play Warren Hastings.

Hair combs (tortoiseshell). *Hairband* (yes even today they can be found. Until the Seventies *all* Sloanes had a navy or black velvet hairband).

Big sunglasses. 'Sun specs', because Sloanes don't say glasses. See-through, not reflecting.

Suitcase

Battered Loewe/Asprey/Mulberry suitcase, with initials. Sloanes know that A Lady Has Good Luggage. They aren't confident enough to travel with only a dress bag: so they always have to wait for the turntable at airports.

Maternity clothes (see pp 39 and 140)

The Golden Hoard—Sloane jewels

Sloanes are the jewellery classes. They are given it throughout life, as office workers get rises. The pieces are kept in 'my jewel case', either a leather case or an inherited wooden box. For holidays and weekends, Sloanes are very keen on those little travelling roll-ups of suede or satin. Emeralds, sapphires and rubies are the most popular Ranger stones. Gold not silver. Hawkes, Hooper Bolton or Sloane Pearls are the family jewellers who regularly restring Caroline's pearls, clean her good pieces and advise her.

All Sloane jewel cases contain the same things, acquired at recognised stages:

0 months	*Christening presents:* the baby dowry. Pearls, corals.
12 years	Daddy's regimental brooch.
15 years	*Confirmation:* the pube dowry. A gold watch. Earrings from Butler & Wilson. String of pearls if you didn't get one at your christening.
16 to 20	Caroline's ears pierced at 16 or 17, letting in a swarm of gold studs, little gold rings, pearl studs, tiny bows or bees from Jones. If Caroline buys her own jewellery it is gold from Jones or Don Cooper, pieces so small you can hardly see them. Bees are pinned through countless collars and forgotten in the wash. These midgets do nothing to enhance her appearance: they are like the Jaeger labels sewn into the back of her velvet jacket, *symbols* of security. All is in much too good taste, with two aberrations: a gold chain which incorporates her name; a large ugly wristwatch from Fenwick's. Caroline also acquires chokers of all sorts—velvet ribbons, satin ribbons (the Victorian heroine again), three or four rows of inherited pearls with an emerald and diamond clasp. The Cartier ring is essential to the uniform. Gold chains (match the gold on her shoes); perhaps from Florence if she's studied there.
17 to 30	*Presents from boyfriends.* The school makyth the present-giver. Etonians are best, might give you le Cartier watch (le must), gold bangles and rings (rich fathers). Ampleforth, Marlborough very good,

offbeat: Ken Lane earrings, gold chain and pendant from Fior's fun jewellery department, perhaps Jones' gold midgets to dangle from your chain; gold luggage tags, hearts, shells, butterflies. Oundle and Radley good: perhaps give Butler & Wilson ivory, jade and turquoise. Tonbridge good to excessive: monogrammed cufflinks from Apsrey, basketloads of Gucci. (It's no good looking to Harrovians—Harrovians don't give presents.)

21	Double long rope of pearls from Daddy. Diamond or other valuable antique earrings from the family store.
Great-aunt dies	Tiny diamond star brooch.
Grandmother dies	Fine Georgian brooch. Victorian pendant, good old rings, drop earrings, an antique clasp that moves from necklace to brooch to pendant.
Marriage	The proper dowry. Earring studs of diamond and sapphire from Henry—by way of Tessiers. Diamond and sapphire engagement ring and gold wedding ring from Collingwood's or Garrard's.
Birth of child	Sapphire and diamond eternity ring from Henry. Next baby, another ring to tone with the first.
Birthday or Christmas	Gold racehorse brooch from Henry from Tessiers.
Mother dies	Her pearls. Have them remade with coral and crystal knots. She *might* leave you a tiara. But if not the wily Ranger can always find a Friend who will Lend.

What the jewelled Ranger does wrong

She shows no daring or dash in her

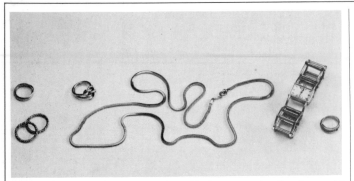

jewels, unlike her general style. She would rather have a ring set with minute diamonds and blue sapphires than a large gorgeous yellow sapphire ring or a pink diamond. She eschews the beautiful semi-precious stones, the turquoises, lapis, garnets and amethysts, in favour of the right thing in the accepted colour.

She would not wear Art Nouveau jewels (too way out) or Art Deco Cartier, which might remind her of a Bolter in the family.

She will wear her jewels in an utterly conventional way. Unlike Princess Michael of Kent, she would not pin a huge diamond brooch on a black velvet bow round her neck or on a cummerbund round her waist.

She is afraid of the big jewel (might look fake).

She is afraid of bracelets.

She is afraid of necklaces, except for chains, pearls and borrowed finery for dances.

The jewel pool

Friends make up a jewel pool and borrow from each other for bollocks. 'Yes, I might be able to get Selina's tiara for the Hopetoun party, and perhaps I can persuade Sophie to lend me her necklace.' A dance is the one occasion on which Caroline will wear large antique jewellery.

IN: pearls, diamonds, dark blue sapphires (like Princess Diana's), cameos.

OUT: amber, coral, topaz, aquamarine, enamelled jewellery, jet.

Caroline's London sources

London Sloane shops which have served the Princess of Wales

BELLVILLE SASSOON, 73 Pavilion Road, SW1 (235 5801). Evening and day clothes.

JOHN BOYD, 19 Brompton Arcade, SW3 (589 7601). Gorgeous hats.

BRADLEYS, 83 Knightsbridge, SW3 (235 2902). Pretty underwear.

DONALD CAMPBELL, 8 William Street, SW1 (235 3332) and at CHATELAINE, 78a Chelsea Manor Street, SW3 (352 2332). Day clothes and dressy outfits.

CAROLINE CHARLES, 9 Beauchamp Place, SW3 (584 2521). Suits, coats and sophisticated 'fun' clothes.

JASPER CONRAN at PIERO DE MONZI, 72 Fulham Road, SW3; TAYLOR & HADOW, 37 Beauchamp Place, SW3; ROXY, 25 Kensington Church Street, W8; SHAW's, 48 Beauchamp Place, SW3. She has worn *sooo* many of his evening and day clothes.

DAVID and ELIZABETH EMANUEL, 26a Brook Street, W1 (629 5569). The Wedding Dress, That Black Dress and more.

DAVID NEIL & JULIA FORTESCUE, 38 South Molton Street, W1 (408 1021). Pretty, flouncy silks and taffetas.

FREDDIE FOX, from FORTNUM & MASON, 181 Piccadilly, W1 (734 8040). Hats again.

GUCCI, 27 Old Bond Street, W1 (629 2716). All those accessories.

BILL PASHLEY, 7 Juer Street, SW11 (228 8721). Mummie's couturier, now daughter's too. Dress and day clothes.

CLIVE SHILTON, 58 Neal Street, London WC2 (836 0809). Ivory silk slippers for The Wedding, leather pochettes.

TATTERS, 74 Fulham Road, SW3 (584 1532). Edwardian and Victorian frills and flounces.

ZAPATA, 49 Old Church Street, SW3 (352 8622). Footwear by Manolo Blahnik, shoemaker extraordinaire.

Coats

AQUASCUTUM, 100 Regent Street, SW1 (734 6090)

BORN & BRED, 85 Bourne Street, SW1 (730 4944)

BURBERRY, 18 Haymarket, SW1 (930 3343)

HUSKY, Stowmarket, Suffolk (04492 4471)

GORDON LOWE, 173 Sloane Street, SW1 (235 8484)

Jerseys

BURLINGTON ARCADE, Piccadilly, W1 (Peals's and S. Fisher, like Henry)

GUERNSEYS GALORE, 49 Moreton Street, SW1 (834 6141)

INCA, 45 Elizabeth Street, SW1 (730 7941)

SCOTCH HOUSE, 2 Brompton Road, SW1 (581 2151)

THE SCOTTISH MERCHANT, 16 New Row, WC2 (836 2207)

WESTAWAY & WESTAWAY, 29 Bloomsbury Way, WC1 (405 2128)

Shirts and blouses

JAMES DREW, 3 Burlington Arcade, W1 (493 0714)

Suede and leather

JANET IBBOTSON, 7 Pond Place, SW3 (584 2856)

Clothes in Indian materials

MONSOON, 53 Beauchamp Place, SW3 (589 7737)

Dressing up/best clothes. Day and night

HARDY AMIES, 14 Savile Row, W1 (734 2436)

BELLVILLE SASSOON, 73 Pavilion Road, SW1 (235 3087)

CAROLINE CHARLES, 8 Beauchamp Place, SW3 (589 5850)

PIERO DE MONZI, 70 Fulham Road, SW3 (589 8765)

CHRISTIAN DIOR, 9 Conduit Street, W1 (499 6255)

EMANUEL, 26a Brook Street, W1 (629 5569)

GINA FRATINI, 2 New Burlington Place, W1 (734 0125)

IB JORGENSEN, 18 Sloane Street, SW1 (235 5626)

ROLAND KLEIN, 26 Brook Street, W1 (629 8760)

MOTO, 7 Sackville Street, W1 (734 4727). Mr Yamamoto was head of the team at Ladies' Habits before it closed down

THEA PORTER, 1a Avery Row, W1 (499 4260)

REGAMUS, 17 Beauchamp Place, SW3 (584 7295)

RODIER, 15 Sloane Street, SW1 (235 3417)

SAINT LAURENT RIVE GAUCHE, 113 New Bond Street, W1 (493 1800)

TATTERS, 74 Fulham Road, SW3 (584 1532)

Underwear and nightclothes

NIGHT OWLS, 78 Fulham Road, SW3 (584 2451)

Shoes and bags

BALLY, 30 Old Bond Street, W1 (493 2250)

BROTHER SUN, 153 Fulham Road, SW3 (581 2976).

CELINE, 28 New Bond Street, W1 (493 9000)

CHELSEA COBBLER, 164 Fulham Road, SW10 (373 6115)

GUCCI, 27 Old Bond Street, W1 (629 2716)

CHARLES JOURDAN, 47 Brompton Road, SW3 (584 3258)

RAYNE, 57 Brompton Road, SW3 (589 5560)

RUSSELL & BROMLEY (main branch), 24 New Bond Street, W1 (629 6903)

SUSAN, 92 King's Road, SW3 (589 9084)

Jewellery

ASPREY, 165 New Bond Street, W1 (493 6767)

ATKINSON, 4a Sloane Street, SW1 (235 3481)

BUTLER & WILSON, 189 Fulham Road, SW3 (352 3045)

CARTIER, 175 New Bond Street, W1 (493 6962)

COLLINGWOOD, 46 Conduit Street, W1 (734 4182)

DON COOPER, 40 Beauchamp Place, SW3 (584 2656)

EMELINE, 45 Beauchamp Place, SW3 (589 0552)

FIOR, 22 New Bond Street, W1 (491 4119)

GARRARD'S, 112 Regent Street, W1 (734 7020)

HAWKES, 50 Walton Street, SW3 (589 2523)

HOOPER BOLTON, 17 Motcomb Street, SW1 (235 5201)

JONES, 52 Beauchamp Place, SW3 (589 3215)

KEN LANE, 50 Beauchamp Place, SW3 (581 2293)

SLOANE PEARLS, 49a Sloane Street, SW1 (235 9163)

TESSIERS, 26 New Bond Street, W1 (629 0458)

Maternity clothes

ELEGANCE MATERNELLE, 198 Sloane Street, SW1 (235 6140)

GREAT EXPECTATIONS, 46 Fulham Road, SW3 (584 3468)

JUST JANE, 8 Sloane Street, SW1 (235 6639)

YOUNG MOTHERHOOD, 188 Sloane Street, SW1 (235 1795)

Scarves and belts

COUNTRY LANDOWNERS' ASSOCIATION, 16 Belgrave Square, SW1 (235 0511)

HERMÈS, 155 New Bond Street, W1 (499 8856)

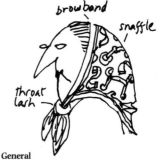

General

LAURA ASHLEY, 9 Harriet Street, SW1 (235 9796)

BENETTON, 23 Brompton Road, SW3 (589 6503)

CROCODILE, 90 Brompton Road, SW3 (584 6257)

FENWICK'S, 63 New Bond Street, W1 (629 9161)

FORTNUM & MASON, 181 Piccadilly, W1 (734 8040)

HARRODS, Knightsbridge, SW1 (730 1234)

HARVEY NICHOLS, Knightsbridge, SW1 (235 5000)

JAEGER (main branch), 204 Regent Street, W1 (734 8211)

JOSEPH, 6 Sloane Street, SW1 (245 9139)

LIBERTY'S, Regent Street, W1 (734 1234)

LILLYWHITES, Piccadilly Circus, SW1 (930 3181)

MARKS & SPENCER (main branch), 458 Oxford Street, W1 (486 6151)

PETER JONES (Young Chelsea department), Sloane Square, SW1 (730 3434)

SHAW'S, 48 Beauchamp Place, SW3 (584 7270), for jeans etc; in fact almost all shops in Beauchamp Place almost all shops in South Molton Street, W1

WAKEFORD'S, 102 King's Road, SW3 (589 2126)

Henry's Clothes

Wearing the uniform

Henry knows the form, which means no fashion and limited self-expression in the kit. Sloane men's clothes are a uniform. There really *are* rules, still. Henry's clothes, like everything else, relate to What Really Matters. WRM has altered little in the last twenty years, except for the arrival of Guccis and jeans (currently worn with tweed jacket) and the departure of the bowler hat.

Everything is worn until it falls apart. Henry wears outerwear indoors, country wear in London, and many of his clothes closely resemble his old school uniform, thereby proclaiming him part of that invisible club of Rangerdom. SRMs are annoyed, subconsciously, that foreigners wear *le style anglais* as a look and not as a badge of faith.

Henry, though utterly predictable, is usually the most attractive man on any occasion. He wears the uniform of the City gent, country squire, penguin, as though he was born to it, which he was. The overall look is knowing the form (properly dressed) but not thinking about it (suspect). The aristocratic tradition means that business Rangers are allowed to look more dashing that their inhibited over-careful American cousins the Preppies. The basics of Ranger dressing are balanced by historically sanctioned flash. Real Ranger clothes, like Tory hair, look a bit *cavalier*. Henry adds colours and Sloane glamour which other classes wouldn't risk—foppish snuff handkerchief, rakishly tilted Herbie J cap, broad scarlet or mustard box-cloth braces. WRM for Henry means:

Rus in urbe. Henry brings the estate to London with his Barbour (qv), his Husky (ditto), etc.

Provenance. Really ancient tweeds and dinner-jacket, archaic but excellent cut, made for his father or even his grandfather. Similarly a shirt from school or Oxford/Cambridge, well worn at the

City Swinger

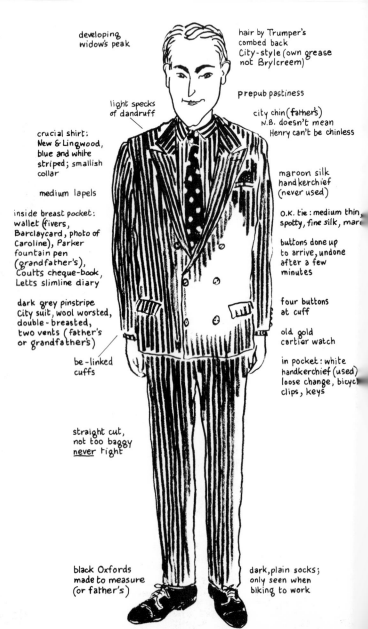

developing widow's peak

hair by Trumper's combed back City-style (own grease not Brylcreem)

prepub pastiness

light specks of dandruff

city chin (father's) N.B. doesn't mean Henry can't be chinless

crucial shirt: New & Lingwood, blue and white striped; smallish collar

medium lapels

maroon silk handkerchief (never used)

O.K. tie: medium thin, spotty, fine silk, marc

inside breast pocket: wallet (fivers, Barclaycard, photo of Caroline), Parker fountain pen (grandfather's), Coutts cheque-book, Letts slimline diary

buttons done up to arrive, undone after a few minutes

dark grey pinstripe City suit, wool worsted, double-breasted, two vents (father's or grandfather's)

four buttons at cuff

old gold cartier watch

be-linked cuffs

in pocket: white handkerchief (used) loose change, bicyc clips, keys

straight cut, not too baggy <u>never</u> tight

black Oxfords made to measure (or father's)

dark, plain socks; only seen when biking to work

Rus in Urbe

Army Smarmy

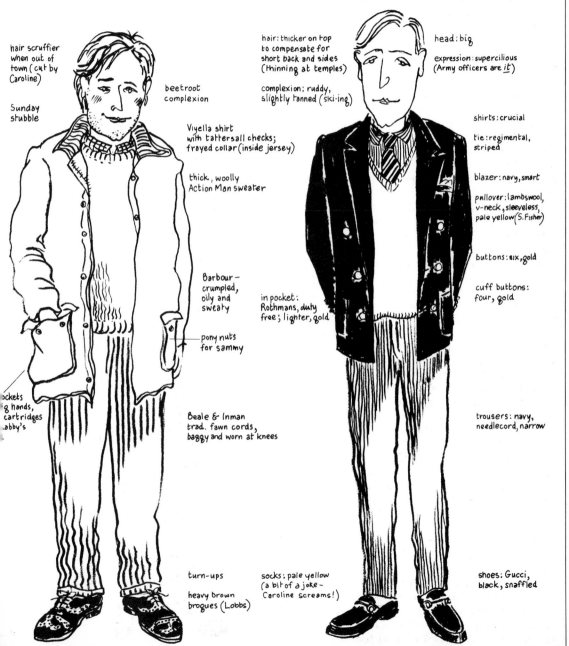

hair scruffier when out of town (cut by Caroline)

Sunday stubble

beetroot complexion

Viyella shirt with tattersall checks; frayed collar (inside jersey)

thick, woolly Action Man sweater

Barbour — crumpled, oily and sweaty

pony nuts for sammy

...ockets ...g hands, ...cartridges ...obby's

Beale & Inman trad. fawn cords, baggy and worn at knees

turn-ups

heavy brown brogues (Lobbs)

hair: thicker on top to compensate for short back and sides (thinning at temples)

complexion: ruddy, slightly tanned (ski-ing)

in pocket: Rothmans, duty free; lighter, gold

socks: pale yellow (a bit of a joke — Caroline screams!)

head: big

expression: supercilious (Army officers are *it*)

shirts: crucial

tie: regimental, striped

blazer: navy, smart

pullover: lambswool, v-neck, sleeveless, pale yellow (S. Fisher)

buttons: six, gold

cuff buttons: four, gold

trousers: navy, needlecord, narrow

shoes: Gucci, black, snaffled

collar. He's a little acorn from an old OK tree.

Membership. Something (*not* an OE tie, that one's too obvious) that signals belonging, eg crested signet ring or cufflinks.

Kit inspection
Suits and jackets

The right suits are dateless—except when you show the date label in the pocket which all proper tailors include—but they often hint at the archaic (eg the classic double-breasted pinstripe still says 'Anthony Eden, 1939'). The cut's never exaggerated though it's basically a bit baggy and easy. Suits should never look cardboard. Better be rumpled than Flash Harry. A buttonhole is essential (we're the morning-coat classes). And all but the most formal of a Sloane's suits (no vents) have two vents, for two reasons: he can put his hands in both pockets, and when he moves fast or dances, the skirts fly up, showing the silk lining (raspberry is a *bit* charlie, but it does look fine).

That great Sloane species the waistcoat is threatened—only one out of three suits has them now: warmer offices. A rough guide for a best suit is: double-breasted, no waistcoat. Single-breasted, waistcoat.

Key notes. There are a few basic lines that continue practically for ever, like the pre-war wraparound double-breasted and the basic City three-piece. The worst, *most charlie*, thing is bad imitations of these.

Younger Sloanes often go for something lower-profile, grey flannely, if they can't afford the real thing. Younger Sloanes are dressing that bit lower-profile in general, just keeping a few key things. These suits are eternal:

The dark blue pinstripe. The famous 'dark suit' or 'City suit'. Also the cocktail party suit. In wool worsted. The fabric *must* be right: the texture, distance between stripes. Anthony Eden was here.

The dark grey with chalk stripes. Same

uses but looks better than the blue in sunlight. Henry has it in worsted. Chalk-striped flannel is what Italians wear.

The low-profile grey worsted/flannel. Two vents. Single-breasted. What young Sloanes are wearing. Minimal cut, vaguely 'modern' but no fashiony details.

The summer suit. Summer suits are pretty much like winter ones in the Sloane wardrobe, just lighter fabrics.

The tweed suit. Ideally old (even the old man's). For church (with brown Oxfords), weekend midday drinks parties, Sunday lunch (perfect in London, if Henry needs to look pukka). Made of Donegal, Harris or other tightly woven hard tweed. Too new, too soft mock tweeds with ready-made leather patches look very charlie.

The tweed jacket. Army Sloanes call it a change coat. Etonians call it half change. Worn in all situations, particularly with jeans. Must be real tweed, seriously made by an English maker. Never in a fashion cut. One vent.

The blue and white striped seersucker jacket. Entirely inessential but looks charming on Sloanes in the summer (good things come in blue jackets, as Tom Kitten's mother believed).

The blazer. Watch it. A good (old) blazer can be wonderful if you're Free Foresters 'united though untied'/Leander/a general/over 50, etc., but a natty blazer with the wrong buttons can slip into caricature. Two vents.

The velvet smoking-jacket. Very popular with county SRM entertaining at home: plum faces atop plum velvet, bottled faces atop bottle-green velvet. Worn with embroidered slippers—see Shoes.

Trousers
Trousers should never be exaggerated. They shouldn't be sexy and they shouldn't be fashiony. No Sergeant Pepper look, no drainpipes. Nothing emphatic round the crotch. Not freshly pressed. A gentleman is not seen to pull his trouser-knees

oo adore the egg motif

when he sits down. Pleats are dubious except on old suits. Straight leg or, more traditionally, a slightly peg effect achieved by turn-ups on trousers that are fairly baggy at the knee. Plain side-pockets, of course. Turn-ups are usual, on formal trousers anyway: at a standard depth of about an inch. On formal trousers, six buttons for the Albert Thurston box-cloth braces. Little extra pockets are nice because they demonstrate tailoring; but never any contrast piping or tacky detail. And yes, worn a bit short—looks boyish and shows the Sloane ankles and socks.

1) Off-duty trousers

Needlecord jeans. Never fashion cut. Baggy at the seat. Straight legs. Fawn and navy are the basics but silly colours too, like dusty pink. Worn with Guccis or other black moccasins.

Proper (trad) cords. The Beale & Inman cut. Very plain correct cord in a rainbow range including the classics, plus maroon and olive. Worn with a Tattersall check shirt and—traditional dash—an Indian neckerchief (a bit pastiche Cambridge, this). The drawback is the horizontal pockets in front, hard to rest your fingers in nonchalantly. Sloanes are great fingers-in-pockets men.

Thick cords. A newer look. A bit après-ski.

Moleskin. For traditional country pursuits (like going to the pub).

2) More serious trousers

Cavalry twill (the real thing). A key uniform (mufti) look for older Sloanes.

Grey flannels. Sunday-best still when not wearing the tweed suit. Turn-ups optional. Cut as every other trouser.

3) Summer trousers

Pale khaki cotton bags. Shades of the Raj.

Jeans. Must be worn with Guccis.

Coats and outerwear

Your coat has to suggest a lot: that you've given up caricature things like the bowler, the umbrella and the hogskin gloves (all hibernating in the 1780 Cuban mahogany press), but that that's the class you belong to. So two or three symbolic styles are essential:

The City coat. Worn over the striped suit, and on all formal occasions. Usually navy blue or black, or very dark grey,

A meeting of Sloane coats: the Bullingdon point-to-point.

The covert coat.

single-breasted, good plain fabric. Velvet collar optional now (post-war Edwardiana). From Aquascutum, Simpson's, Harrods, or made by Henry's tailor.

The big tweed coat. Ancient country coat, preferably inherited from a grandfather, though a father will do. Alternatively, this type of coat can be bought second-hand (with no shame attached) via advertisements in the Country Landowners' Association magazine. Good worn over jeans as counterpoint.

The covert coat. Pronounced cover. Comes from covert (thicket) and is the old shooting/riding coat. A vital garment because *only Sloanes wear it*. Fine pre-aged-looking mud-coloured worsted, cut slim, with mole-coloured velvet collar (optional) and four rows of stitching at the bottom. Daughters like borrowing it.

The British Warm. Saturday wear for older Sloanes: the Army camel for post-war gents (available to civilians). To be worn with brown suede brothel creepers.

The sheepskin jacket. Part of a sports car. This or the British Warm for point-to-

points. Hugely practical but avoid the football manager look by wearing the right accessories (see Accessories) like the neckerchief and the Herbie J cap tipped forward.

The riding mac. Very Sloane with its pale stone colour, tabs, belt and dashing full skirt with the vents. But a bit bulky and rubbery if you don't actually ride.

The Burberry. The Sloane mac for the non-rider. Respectable, stone-coloured.

The Barbour. The country jacket for shooting, etc., though of course it does appear in London. The Barbour appeal is its green *oily* pre-synthetic look. Surprisingly expensive (they've got the Royal Warrant). Smells of dogs and has a couple of spent cartridges in pocket.

The Husky. Last and greatest. It's like wearing a Land-Rover. The Cotswold Mink. Green, with navy coming up fast. The Sloanest garment ever invented— but it was only invented in the early Sixties. Sloanes have spent the winter in its snug insulation ever since. Deserves its own box (which it gets—p 34).

Shirts

Shirts are crucial, particularly the collar. The Jermyn Street *shirtmaker* collar is instantly identifiable. It's never giraffe or tiny (half an inch change in a decade is a revolution). Look for the tightly woven proper poplin texture, the slight *concave* curve to the collar-bone (cardboard shirts go convex easily because of the cheap stiffening), the fine stitching inset precisely $\frac{3}{8}$ of an inch from the collar edge. The New & Lingwood/Harvie & Hudson/ etc. shirts all have *the* look. These collars need ironing. Hard-core Sloanes often let a good shirt like this get frayed at the collar.

The key shape is unshaped (body-hugging jobs with darts are strictly for John Travolta) with a long tail (for when you send them back to be given new collars and cuffs).

1) Town shirts

The key pattern is striped—particularly the simple Bengal or ladder varieties (end on end: meaning the stripes are woven in, not printed)—in dark red, dark or mid blue or grey, all on white. Research shows that 80 per cent of Sloanes wear one of these crucial striped poplin shirts 60 per cent of the time. Figurative—or abstract —patterns are not trusted in Sloaneshire—sailing ships, Art Deco derived motifs or things of the kind.

The alternative everyday material is Oxford—a softer thicker flannely cotton with the same stripes—and the alternative pattern is plain. Key colours are white, classic light blue (for the Can't Fail blue shirt/dark red tie combo, see Accessories), dusty pink. The light blue cloth once issued to policemen and certain other Service personnel is also particularly reassuring.

Some Sloanes have their initials embroidered on their shirts, low on the left breast, where it is normally hidden by a jacket. This is *not* so the laundry won't lose them. But it's a bit charlie unless you have a coronet to put above your initials, or very distinguished initials.

2) Country shirts

For the actual country and rus in urbe, Tattersall checks are *the* design, and Viyella is a fairly crucial fabric. You can buy Tattersalls at shirtmaker prices *or* at Marks & Spencer.

For total off-duty, those loudly horizontal cotton jersey short-sleeved numbers from Jermyn Street are worn by older Sloanes, and the Lacoste sports shirt is OK in white or navy. But it's not crucial like in America.

3) Evening shirts

Evening shirts are a danger point—a Sloane girl will start making plans to scrap a man who destroys her reputation by appearing in a pale blue polyester georgette Engelbert Humperdinck dress shirt with a row of thick frills piped in dark blue. The correct dress shirt is either the waffle piqué kind in thick textured white cotton, or narrow flat pin-tucks or box pleats in plain cotton or silk. Always white or natural tussore colour, and (old) studs.

4) Hong Kong silk shirts

Sloanes love having their shirts (or suits, or jackets) copied by Sam on a business trip to Hong Kong. Two days, and so much cheaper.

Shoes

Sloanes can become hard of hearing if you're wearing the wrong shoes. How can one really understand a person wearing the wrong shoes? Whereas others take mental note of ties or lapels, Sloanes look first at shoes. There they read the bottom line. Shoes are crucial. Hard-up Sloanes will give up several meals for decent shoes. This is because they are instinctively aware that in the days of knights and peasants, only knights wore them.

After the Industrial Revolution, there were boots and shoes, and Sloanes wore the shoes. Henry treasures his father's hunting-boot jack and his great-grandmother's shoehorn and buttonhook. His father distrusted suede shoes ('for cads') but they've crept into Sloanedom now, though Prince Philip still doesn't like them. But Henry would never, ever wear high heels or fashion shoes. Anyone who does is a giant step away from Sloanedom.

There are four golden rules for shoes in the Known World:
—all leather
—black, brown or white
—highly polished (Sloanes don't go in for the natural look and they don't begrudge the polish that is wasted in the holes in their brogues)
—preferably old.

The ideal is a classic from Lobb circa 1965 resoled and patinated over the wrinkles. Sloanes just know you don't wear synthetic-soled formal shoes, patent in the daytime, interesting free-form designs on the welt, or innovative laces... they're against nature.

Henry has a pair of:

Oxfords. One black pair, one brown. Ideally made to order, but Church's and Alan McAfee are standbys. (Not 'jazz' oxfords—cream or grey or two-tone or mid-Seventies disco or Gatsby. Plain ones).

Brogues. Must be right. Ideal is the Lobb pattern. Black and brown again.

Guccis. Eternal because perfect. How clever of Mr. Gucci to provide decorated shoes for gentlemen. The ones with the red and green stripe look regimental, and they all look equine because of the snaffle. Henry would also accept reasonable look-alikes from Russell & Bromley. (Low-profile Sloanes wear black moccasins with some discreet metal across the instep.)

Wildsmith loafers. Black, narrow-cut, low vamp which shows a lot of sock. Some other makers do the same pattern.

Tasselled loafers. Black. (A bit poncy?)

Brown suede shoes or chukka boots (optional). Hard soles preferred by Sloanes—they distrust soft soles: 'treacly'.

Hunter wellies. Green. London Sloanes sprout green wellies in wet weather like a plague of frogs.

Tennis shoes. Green Flash, or Gucci if he's lucky, but probably battered old mongrel.

Moonboots. Skiing symbolism.

Walking boots for Scotland. Ideal for the moors. Studded, firm around the ankles, almost bog-proof.

Evening shoes (optional). Patent leather

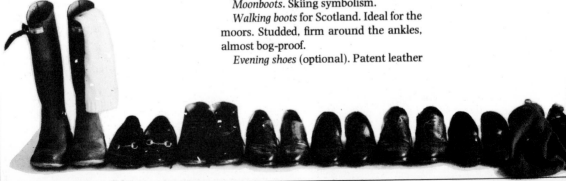

HENRY AND HIS STICK

The rod-and-staff classes

The polished wooden walking-stick, often with ivory trim or silver band, survives in Henry's country life as a symbol of Sloanehood. It is a descendant of the sword, staff, crozier—it is an authority symbol. Henry used to carry a rolled umbrella even when it wasn't raining, and his father had an ebony silver-topped evening cane like Fred Astaire. Cavalry Sloanes must carry a rolled umbrella at the Cavalry Memorial Parade (below). At Eton, only boys in Pop (ie important) may roll their umbrellas, so they all walk about with tightly furled umbrellas all the time.

Watch Henry with his stick—how he likes to lightly change his grip on it, tap the ground as he walks along, point things out with it, slash at a weed. You can see it's a sword. Every Sloane home has an umbrella stand near the front door bristling with sticks, emblems of the knightly class.

pumps with the grosgrain bow are archaic but nice with a dinner-jacket. Patent lace-ups nice too but you can always get away with Guccis.

Velvet slippers with your initials or a motif in gold for dinner parties at home. Black, green, burgundy, navy. Hunting Henry is eligible for slippers with gilt fox (stag thought to be charlie). Married Sloanes are distinguishable by needlepoint slippers which Caroline took years to make: his initials interwoven, his crest; canvas painted for her by the Women's Home Industries tapestries shop in Pimlico Road.

Jerseys

Sloanes need lots of these because they live in cold houses:

The guernsey. Key to the SRM uniform. Rupert is given one on his first birthday. From Guernseys Galore. The navy blue standard.

The Action Man sweater. The Army standard. Olive green—or navy—with cotton patches on shoulders and elbows. Going out—so many at Milletts.

The lambswool V-neck pullover. A waistcoat substitute. In navy, maroon, pale yellow. Can be worn to work.

The Henry Higgins cardigan. This fine-knit V-neck cardigan with two pockets may come from Harrods but it is more likely to be from Marks & Spencer. Henry wears it at home in the evening; or a chunkier knit with leather buttons. When the elbows wear out Caroline darns or patches them. She eventually mounts a campaign against That Cardigan.

Aran and Norwegian jerseys. Much used but rarely washed. They saved Henry in his cold bachelor pad. Still his friends for skiing and sailing.

Shetland and Fair Isle jerseys. Henry wore them as a child of course, but they're suspect now all the foreigners and art directors are in them. (Henry does not aim to look like a northern boy in a Hovis advert.)

The polo-neck. Black, navy, red. From Beale & Inman or other classic source.

Dressing-gown and slippers

Henry is princely in his paisley silk foulard dressing-gown (when he's not wearing his ugly old school camel), but he has to wear cut-away leather backless slippers in which no foot can look good, unless he's an Eton slipper man—coloured corduroy and leather from Gane's. Underneath, schoolboy striped pyjamas.

Socks

Extremely conservative, plain (almost all patterned socks are deeply charlie); finely ribbed wool, length 'long'. Dark grey, dark blue, maroon, dark green. Yellow is daring.

Shooting stockings (socks) are Henry's only chance to be a peacock: they may be mustard or indeed peacock, or any shade of heathery bluey-greeny-purple, as long as they look hand-knitted. From Almost Unwearoutable Socks, Scottish Merchant; or Scotland.

Sports wear

Correct. Sloanes would never defy the great god Sport by wearing other than white for tennis and cricket in public. Henry observes all the myriad rules of dress for riding-and-watching-horses and is surprisingly keen on looking smart on the hunting field. The only sports he wears the wrong clothes for are skiing and climbing *outside his own country*. Epater les woggies. Young skier Sloanes enjoy getting together with other Sloanes to all appear on the hill one day in kilts, or something else unsuitable, and Sloanes like walking blithely up mountains in light shoes, past booted and bepacked pros.

Shooting/stalking/fishing clothes

There's the tweed suit with knicker-bockers which was made for Henry when he was seventeen and he has worn it ever since (though of course he was shooting at fourteen). Otherwise he can call on

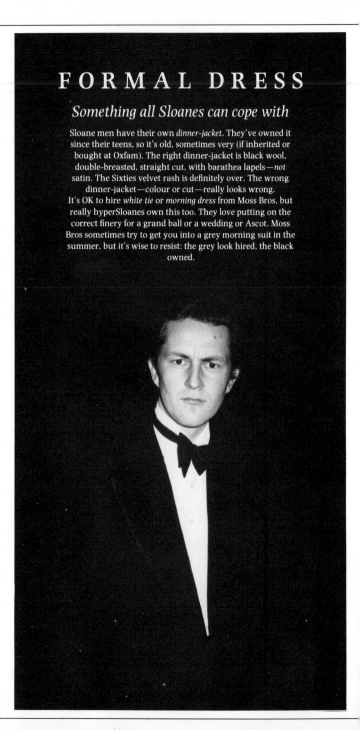

FORMAL DRESS

Something all Sloanes can cope with

Sloane men have their own *dinner-jacket*. They've owned it since their teens, so it's old, sometimes very (if inherited or bought at Oxfam). The right dinner-jacket is black wool, double-breasted, straight cut, with barathea lapels—*not* satin. The Sixties velvet rash is definitely over. The wrong dinner-jacket—colour or cut—really looks wrong.
It's OK to hire *white tie* or *morning dress* from Moss Bros, but really hyperSloanes own this too. They love putting on the correct finery for a grand ball or a wedding or Ascot. Moss Bros sometimes try to get you into a grey morning suit in the summer, but it's wise to resist: the grey look hired, the black owned.

that compost heap of brown and green sporting tweeds which has been in the family for years and which hangs in the downstairs cloakroom at home (ie the house where he was brought up) with assorted fishing bags, rods, binoculars, cartridge bags, deerstalkers and flat caps, all decomposing very slowly but pongily.

Accessories

The principle of Sloane Ranger male accessories is military/historical/symbolic since all these articles stand in on mufti (ie civilian clothes) for the glamorous medals, tassels, epaulettes and bits and bobs that a true warrior gent wears. *But* lots of new gold, bracelets for men, gold coins on necklaces, and other types of Arab prince, Latin lover or Cockney millionaire jewellery is utterly unSloane. Too sexy for a start. Too 'me'. Proper Sloane

accessories are 'we' stuff. Inherited, given, made for you—not just bought. Proper decorations are pinned on you, like medals:

1) *The crucial cuff-links (are there any others?)*
   (i) Gold, thin, oval, usually *double*. Engraved with complete set of initials. *Not* swivel-backed.
   (ii) If you're richer (then they *must* be old) as (i), but can be set with discreet semi-precious stones/ seed pearls or good enamel (ideally dark blue with gold— could be regimental).

2) *The crucial ring.* Plain gold, crested. Good for identifying decomposed Sloane corpses.

3) *Principles of tie choice.* Basic Sloane taste is for 'foulard' or simple little patterns—small animals, spots, pais-

leys on thin woven silk. They are usually predominently red or maroon. Ties should avoid overbearing textures—not silk half-an-inch thick. Brilliant colours are OK sometimes. The odd batik on a Harvie & Hudson shirt can be fun. Swirling paisleys are slightly Oxbridge. Ranger ties tended to be on the thin side when others were fat, but now that thin is New Wave, they are medium ($2\frac{1}{2}$–3 inches wide).

'Striped rep' à l'américain is OK too. School and regimental ties are more of an issue—What school? When? *Really?* The OE tie is even in novels it is such an issue. Go easy on it. A Sloane never wears polyester and is unkeen on wool ties (arty, Michael Foot-ish), except when shooting.

4) *The regulation belt*. This has a *plain* buckle of its *own size*. Large/expressive buckles are dangerous. Crocodile is difficult unless it's the old brown kind. Lizard is more discreet and black calf is safest of all. Brown cowhide is OK with country clothes.

The striped elastic schoolboy belt with the S buckle (Harrods boys' department) is cheap and irreproach-

able. So is the army webbing belt.

5) *Braces are now only worn by Rangers and old men in Scarborough.*

Q. When is a man most like a horse?

A. When he's in harness with red braces.

Harness-like red braces are *the* ones, with proper leather button loops. This kind also come in other clear, bright colours and tartans and such.

6) *The crucial scarves*. These include the blue or maroon polka-dot silk square, the red paisley square (worn like a stock—but be careful, they can look actorish), the double-sided spotted silk and cashmere long scarf (for wearing with covert coats), and the plain cashmere longer scarf. No mile-long knitting, no 'college' scarves.

7) *OK watches*. The ideal watch is old, plain and gold, passed on. A Cartier would *have* to be old, and Rolex is very City New. Battered boys' watches are acceptable if not too pop-y. Lucky Rangers produce gold hunters or half-hunters from their pockets.

8) *Spectacles*. These should not be a feature of a person's appearance. They should be old-fashioned and unexaggerated.

9) *Handkerchiefs are necessary*. Dark red or paisley silk are 'pushed in and puffed out' of the chest pocket to look dégagé. Never folded, or pleated white numbers.

10) *The crucial hats*. The Newmarket cap says horses all over. The brown trilby says 'He's in the running'. Bowlers are now out for most events.

11) *Umbrella*. Only one kind keeps off the rain. The full-size old-fashioned black one with the plain brier handle topped with a gold ring (traditionally from Swaine, Adeney & Brigg).

12) *The case*. Battered brown leather boxes with simple locks and not too much brass. Avoid trendy aluminium things that look as if they've an electric typewriter inside.

Henry's sources

Tailors

ANDERSON & SHEPPARD, 30 Savile Row,
London W1 (734 1420)
BENSON, PERRY & WHITLEY, 5 Cork Street, W1
(734 3113)
BILLINGS & EDMONDS, 22 Princes Street, W1
(629 1266) (the schoolboy tailors: some
Henrys have been going to them for 25
years)
TOM BROWN, 24 Princes Street, W1
(629 5025)—also Eton
DENMAN & GODDARD, 31 Sackville Street, W1
(734 6371)
HAWES & CURTIS, 2 Burlington Gardens, W1
(493 2200)
HUNTSMAN, 11 Savile Row, W1 (734 7441)
(£800 a suit—beyond most Sloanes)
JOHNS & PEGG, 4 Clifford Street, W1
(734 1713) (The Prince of Wales's tailor)
KILGOUR, FRENCH & STANBURY, 33a Dover
Street, W1 (629 4283)
HENRY POOLE, 15 Savile Row, W1
(734 5985)

ROGERS JOHN JONES, 16 Clifford Street, W1
(734 2248)
WARD & KRUGER, 6 Sackville Street, W1
(734 4358)
WELSH & JEFFERIES, 35 Savile Row, W1
(734 3062)—also Eton (Mr Boddy)
HALL BROS, 119 High Street, Oxford
(Oxford 42756)
Occasionally, Henry buys a suit off-the-peg,
from Harrods, Simpson's, Aquascutum,
Jaeger—or Marks & Spencer.

Shops and department stores

AQUASCUTUM, 100 Regent Street, London W1
(734 6090)
HARRODS, Knightsbridge, SW1 (730 1234)

JAEGER (main branch), 204 Regent Street, W1
(734 4050)
MARKS & SPENCER (main branch), 458 Oxford
Street, W1 (486 6151)
MOSS BROS, Bedford Street, WC2 (240 4567)
SIMPSON, 203 Piccadilly, W1 (734 2002)

Shirts, ties, socks, jerseys

ALMOST UNWEAROUTABLE SOCKS, Piper Close,
Corbridge, Northumberland
(Corbridge 2283)
BEALE & INMAN, 131 New Bond Street,
London W1 (629 4723)
BURLINGTON ARCADE, Piccadilly, W1:
especially S. Fisher (cashmeres)
COLE'S, 131 Sloane Street, SW1 (730 7564)
EAGLE SHIRT CO, Sutherland Works,
St Andrews Road, E17 (527 8376)
(Some Sloanes have discovered that this
firm makes the shirts for many more
expensive labels)
GUERNSEYS GALORE, 49 Moreton Street, SW1
(834 6141)
HARVIE & HUDSON, 77 Jermyn Street, SW1
(930 3949)

HAWES & CURTIS, 2 Burlington Gardens, W1
(493 2200)
T. M. LEWIN & SONS, 106 Jermyn Street, SW1
(930 4291) (ties)
NEW & LINGWOOD, 53 Jermyn Street, SW1
(493 9621)—also Eton and Cambridge
THE SCOTTISH MERCHANT, 16 New Row, WC2
(836 2207)
TURNBULL & ASSER, 71 Jermyn Street, SW1
(930 0502)

Huskys

Selected stockists. Information from:
HUSKY OF TOSTOCK, 115 Bury Street,
Stowmarket, Suffolk (Stowmarket 4471)

> outergarments
> should be seen
> and not
> heard

> Surely you
> mean scene
> and not
> herd?

Barbour jackets

C. FARLOW, Pall Mall, SW1 (839 2423)
Otherwise, write for further stockists to:
J. BARBOUR & SONS, Dept CL, Simondside,
South Shields, Tyne & Wear NE34 9PD

Shoes

BALLY, 116 New Bond Street, London W1
(629 6501)
CHURCH & CO, 163 New Bond Street, W1
(629 3371) and other London branches
LOBB'S, 9 St James's Street, SW1 (930 3664)
MAXWELL'S, 11 Savile Row, W1 (734 9714)
NEW & LINGWOOD (they incorporate Poulsen
Skone), 53 Jermyn Street, SW1 (493 9621)
RUSSELL & BROMLEY, 24 New Bond Street,
W1 (629 6903)
TRICKER'S, 67 Jermyn Street, SW1
(930 6395)
WILDSMITH & CO, 41 Duke Street, St James's,
SW1 (930 1623)
J. GANE's (owned by New & Lingwood),
125 High Street, Eton, Windsor, Berks
(Windsor 66284) and Oxford

Hats

HERBERT JOHNSON, 13 Old Burlington Street,
London, W1 (439 7397)
LOCK's, 6 St James's Street, SW1 (930 5849)

Accessories

SWAINE, ADENEY, BRIGG & SONS, 185
Piccadilly, London, W1 (734 4277)

For what Henry wears between 18 and 23, see
Oxford, page 96.

The Sloane Ranger Reads Again

Small words in large print

Sloanes are great and enthusiastic *social readers*. Social reading is the kind that matters: invitations. At parties, Sloanes hover around the mantelpiece or the Bechstein until they have taken in all the embossed siren calls to grand names At Home and Bond Street private views and wonderful weddings.

When you've read the stiffies, you go back to the books you are permanently in the middle of: *Who's Who* (parental 1975 edition—the Family Entry died in 1976 —or the office copy); *Debrett's Peerage*, *Burke's Peerage* (whenever you can; they are so expensive and they weigh *a ton*).

The addiction of Sloane Rangers to *Debrett's* amazes anyone not hooked. One Sloane girl staying in the country broke the glass of her host's bookcase to get at it. And when Mrs Kenward of *Jennifer's Diary* said on *Desert Island Discs* that it was *the* book she wanted to be marooned with, a number of Radio 4 listeners—the dominant Sloane contingent—felt their ears burn with amused recognition.

Newspapers

With the exception of the *Mail* and a scan of Henry's *Times* or *Telegraph*, Caroline doesn't go a bundle on newspapers. She has to read the Personal column, and hatched, matched, dispatched in *The Times* and the *Telegraph* so that she can fire off a request for a countrywear catalogue or congratulations to Simon on securing *such* a sweet girl. But Caroline does adore her *Daily Mail*—especially Nigel Dempster. She says he's appalling. He's caused friends *untold misery*. She always reads him.

Current affairs are given short shrift, unless there is a royal birth/engagement/marriage/death/scandal; 1981 was a vintage year. The racing page may be studied —homework for Ascot and Goodwood, or for punting. You have to have 'a bob each way'.

London Sloane girls buy the *Standard*—

skim through Londoner's Diary; glance at the spot-on TV listing and sigh for the return of Sebastian Flyte/Lady Astor/Edward VIII—'there's *nothing* on'; a read of Patric Walker's predictions. You are keen on horoscopes despite a lack of imagination and the fact that the zodiac is American. But your favourite Stars are by Celeste in *Harpers & Queen*: 'It's *frightening* how true they are.'

Glossy magazines

Sloanes love the glossies of course, because they're solid temptation: the social glamour and gossip of *Harpers & Queen* and the *Tatler*. You like the expensive shiny paper and the subtle smell. You believe every word about health and hem heights. But mostly you see them as picture-books assuring you that all is well, the Wicked Witch won't win, the world is safe for Sloanes.

Since your parents live somewhere like Sussex, you buy the occasional *Country Life* and *House & Garden*. The downstairs loo in the country is lined with the *Field* and *Horse & Hound*.

Sloanes are so keen on glossy magazines that they support two Is-It-A-Book-Or-Is-It-A-Magazine categories: the Smart Catalogue and the Coffee Table Book. ,

The smart catalogue

Sotheby's and Christie's catalogues make a natural addition to the Sloane home, together with the annual yellow *Gardens Open to the Public in England and Wales* and *Historic Houses, Castles and Gardens*. Recently, other parts of Sloanedom—such as Harrods, Liberty's and Laura Ashley —have joined Habitat in realising that Sloanes will pay a pound or so for a catalogue that looks like a magazine. You love news of your favourites and don't notice the salesmanship in the velvet glove.

Private Eye

Richard Ingrams is a Sloane hero. His mag exactly expresses Henry's views. It

has Henry's puerile sense of humour, suspicion of the arts, wariness towards anyone called Geoff or Dave, hatred of pseuds, dislike of suede shoes, love of insider gossip about the City. It's the Sloane school magazine.

Books

Reading needs concentration. It also helps to sit still. Sloanes haven't mastered either. You like books in short sections or broken up by pictures—easy to stop and restart between outings. If a book is solid text it has to be fascinating enough to pin you down. 'I was *riveted*.' Both Henry and Caroline can be suitably riveted by the following Sloane books:

THE COFFEE-TABLE BOOK. The hard-cover version of a glossy magazine.

THE HISTORICAL ROMANCE. Caroline loves period pastiche—her own view of the past played back: Georgette Heyer (re-reading: she's read them all), Jean Plaidy (becoming rather passé), M. M. Kaye and the jolly super romances of Jilly Cooper. A fierily independent heroine, restrained by the strong forearms of a dashing dark hero, literally *transports* Caroline, stuck on a No 14 bus in Piccadilly.

THE BLOCKBUSTER. Sloane men like *full-blooded* books: Harold Robbins, Jeffrey Archer, Alistair Maclean, (the late) Nicholas Monsarrat and Neville Shute. Henry gets every Frederick Forsyth,

Wilbur Smith and Dick Francis as it comes out. He is stuck on *spyland*. Le Carré, Forsyth, Deighton all suggest that Sloaneshire has secret international depth and connections. And books about the Green Berets, Red Berets and black bala-clavas (SAS) suggest it has muscle.

THE CLASSIC. Sloanes have read the *short* classics—*Animal Farm, Brave New World, Brighton Rock*—in the Breakaway Period. Also Tolkien and Gerald Durrell. H. G. Wells's science fiction still finds a Sloane readership. Those enjoying a late-night wallow in the bath widen their literary horizons with one ear tuned to A Book at Bedtime.

Anyone who has read Proust is not a Sloane Ranger.

KNOWN WORLD BOOKS. Sloanes read books about Sloane milieux: the racing thrillers of Dick Francis, James Herriot's vet experiences, Richard Adams's *Watership Down*—they're not interested in the allegory but it *is* set in Berkshire. Nancy Mitford's books are essential to SRs even if never read; Evelyn Waugh is another key author.

THE SEXY BOOK. The Sloane mind is often a dirty one. You search *Lady Chatterley's Lover* and Xaviera Hollander's *Happy Hooker* for exciting bits. Illustrated manuals like *The Joy of Sex* cause Caroline and her friends many girlish giggles (alas: 'Caroline works hard but lacks aptitude').

The Right Lines

Sloane communications

For people who don't read much, Sloanes write like maniacs. They all scrawl exactly the same things in identical handwriting—but they see it as an expression of uniqueness. They have My Pen, My Paper and My Desk. If you are a true Sloane you:

1) kept a diary in your youth;
2) still write to the friends of your youth (Jonty, Mary-Anne, Harry, Catkin);
3) support the Christmas card trade (but not the Mother's Day trade);
4) thank for dinner parties and weekends the day after (spreading the bread-and-butter with a trowel).

The Richardson Method

All this putting Pentel to paper begins at about the age of eight, when Caroline is set to the copy books of Marion Richardson. Between the lines of MR writing there are blank lines; soon the alternating SR script becomes indistinguishable and unmistakable—simple, rounded and 25 words to a page.

...and the value of EMPHASIS

These words are liberally dashed— and dotted with CAPITAL LETTERS and underlinings, finished with a flourish of double exclamation marks—sometimes treble!!! It is a curious fact that as letter writers Sloane Rangers have more in common with Queen Victoria than with the twentieth century:

Henry's writing is smaller but also distinctive:

Desk ants

Sloane desks are old, undersized and full of things that Sloanes like to close the lid

---

DESKY MAIDEN

Caroline loves additions to her desk (with its inner secret of letters from her three attachments, starting with Susannah at fifteen). She has lots of little joke accessories—a sharpener like a Coca-Cola can, a rubber like a piece of chocolate, a bill-holder like a clothes-peg, a biro like a banana—as well as feminine bits such as many coloured drawing pins and marbleised paper sets with matching files from Nina Campbell. She likes giving desky presents and can spend happy hours in London choosing them at:

NINA CAMPBELL, 48 Walton Street, SW3 (584 9401)
PAPERCHASE, 167 Fulham Road, SW3 (589 7873)
PARROTS (bits and pieces, no paper), 56 Fulham Road, SW3 (584 5699)
SCRIBBLER, 170 King's Road, SW3 (351 1173)
WALTON STREET STATIONERY COMPANY, 97 Walton Street, SW3 (589 0777)

on: dog combs, children's clay sculpture, seed catalogues, Spanish postcards. A Sloane home contains Daddy's Desk and Mummie's Desk. These are not working desks. They are desks of character and show the Sloane view of work. Mummie goes to her desk most days, at 9, 12 or 2, depending on bondage for the children. She pays her bills the day they arrive, and often twice. (The shop, used to procrastinators, sends a reminder automatically. Caroline says 'I'm sure I paid this...' but fires off another cheque.)

Daddy goes to his desk in gardening clothes on Saturday, swearing and muttering about how these bills are RUINING him. They both write to the children at school, who are writing them the junior version of stiff-upper-lip-plus-sports news.

Engraved on the Sloane heart

On to the Sloane brush mat fall stiffies announcing that a hostess will be At Home or Requests the Pleasure of Your Company. The wording is exactly as in the nineteenth century. This is crucial. No one but a duke dare deviate.

But there is still an area of doubt. You apply Sloane Braille, feeling for the bumps of engraving. A true Sloane card always has them. (To detect the cheaper bumps of the modern process, thermography, scratch it with your nail. Thermography is brittle.)

After the card is vetted and answered in the third person—also in nineteenth century idiom—it is displayed as a trophy on the drawing-room mantelpiece. A litter of invitations two months old is not desirable—but it is acceptable. A mantelpiece *needs* at least three white cards engraved in black script, or it is underdressed.

Paper tiger

Sheet for sheet, Sloane paper gobbles up more trees than other people's paper. It looks as if it had been made by the estate printer, using nineteenth-century type.

There are four Sloane places to buy your engraved paper and imitation paper in London: Harrods, Knightsbridge, SW1; Smythson, 54 New Bond Street, W1; and Truslove & Hanson, 205 Sloane Street, SW1. There is also the Granary Press, at Pluckley in Kent, and because it is owned by a Sloane who doesn't engrave, Kent is the one county where flat invitations will do.

Before 25, you might write on flowers or pastel colours, but after that you come into the straight. (Lady Diana Spencer went Smythson-sensible before 20.) Caroline goes in for bordered paper, say blue with a navy edge (Smythson's most popular is cream with brown), while Henry likes plain blue or white. Truslove & Hanson find that the paper of theirs which is most popular with Sloanes is, conveniently enough, called Sloane. Knightsbridge comes second. In the die-stamping of the address, A77 to 80, the very first samples in the T & H book, are the ones Sloanes inevitably choose.

Sloane marrieds have a postcard each (always called a pc). Henry's is headed (all in one line):

> Mr Henry Bloggs,
> The Old Vicarage,
> Blogton, Berkshire

and Caroline's is headed:

> Mrs Henry Bloggs,
> The Old Vicarage,
> Blogton, Berkshire

Their *real* postal address is The Old Vicarage, Tiggleton Road, Blogton, Hungerford, Berkshire RG17 0TL, but 25 per cent of Sloanes will not use the post code and country Sloanes hate to admit they live on a road. As a result, some letters never reach them.

When the Post Office achieves 100 per cent mechanical sorting, the Sloane stationers will be busy. In a battle between conformity and romance, conformity, sadly, wins.

THE
SLOANE
IN EMBRYO

Christening and beyond

Older Sloanes know God better than they know the Queen. He is their friend. They often talk to or about him, jocularly. 'Listen, God, if you don't send some rain, the flower show will be a wash-out'. 'I let God heat the swimming pool—but I help him with my solar blanket.' One would never talk about true feelings—excessive piety is rather squirmy—any more than you would about your love for your human friends. Caroline knows God even better than Henry does.

To the Sloane, *religion* is separate from God. The former is best left to the experts, who sometimes make life rather uncomfortable and don't do what they're asked. They can refuse to celebrate your second marriage in church, for example. However, God understands your renewed faith in permanence, even if the vicar doesn't.

The Christening: one's first public appearance

The sprog is introduced to God and Mammon at about six weeks, or when the baby fits the family christening robe. Sloppy types don't much mind at what age their children are christened, and sometimes even leave christening until just before confirmation. But usually Sloanes want their child to start off right, with the godparents contracted into their job and with the collection of valuables, from silver mug to Treasury bond, that distinguishes a Sloane from an unprivileged child. The self-respecting Sloane baby expects to be 'born with a silver spoon in his mouth'—in other words, with a dowryette.

Bedecked in family robes and two hats (one lace and one net), the flannel-petticoated Sloaneling screams lustily throughout. Fearful of offending, the first-time parents have over-invited and feel like the royal family in that film about them—if only someone would provide amusement.

Tea (or drinks: christenings are getting

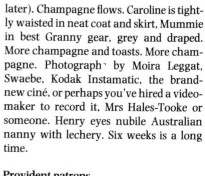

later). Champagne flows. Caroline is tightly waisted in neat coat and skirt, Mummie in best Granny gear, grey and draped. More champagne and toasts. More champagne. Photograph˙ by Moira Leggat, Swaebe, Kodak Instamatic, the brand-new ciné, or perhaps you've hired a video-maker to record it, Mrs Hales-Tooke or someone. Henry eyes nubile Australian nanny with lechery. Six weeks is a long time.

Provident patrons

Poor priest—he's at a semi-pagan ceremony today. The most important people in the church were not his Trinity, but the godparents. Three or five. The Sloanes have worried and worried about who to appoint. Their good hearts said 'Our dear old chums', their ingrained beliefs 'Put the child under the protection of a powerful patron'. The choice reflects the dichotomy. One or two of the godparents will obviously have been chosen not for their spirituality, nor indeed for their conformity with the family denomination, but for their future usefulness ('two rich and one honest'). Some ambitious Sloanes go up to six godparents, but this does dilute the sense of obligation. Godfathers are chosen for boys with a wide spread—as they say of unit trusts; for one never knows how young Henry will grow up. A grouse moor vested in one, partnerships in the City in another, would be very useful contacts for him. A discreet homosexual is another good choice; he will not have the competitive patter of filial feet towards his cheque-book. Peeresses and society hostesses are popular as patrons for girls, with an elderly spinster added for good measure. Most of these have no illusion about the kind invitation and limit their godchildren to twelve. It is never too early to join the Old Boy Net, and any managing director knows the sentence beginning, 'A godson of mine is about to leave school/come down from university, and . . .'

So who is that pleasant, unsmartly dressed, fresh-faced man or woman who is standing with the godparents? The one who seems to know the words of the prayers? It is the Good Godparent, the Old School Chum, chosen by the nice side of Caroline and Henry (the side that will prevent them ever rising to the top of the heap). If the Rich godparents represent secular success and the promise of future rewards on investment, the Good Godparent is the spiritual insurance policy in case of default.

But the very brief appearance of God at the christening isn't so strange. Sloanes

Sloanehood confirmed

After being enrolled in Your Religion, the next formal ceremony is around fifteen. Then Sloane children join a confirmation class and after a few weeks' tutoring are ready to make their own vows in the school chapel or local cathedral. Confirmation has great tribal significance and is certainly less painful than some of the initiations imposed on African and American Indian children.

The Good Godparent has sent 30 presents since the christening. One of the grand godparents has sent fifteen cheques, but the other has ignored your

Wise Men Bearing Gifts

The dowryette

Silver christening mug still de rigueur, four initials and date—girls hide them around 27. Silver napkin rings (check for hallmarks). Pencils, always initialled and sometimes gold. Ivory hairbrushes are almost over for 'the little man' (he's almost killed off the elephant). For boys, flasks (Mappin & Webb), pewter beer mugs, and 1975 port (a case, not a pipe nowadays). For girls, pearls would be wonderful (Collingwood or Cartier) but they don't always materialise, so they get teeny silver thimbles. Premium bonds and building society accounts for both sexes.

The pube dowry

A tape recorder. A gold watch. For boys, a shotgun (not a Purdey—now £9,500, 30 months' wait—something from John Rigby & Co or J. Roberts & Son for £350 upwards or a Spanish AYA). For girls, sundry pieces of antique jewellery or some modern earrings from Butler & Wilson. From the spinster, Robert Bridge's *The Spirit of Man* or Lord Wavell's anthology *Other Men's Flowers*. The Good Godparent gives a Bible, as well as something secular: a Waterman pen, a good wallet, the *Dictionary of National Biography*, the *Oxford Dictionary of Quotations*, a print or two.

are versed in Andersen and Grimm (so cruel and grim) and the much nicer English collections, Andrew Lang's twelve coloured Fairy Books, and the best of the lot, *English Fairy Tales*. So the christening *means* tokens and portents. It's one reason you never enthuse about your offspring's beauty or brains: young Henry 'looks like a boxer puppy' and baby Caroline's 'nice but a bit post-like in the brains department'. You want to ward off the envious attentions of the Bad Fairy.

Thus in every Sloane's life, the kind intervention of a richer older female Sloane is almost expected. When you are most in need of a new coat or a deposit for the house, hey presto! enter 'My fairy godmother'.

existence. Your parents have this one more chance to make the point. You receive the Holy Spirit, yes, but you also receive the Sloane child's second beneficence, the pube dowry: some of the expensive necessities with which to start grown-up Sloane life.

A Sloane by any other name

Acceptable girls' names include Emma, Lucinda, Sarah, Diana—and almost any name ending in 'a' except Tanya. Feminine derivatives of Henry, George or Charles: Henrietta, Harriet, Georgina, Charlotte, Caroline. Jolly-hockeysticks names: Jennifer, Jill, Judy (Gillian, Judith). Jane, plain or in combination (Sarah Jane, Eliza Jane). Mary and Anne are not very Sloane, more old dull aristocracy—Sloanes like some style and dash. Scottish names: Kirstie, Catriona, Fiona.

Boy Sloanes are called Henry, Charles, Mark, Peter, Simon, Christopher, Richard, William—what they call 'plain English names' (actually, Norman Conquistador names). Scottish Sloanes are called plain Scottish names: Andrew, Alistair, James, Alexander, Robert, Archie. Rupert came top in 1977, but Charles is the all-time favourite. Timothy and Jonathan are liked (John's a bit dull).

Sloanes don't go in for James Charles Sloane II, but they do usually have a 'family name' among their three. This can be that of a rich great-aunt or uncle, and do the same work for the child that making them a godparent would ('To my namesake . . .').

British Sloanes do not go in for nicknames with the fervour of their American cousins. They are usually nursery: Billie, Catkin; or prep-school surname nicknames: Smitty, Dodders, Tolly, Cobblers. Girls do *not* spell their nicknames to end in 'i'. In the garden of live flowers, Daisy, Flora and Pansy are Sloane, Lily and Heather are very unSloane. ('They christened her Marigold and hoped she would.')

Names Sloanes are not called

Sloane Rangers have not yet reached the Days of Waynes and Roses. Nor do they like anything beginning with T for a girl —Theresa, Tara, Tanya, Tracy. Thinking about lists at school, they are very initial-conscious. Parents whose surname begins with C don't call their son William. Sloanes are never called Celtic names unless Irish or Scottish, and then few: never Kevin, Keith, Sean, Blodwen, Kelly, Brigid. Nor Saxon names: Walter, Harold (except Harold Macmillan).

They are never called the poncy names that intellectuals saddle their children with: Lancelot, Torquil, Peregrine, Jennet, Io, Perdita, Hepzibah.

Never called film star names: Dawn, Marilyn, Rock, Merle, Kim, Tab, Clint, Charlton.

Though they scorn lower-middle class names (which is to say Celtic names and film star names), Sloanes perversely rather like housemaids' names: Mollie, Polly, Kate, Betsy, Betty, Elsie and Alice.

Never called footballers' names: Bobby, Frank, Ron, Les, Terry, Dave.

Never never called Sixties psychedelic names: Galaxy, Jet, Harmony, Willow, Saffron, Jade. Sloanes *hated* the Sixties.

Never called after jewels: Emerald is too grand for Sloanes, Ruby, Pearl etc. are for cleaning women. Amber's a joke.

Finally, they are never called names which are 'too' biblical, smack of flagrant Popery or otherwise go off the deep end of ecumenism: Bernadette, Marie, Annunciata, Ignatius (RC); Samuel, Leah, Ruth (Jewish); Dora, Patience, Christian (Quaker).

Let's call her Marigold and hope she will . . . .

The Sloane Child's Training

Practice makes perfect

Sloanes don't question authority—those who do have taken a giant step out of Sloanedom—and they have an awful lot of authority not to question. As a Sloane, you are *taught* everything, from walking to French to reels, mostly by hired teachers. The Sloane mother is endlessly busy. There's her charities and the Party, but most of her work is *the travelling entailed in being a Sloane*: the country/town shuttle, the children taken to and from Brownies/dancing/swimming/music/parties/school/gym/smart church ('Where we were married')/Queen Anne Street. The Renault engine lurching into life punctuates young Henry and Caroline's early days. Running to stay in the same place. Sloane children don't go to the local places, they go to the Sloane places. Only a few centres transmit Sloane culture. Only there will you meet your contemporaries. Sloane speech is punctuated with 'I know him/her—we went to the same Brown Owl/dancing class/swimming class/piano teacher/parties/school/gym/Sunday school.'

The result of always going to *the* place and of having lessons in everything is that Sloanes grow up feeling there is a Right Way (and a Wrong Way) and they know it. They may stand in a room nervously clinking coins and keys in their pockets, but the *way* they stand is an approved way, the way they *walk* has been approved (every Sloane has his/her own walk, it's part of the importance of Shoes). When they see non-Sloanes thrown into social panic and suddenly conscious that they don't know how to *stand*, let alone walk, it's cringeingly embarrassing. A Sloane has been taught how to be natural.

A Sloane, it follows, is subject to all the emotional pressure and heartache of being highly trained. You are the son/daughter of the person who pays the training fees, and that realisation stays snobbishly with you throughout life. But you aren't spared. Your nanny, if she's good, is fiercely proud of you, pouring hopes into you—you are liable to love a long-term Nanny more than Mummie. (The same unfortunately is not true of the *au pair*, who nevertheless teaches you resourcefulness by leaving you to fend for yourself.) But you are also at the mercy of people who bully you or do not like you. And Sloane teachers tend to *care* deeply, since it's an ethos. For a sensitive child it's a daily agony. The great Sloane people-network of family, family friends, 'help', teachers and fellow-pupils has always been a demanding, disciplining place to live.

The Sloane child is the one person left in the world who is told 'Don't answer back'. He/she has at least fifteen people (relations, nannies, teachers of its various classes, Madame in the French family) saying '*This* way not that way. You can't do *that* in Polite Society.' Instruction rains down on the Sloane child, and often comes out again in a bossy Sloane grown-up.

No wonder young Henry/Caroline feels that toys and the dog are the only real friends, and develops an unnatural fondness for the Outdoors, My Room and the nursery—anywhere as long as it's away from the grown-ups.

All that said, psychiatrists consider that Rangers bring up their children well. Mummie is firm and fair. She believes in routine: afternoon walks, laid tea-table, bedtime stories, things kept up with: 'Please sit down *now* and write your thank-you letter to William's Mummie.' Manners are practised by having people to stay. In the holidays, London Sloane children go and stay in the country themselves, with cousins, grandparents or friends (country roots must be kept strong; no one wants nervy London children). A Christmas pantomime and Verbier, Pony Club camp and Scotland all come round like clockwork. Soon there will be swaps with children in France, Italy or Spain. In January, the Corfu villa is booked for July, or the same house taken for the umpteenth time on the coast of Norfolk, Cornwall, Kent, Wales or Devon.

YOUR NURSERY
(as strong-minded Mummie calls it)

You live there with your bears—Teddy, Paddington, Bunyip Bluegum—your golliwog and your dolls (Sloanes of both sexes prefer animals to dolls).

Also:

your collection of cars, china mice etc.
your baby musical box
your first portable
Peter Rabbit china
Galt bricks
Fisher-Price toys
Designers Guild wallpaper
posters of Winnie the Pooh and Tom Kitten
a Walt Disney mobile
Laura Ashley curtains
Kermit
Your rosettes (leading-rein classes at first)
But above all, your books

YOUR BOOKS

The crucial childhood influences on Sloanes—even in the 1980s—are Edwardian. All Sloane children (of many nationalities all over the world, which makes it cultural imperialism) are brought up on British Edwardian children's books. They read about Edwardian heroes like Bulldog Drummond, Richard Hannay and Sir Percy Blakeney (that damned elusive Pimpernel).

Edwardian equals 'classic' in Sloane. Everyone knows A. A. Milne (*Winnie the Pooh* in Latin is Sloane compounded—shows classical education too). Kenneth Grahame, Beatrix Potter and Peter Pan (Kensington Gardens is near the epicentre of the Known World). Sir Henry Newbolt is the public-school poet; well—you laugh, but you don't really mock.

Sloane mothers like the Edwardian pantheon in the battered handed-down books: they reinforce everything that's *right*. Many say things that one wouldn't want to say out loud today. Those books strike the Sloane nerve: all the maids, dashing gents, common villains and Fauntleroy childhoods that radicals so hate. They do encourage your childishness: the unspoken belief that animals are people; that good things come in blue jackets; that every hill has a golden treasure inside it. There is an unmistakable *nostalgie de la Victorian* kitchen range (every Sloane loves an Aga). Sloane girls thereafter go through life predisposed to pig-like men with red and white spotted handkerchiefs.

Sloane children, while they're watching TV, eating fish fingers and going to see Adam Ant at Christmas, are still plugged in to the Great Nanny World of *Upstairs, Downstairs*; a world reinforced through their reading matter. Once upon a time everyone—in sway to ruling-class values as Marxists would say—read these books. Now it's Sloanes who cling to them.

The Small Sloane's Uniform

Just like Granny and Grandpapa at your age

Your first clothes are chosen on the same principle as your parents' clothes. They are classic, sensible, in natural materials, made to last. Your party clothes and bridesmaid/page outfits take a leaf out of Gainsborough's or Reynolds's sketchbooks. You may be allowed into the modern world for 'run around' clothes, but not otherwise.

Your everyday clothes

Caroline is on a line of hand-me-downs for all those Sloane children's classics: Fair Isle jerseys, a guernsey, a size 2 Husky, Viyella shirts, Viyella dresses, a kilt (every Sloane has 'our tartan' either near or far in his ancestry), pinafore dresses, corduroy trousers, dungarees, jeans, Rob Roy socks. French clothes (particularly Le Bourget jeans) are much admired, but generally considered too expensive.

Mummie is clever about shopping for you: if she wasn't she'd be broke. She uses Mothercare, Marks & Spencer and C & A with great discretion for jerseys, underwear, coats. When she is feeling *very* 'pushed', she goes to Save the Children jumble sales (she is on the local committee herself) and buys not-quite-worn-out Shetland jerseys or riding breeches (*never never* second-hand shoes). Children's Bazaar is another of her second-hand haunts (babies to teenagers), and Walton Day Nursery for new clothes (0 to 8) by leading manufacturers in England and Europe sold at a low mark-up.

Your nightclothes

Viyella nighties, Rob Roy pyjamas.

Your best clothes

You have (though seldom wear because you prefer jeans/T shirts/nylon anoraks, like everyone else) one of those beautifully tailored heather-smelling Harris tweed coats with a velvet collar from Rowe's, *the* classic shop (who get your co-operation through the treat of sitting on their wooden horse), or Harrods (they have a horse too, but you sit on him when you get your certificated first haircut). This coat is identical to the one both your grandparents wore. Little Caroline in hers, with her long straight hair pulled back into a ribbon each side, her one-button shoes and beige leggings, does in fact look exactly like Granny at the same age.

For the other bests, Mummie goes to sales at Harvey Nichols, the White House, Simple Garments, Little Horrors, Mome, Chelsea Design Co, Great Expectations. She likes to see her daughter in smocking —which she wore herself, and Granny wore, and the ploughman wore before that.

Your shoes

Peter Jones (of course) to be fitted with Clarks or Start-Rites. A Sloane mother never minds the queue, because she always sees someone she knows or strikes up a conversation with a similar mother-child combination with a view to enlarging your circle of little friends. She goes to Kickers for young Henry's tough lace-ups. The children also have cowboy boots (a present from an itinerant godmother) and yellow wellies, from Woolworths.

Your clothes shops in London
CHELSEA DESIGN CO, 65 Sydney Street, SW3 (352 4626)
HARVEY NICHOLS, Knightsbridge, SW1 (235 5000)
KICKERS, 183a Brompton Road, SW3 (589 2211)
MARKS & SPENCER (main branch), 458 Oxford Street, W1 (486 6151)
MEENYS, 241 King's Road, SW3 (351 4171)
MOME, 27 Harrington Road, SW7 (589 8306)
ANTHEA MOORE-EDE, 16 Victoria Grove, W8 (584 8826)
PLEASE MUM, 69 New Bond Street, W1 (493 5880) and 22 Sloane Street, SW1 (235 5303)
ROWE, 120 New Bond Street, W1 (734 9711)
SIMPLE GARMENTS, 39 Sloane Street, SW1 (235 4727)
THE WHITE HOUSE, 51 New Bond Street, W1 (629 3521)

Sophie

plaits by nanny or the au-pair

velvet collar

Rowe's Harris tweed for sunday best

hand-me-down Fair Isle

Viyella graphpaper checked shirt like daddies

kilt in your tartan (or Black Watch) it goes so well with all your navy blue

ribbed woolly tights

sensible Clarks button-ups

Jamie

no-nonsense pudding basin by Miss Laird

teeth will be taken to the orthodontist soon

angelic expression highly misleading

navy guernsey (mini version of mummies' and daddie's)

in pocket: Mars bar wrapper

rather battered dungarees

Kickers (from the sale for his birthday)

How they teach the young elite

Even Sloanes don't like to say 'He's common' or 'She's not a lady' any more. NQOCD (not quite our class, darling) is an American joke. You might say 'He's a bit ordinaire...'

PLU (people like us) was the euphemism for Sloanes in the early Fifties, forerunner of the contribution of Nancy Mitford and Professor Ross to class definition in speech. For years after they published *Noblesse Oblige* in 1956, all Sloanes used exactly the same words and pronounciation as Nancy Mitford. But today they harbour a few weeds she wouldn't have because the Mitford approach seems a little excessive. For instance, 'mantelpiece' and 'mirror' ('if it's *me* it's U!'). A crowning irony is that now Sloanes don't like to say 'that's non-U'.

So how are Sloane children of the Eighties taught that they are not as other children? It is subtle. The word is passed on in inflections, tone of voice, hints. In remarks like:

'I don't think Kevin would enjoy your birthday party. None of his friends will be there.'

'Not toilet, darling—it's lavatory. Yes I know they do, but *we* don't.'

'Granny used to say ...' (whopping pieces of snobbery are wheeled in behind *her* skirts).

But the great expression that says it without anyone else knowing is 'de rigueur'. 'De rigueur' is constantly on Sloane lips. It means one *does* it. Infra dig is the opposite: one doesn't do it. In fact, the vernacular comment is used probably more: something is 'done' or 'not done'; 'the done thing' or 'not the done thing'.

Party Time

First birthday party

You are the birthday boy or girl for the first time. You are too young to hate it. (You may hate all the other parties you go to from two to 20, but even while paralysed you are forming Sloane bonds, collecting companions in shyness.) Mummie has been assembling a circle for you, boldly approaching Sloane Ranger strangers with 'Is Louisa's birthday in May, too? Then she'd better come to Henry's party.'

Actually it's not just fun: it's a walking race. Can little Henry or Motty take their first step by twelve months? The competition is horrific. Little girls wear the coral necklaces/seed pearls/gold chains they were given as christening presents. For after tea, a row of potties has been kindly set out by the hostess, together with Snugglers.

Presents to the birthday boy or girl and little going-away presents to the tiny guests are essential; you are given Fisher-Price toys. Your name is up among flowers and animals on a hand-painted poster; and on the cake.

Second birthday party

This one's a talking race, plus who's-out-of-nappies? race. You are getting sophisticated in the ways of parties. Balloons are a must. You are given Beatrix Potter books and figures.

Three and four

Mummie and Trudi (your nanny or mother's help) have collected little Henry a good circle by now, picking from dancing, gym, swimming and school. Mummie has renewed long-lost friendships ('Weren't you in my batch? Didn't we come out together?'). Trudi has struck up with another surrogate mother, and you are whirled from house to house on the tea-party roundabout. You know what to expect. Hats, tooters, masks (optional). Blind man's buff, pass the parcel, musical chairs; games are de rigueur. Paper plates, crisps, orange juice, chocolate cakes in paper wrappers, sausages, Smarties, jellies (green is best), hundreds and thousands. When it's your birthday, you are given Galt toys in wood ('proper toys') and Lego.

God, girls are hard to talk to ...

Five to seven

Now is the time for a jolly good jester to come to the aid of the party. There is a small band of magicians, conjurers, entertainers who can control young Sloanes and give them a lovely afternoon. Smartie Artie is the famous name (there are seven of him), but the following have all been tested in the fire by Sloane tinies:

Barney the (slapstick) Clown, has worked in the circus; 24 Sanderstead Avenue, London, NW2 (452 9505)

Click, amazing woman who involves the children in plays; Field House, Meysey Hampton, Cirencester, Gloucestershire (Poulton 743)

Peri Aston, actress and mime artist, 37 Gunmore Road, SW20 (946 3152)

I know! *I* know! *I* know!

Rhubarb, totally silent clown, 10 Shelburne Road, N7 (607 9829)

Smartie Artie, 4 New Greens Avenue, St Albans, Hertfordshire (St Albans 50837)

Puppeteers, over 60, listed by area: the Puppet Centre, Battersea Arts Centre, Lavender Hill, SW11 (228 5335)

Eight

At eight, or even seven, Henry wises up, and wants to be taken, with a group of intimates (*no girls now*), to an Italian restaurant or McDonald's, followed by the latest sci-fi movie or the theatre. Young Caroline has decided that boys are horrid and that you can have more fun with your five best school friends.

Your dancing class

Dancing class is essential for Sloane boys and girls. The younger they begin, the better. It starts the training that will keep you permanently on the guest list and bring you to the doorstep on time with your clean handkerchief and shiny shoes, and polite if predictable conversation. No self-respecting Sloane nanny would take a job that did not include a weekly visit either to Miss Ballantine or Miss Vacani's, the two schools which have had generations of Rangers and the royal family through their hands. Children learn to bow, curtsey, skip, show off, wear their best dress—and possibly even to dance.

Miss Violet Ballantine,
12 Herbert Crescent, SW1 (235 8271) minds madly about manners. Starts with babes-in-arms, ends each class with a star on the shoe and a sweet (good children only). She is famous for her annual Matinee, where pupils perform at the Drury Lane Theatre (a red-letter day in the Sloane Ranger calendar) and raise astonishingly vast sums of money for the NSPCC.

Miss Vacani,
159 Brompton Road, SW3 (589 6110), known for 55 years of service, was the niece of the famous Madame V who started the school. It has always been the royal family's favourite: very professional, very traditional. Its new proprietors, Elfrida Eden and Mary Stassinopoulous, have taken over with the blessing of the Vacanis.

Dorothy Ind,
6 Upper Cheyne Row, SW3 (351 4117) is newish on the scene, much loved by younger Rangers for her imaginative and zesty teaching (no underlining of

Good afternoon, Miss Ind!

social graces). Mrs Ind has a team of fourteen who give lessons at 24 top private schools in and near London, and at St Barnabas Church Hall, Pimlico.

Your swimming class

And that was the lesson she taught her —for she was an admiral's daughter: the class that swims together, wins together.

Miss Asher-Summers,
17 Coleshill Flats, Ebury Street, SW1 (730 6704). The favourite with London Carolines, though Sloane fathers gasp at the price (currently £40 a term). Her pupils learn to swim superbly, and they adore her. Their bathing suits are covered with badges flaunting their achievements. Miss Summers believes in warm water. Teaches (mixed classes) at Porchester Hall, W2, after school hours (also teaches the top year of Eaton House at Queen Mother's Sports Centre). Long waiting list.

Mrs Heron,
Chelsea Sports Centre, Chelsea Manor Street, SW3 (352 6985). Mrs Heron belies her aquatic name and does not enter the water herself. Teaches small groups (twos or threes, six at the most) at Chelsea's Small Pool. Teaches children from scratch (Miss Summers' pupils must be afloat already); 85p a lesson.

Gym shoes

London Sloane children go to gym, particularly the boys. It doesn't make them more athletic than other children, it makes them more sociable, disciplined and determined not to be a cry-baby.

Edward Sturges,
106 Pavilion Road, SW1 (235 4234) is the revered name. Boys $3\frac{1}{2}$ to 9; girls 4 to 9. Sexes segregated. Children are initially terrified of Mr Sturges, the original Mr Stiff Upper Lip, but they end up by respecting him like no one else. Discipline is strength here; weaklings and cry-babies spend much time in the corner; Caroline trembles lest little Henry weep or fail to make it to the top of the wall-bars (she has stocked her bag with Mars Bar bribes and rewards,

like the other mothers). The remarkable Mr Sturges, now in his seventies, a wartime Commando, teaches grown-ups from 8.30 am to 8.30 pm, children in the afternoons. £32 per child per term. Sloane mothers love to hate him.
The Gym Club,
23 Kensington Square, W8 (in the garden of Maria Assumpta Convent). Enrolment 17 Cottesmore Gardens, W8 (938 1931). Run by Miss Nikki Avery, the young gymnast who teaches at Thomas's Schools. Splendid equipment, gentle and fun gym for boys and girls (no segregation) of 2½ to 12, after school hours. Up to the age of four, mother/nanny accompanies children through the exercises. Under 5, £12.50 a term, thereafter £35 a term.

Your table manners

\ milk?

...obviously Breaking Away...

The table is where the differences show. What's done and not done has been so instilled in a Sloane that their opinion plummets of anyone who polishes his plate with the back of his fork or holds his knife like a pencil (Sloanes of course don't own those pencil-shaped steel knives: they were a Fifties Scandinavian invention—post Sloane sets of silver).

Sloanes tell stories of the guest drinking the finger bowl and the hostess politely copying him, but this grossly oversimplifies the test that a Sloane meal is. A non-Sloane sees the ranks of glasses and silverware and feels menaced, but that's not where the menace lies. The glasses and silver are arranged in order of use and the finger bowl is what it says. The Sloane do's and don'ts are non-functional, absurd, invisible to the non-Sloane. He breaks the rules without noticing but the Sloanes are all aghast.

● *Napkins.* Supposed to be linen. Put it on lap on sitting down. Fold at end of meal in a house where you're staying, leave crumpled in a hotel. *Rule holds.*

● *Starting.* The rich start ostentatiously the minute the food is on their plate. Sloanes wait for the still-serving hostess to say 'Do start, don't let it get cold'. Waiting for the hostess to eat is middle-class, but starting at once seems barbaric. *Rule confused.*

● *Soup.* Tilt plate and spoon away from you. *Rule holds.*

● *Salt.* In a heap, not sprinkled. *Rule holds.*

● *Fish knives.* Sloanes make a joke about owning these. They're not supposed to—the Georgians didn't—but many do, because Sloane fortunes were *Victorian* fortunes. *Rule relaxed.* (N.B. The Great Sloane Question: Does the Queen have fish knives? Answer: No.)

● *Fork.* Use fork only, if possible, for pudding—otherwise spoon and fork. These are placed along with the rest of the knives, forks and spoons in order of use on either side of the plate. They are *not* laid at the top. Never use spoon without fork. *Rule holds.*

● *Jelly and ice cream* (Nancy Mitford: ice). Spoon and fork still among really dyed-in-the-wool Sloanes, but *rule wobbly.*

● *Fruit.* You can peel with your fruit knife and fork or eat in your hands. *Rule relaxed.*

● *Elbows.* Sloanes are all taught 'All joints on the table will be carved', but they all end the meal leaning on one elbow, drinking and laughing. *Rule relaxed* (for older Sloanes, *not* for children).

● *Port.* Pass clockwise. Sloanes love stories about the port getting stuck because someone Didn't Know. It's not just a rule, it's traffic sense. *Rule holds.*

● *Milk jug.* Sloanes do not put the milk on the table in a bottle or carton, except in the Breakaway Period, 16–19. *Rule holds.*

● *Butter knife.* Do not use your own knife. Same goes for jam spoon. *Rule holds.*

● *Tea.* Milk in second. *Rule holds.*

● *Avocado.* Do not scrape every morsel out of the skin as though you were scraping skis. *New rule,* but on same principle as 'leave something for Mr Manners'.

● *French bread and rolls.* Break with the fingers, never cut with a knife. *Rule holds.*

● *Pudding.* This is what comes after the main course. It is not referred to as 'the sweet', 'afters' or 'dessert' (American Sloanes excepted). *Rule holds.*

● *Children.* Should ask to leave the table: 'Please may I get down?' *Rule relaxing.*

But the au pair usually has to do

As Lord Weymouth wrote in a song about his nanny (who died in 1971): 'When the world was but a cradle, Nanny Marks, when our jelly faces called within the dark, it was you that made us happy—shook the rattle, pinned the nappy. It was you we really cared for, Nanny Marks.' Sloanes regret the loss of the institution called Nanny more than the loss of the Empire. They feel a cultural ache where Nanny used to be. Sloanes over 50 feel embarrassed if they didn't have a nanny —or an ayah or an amah—it's like not having gone to public school. Sloanes under 50 experience double deprivation: they probably didn't have a nanny and now cannot afford to provide one for their children. Guilt is aroused every time the conversation turns to her (which is

often, with Sloanes). Nanny—with her nursery fire and crumpets, nursery fender and Chilprufe, Swan pram, sober uniform, common sense, grandness—is the very symbol of the cosy home life and high status of the idealised Sloane household.

Actually, the modern Sloane couple secretly know they couldn't cope with an old-fashioned, middle-aged nanny in their little house, cheek by jowl with Henry's intake and habits. Things have changed; they sometimes have a full-timer, a young Norland or a Princess Christian (see p 88), at the beginning, but even they often don't wear the uniform now. After the children go to school, it's the downhill slope to cheaper assistance: mother's helps or The Dreaded Au Pair. These girls are called 'the children's keeper' to acquaintances and 'my nanny' to rivals.

Then and now. Above, Nanny Marion Crawford ('Crawfie') with Princess Elizabeth; below, Prince William of Wales's nanny Barbara Barnes with former charges May and Amy Tennant.

SAWS YOUR NANNY TAUGHT YOU

If you have a Northumbrian nanny you might get some even older proverbs, but if you have a foreign au pair, Mummie feels the burden's back on her to give you the oral culture. Sloanes are exceedingly fond of old sayings, because they prove their links with tradition: 'A keeper of my grandfather's said (pithy saw)' or even '(proverb), as they say in Yorkshire...' The nugget of homely wisdom is like an old school tie.

Some Sloane proverbs are not universally applicable. Sloanes find it very awkward dealing with modern people who don't know proverb number 16 and keep using your Christian name and commenting on your clothes as though you were in Madame Tussaud's. The concept of personal 'space' and distance, though it wasn't formulated when the Sloane rules were made, was and is prized. The favourite Sloane nanny sayings are:

1 Go after breakfast.
2 If a thing's worth doing it's worth doing well.
3 Waste not want not.
4 Pride's painful (as she pulls your hair when washing it).
5 Don't care was made to care
   Don't care was hung,
   Don't care was put in a pot
   And boiled till he was done.
6 A stitch in time saves nine.
7 Evil communications corrupt good manners.
8 A prince is the first servant of his people.
9 Noblesse oblige.
10 Don't be beholden to anyone.
11 There's no such word as can't.
12 If at first you don't succeed, try, try, try again.
13 Punctuality is the courtesy of kings.
14 If you go by the road of By and By you'll never arrive.
15 Only servants whisper.
16 Personal remarks are odious.
17 Who's *she*? The cat's mother? (When you call someone 'she', as everyone else does now, instead of 'Mrs Blank'). But Sloanes are taught not to say 'Good morning. Mrs Blank', just 'Good morning' (if you're a woman) or 'Good morning to you' (said by men).
18 The road to hell is paved with good intentions.

No such word as "can't"...

The Dreaded Au Pair sees the children as a job, not a cause. And she has her own lessons to learn—always at the most inconvenient times. Caroline has to come in with The Culture all the time, trying to combat the foreign/local accent, banning Words We Don't Use, being firm about conduct, mothering the girl ('28 is *too young* to have a lovesick daughter of 18...'). So much that used to be almost telepathically transmitted now has to be spelt out. Meanwhile the au pair knows that the video is much nearer than the park and lets the children watch and watch and watch.

Sexy Marie-Louise succeeds idle Ingeborg, succeeds nice Heather, succeeds bad-tempered Martha, succeeds drug-taking Mary at intervals of six months or a year. A good helper is a Sloane mother's most prized asset, and when you put an ad in *The Lady*, the biggest response is other mothers asking you to pass on any good girls you don't need (a telephone number in the advertisement gets six times the response of a box number).

Good or bad, the girls eventually move on. Caroline has to teach each one all the rules: *not* here but *there*...my husband likes...my husband doesn't like...I know it seems old-fashioned but...it's better to do it *straight* away...we use a *jug*...*not* in the house...*could* you please...the children must be allowed to...the dog must not be allowed to...my husband has a *particular aversion* to...I'm afraid this JUST WON'T DO. Caroline's voice rises to a shriek.

Next Thursday The Dreaded searches the ads in *The Lady* in earnest (they always read them anyway to see what they're missing). Caroline composes a new *Lady* ad of her own, with perhaps a duplicate in *Nursery World*. Or she applies to an agency.

Sloanes bring up their own children between help but it's hard. What do you do with the baby when the toddler has to be chauffeured to at least three appointments a day? (Sloanes look askance at those slings earth mothers carry their babies in—it must be bad for the bust.) And one has to go out to dinner sometimes.

The Dreaded is useful at the dinner table at least, providing amusing stories: 'I Came Home to Find...', 'Do you know what she had been Doing?' There's the story of the randy Italian au pair who was an *indelible* character—on holiday in Corfu, the imprint of her bare bottom was found on the bonnet of the car every morning. There's occasionally a scandal nearer home: some Naughty Nanny has run off with a Horny Husband. This does not fall sweetly on Caroline's ears. (Sloanes always foul their own nests when it comes to adultery. If it's not Henry's secretary, the nanny or your best friend, he's faithful.)

Caroline is constantly flaked—nerves frayed by the sound of the Renault, of her own voice rasping, of the children squealing, the dog barking, the au pair using low expressions and the dinner guests braying. These are the *heroic* years. Caroline has lots of reasons why they should move from Hurlingham to the country, and starts hurling 'em at Henry. For one, the children are almost old enough for their first pony. All's well that Thelwell.

Where to find help
The colleges
See p 88.

The nanny agencies

Caroline knows from friends' experience that you must make sure the agency has met the nanny, and you must take up all references yourself. A telephone call elicits more from another Sloane than a letter, because fair play and No Sneaking guide letter-writing, whereas on the telephone you can hear the hesitation.

Babysitters Unlimited (584 1046), *London Domestics* (584 0161), *Nannies Unlimited* (589 8482), 313 Brompton Road, London, SW3. They send very good-quality people, all Lady Di manners and very pleasant. Nanny department run by young ex-nanny, very hot on checking refs, all nannies personally interviewed. Mother's helps supplied too.

Babycare Childminders, 67 Marylebone High Street, W1 (935 4386). London's biggest babysitting agency with 1,000 minders on the books (student nurses, mothers among them). Cover a 20-mile radius outside London.

Belgravia Bureau, 35 Brompton Road, SW3 (584 4343). Housekeepers, cooks, married couples, chauffeurs, chefs, butlers, dailies, nannies. Three-month guarantee (if staff leave within that time they are replaced free of charge).

Knightsbridge Nannies, 5 Beauchamp Place, SW3 (584 9323). Supply nannies all over the world. Norlander on staff helps place girls. Babysitters, too, and some maternity nurses, often New Zealanders.

Nannies (Kensington), 16 Stratford Road, W8 (937 3299). Top end of market. Some swear by them.

Northumbrian Nannies, 8a Gilesgate, Hexham, Cumbria (Hexham 605071). Sheila Bell is a young NNEB with five years' experience as a nanny. Particularly good at matching families and nannies; young nannies like to be on her books. Lots of 'hard-working' northern girls. Mother's helps, too.

Occasional and Permanent Nannies, 15 Beauchamp Place, SW3 (589 3368). Hot on references. Take on trained or experienced nannies/mother's helps. Have a 'Nannie Advice Bureau'—a 'sort of mothers' panic button'—which is a free telephone service for those wanting instant advice on a baby/child problem.

Rospigliosi Bureau, 8 Charing Cross Road, WC2 (836 2015). Domestics of all sorts and nationalities, for Central London only. Lots of au pairs (girls who are already over here), some mother's helps (usually Australian/New Zealand).

Search Agency, 25 King's Road, SW3 (730 6185). Domestic staff of all kinds, foreigners and British—Thais, Filipinos, Italians, Portuguese etc. Lots of Norland and NNEB nannies (almost all under 40). Search place staff abroad and in Britain, are proud of serving titled families abroad. Year's guarantee (staff who leave within that time replaced free).

Universal Aunts, 36 Walpole Street, SW3 (730 9834). Well-known and old-established agency, employing mostly regulars, but all new workers have two references taken up and go through 'exhaustive' interview. Temp housekeepers (resident or not); proxy parents (take over the house if parents have to be away); babysitters, mother's helps; nannies; escorts (cart children across London for school trains, dentist, etc). Cover the whole of Britain.

LEARNING
TO BE
SLOANE

Schools—a Ladder to Success

School is where you learn crucial basics: bits of Latin and cricket-pitch patriotism (Henry Newbolt, 1862–1938, the public-school poet: 'Play up, play up and play the game'). School is where you learn Sloane instincts: knowledge of who's above you and who below you and who equal and how to behave towards them, and that mixture of pomposity and hilarity that's taught by assembling every morning and waiting for the Head to start the day. School is where you meet people you'll go on meeting and they'll *know* you. Nothing need be said. *School is where you join the Old Boy Net* (Old Girl Net), which extends far beyond personal acquaintanceship. You don't need to have been at the same school; as long as you went to public school, the bond is there up and down the generations, linking all the races and nations. The fellowship is truly lyrical (and *very* useful). That's why your school is the first of What Matters.

School is where the *good* Sloane things are learned:

1 Team spirit ('Pull, pull together').
2 No sucking up.
3 No sneaking.
4 No showing off.
5 No crying or whining (a great Sloane dislike).
6 Never say die.
7 Serve God and His institutions (the school).

School is where the *bad* Sloane things are learned too:

1 Don't try too hard: swots are weeds (at Eton: 'tugs don't wash').
2 Don't trust the opposite sex.
3 Young sexual thrills are best (eg buggery and being beaten—*le vice anglais*).
   (Not all male Sloanes learn this lesson now, luckily for female Sloanes.)
4 And, last and worst, snobbery and contempt. This is hydra-headed, as

public-school people say:

a) Most other schools' pupils are *yobbos* (you talk about '*minor* public schools').
b) All the other people in your village are *yobbos* (Kevins and Sharons).
c) Everyone in towns except the Sloanes and the grand is an *oik*.
d) 'Foreigner' is a contemptuous word like yobbo and oik. (It means European. Canadians, Australians etc are Colonials. Americans are Former Colonials.)
e) 'Jew' is a contemptuous word like yobbo and oik. Going out.
f) Non-white people are different again. One can love them as a species ('I *adore* Indians').
g) Soft people are *weeds*, *wets* or *twerps*.
h) Stupid Sloane men (stupid in the Sloane sense of unpredictable and ill-intentioned) are *berks*, *nerks* or *jerks*.
i) Men in expensive but non-Sloane clothes are *berks*, *nerks* or *jerks* (wearing a jerkin makes you a jerk, coincidentally).

All these unattractive traits persist in the Sloane character, more half-hearted now perhaps than at the turn of the century.

A study in Sloanemanship

School is where Sloanes learn that they are the ones who help the people who run the world. If you spend approximately ten years of your life in a very large house with its own chapel, in a closed society where the Cabinet and heads of the armed forces are just ahead of you—Old Boys or Girls—you identify with the powerful. *Gothic suits you*: you feel physically at home in the Law Courts or the Houses of Parliament or the Pavilion at Lord's. You see yourself as a small person in a huge hall where history is being made. You may be small, but you share in the great enterprise. Sloanes put tradition top because it keeps them top.

Nerk

School is the major Sloane investment; private, of course. Sloanes practically starve themselves to cough up the school fees, are on to every sort of school-fee insurance scheme (eg Howard & Partners) and often get help from grandparents. And 'they really want to get their money's worth,' according to one headmaster. Today's Carolines and Henrys are much more on the ball about the actual *education* part of school than were their counterparts before the mid-Sixties education revolution. They realise that because of unemployment, because of tightened regulations about the public-school entry to Oxbridge, because of specialisation, it is no longer good enough to be the child of an Old Boy/Girl, or merely to be able to afford the fees. Getting into the right school is academically tough now. Competition is terrific. That is why the preparatory stage, and the pre-prep stage, matter more and more.

Henry and Caroline join ISIS, the Independent Schools Information Service (26 Caxton Street, London, SW1) which keeps them up to date on private schools from pre-preps upwards. ISIS calls public schools 'independent schools' now to emphasise initiative and enterprise rather than snobbery. And 'things have changed since my day'—few uniforms are apparent (jeans are seen), fagging has been abolished and, in a fifth of boys' public schools, so has beating. Economics is an important subject, as are crafts, sciences and social studies. Where, Henry sometimes wonders, has the discipline gone? The old joke that if you've been through public school you won't find prison life hard falls flat now. The gulf between home life and school life has narrowed alarmingly; exeats are so plentiful that the geography of schooling is vital. Although conscientious parents feel that the school must be accessible from home, somehow the great public schools are booked up with pupils from all over the world.

Very few Sloanes can bear to send their children to state schools. When they do the reasons are always money or geography ('The village school is fine for Henry until he goes away at eight to prep')—never idealism. London state schools favoured by Sloanes are: Bousfield primary (Bolton Gardens); St Michael's secondary modern; the Greycoat school, Graham Terrace very near Francis Holland, with a very similar grey uniform; Hallfield primary (Porchester Gardens, W2); St Peter's Eaton Square (often the first step to Westminster Under).

Sloanes believe that in the end the private system will have to go. But not until their children are through, if they have anything to do with it. Though there are 2,417 private schools in England and Wales from pre-preps upwards, creaming off the top half million children, the choice for Caroline and Henry is, actually, surprisingly slim. A *good* private school is not necessarily a *Sloane* school.

Our first real school: Eaton House.

The first rung of the ladder for girls and boys

The first schools (in the country, play groups) are often started by Sloanes themselves. Montessori methods are widely used (particularly fashionable since the Princess of Wales). Generally, the two-and-a-half to five-year-olds paint and do 'numbers' and learn to mix. In London, Henry gets in early on the party round, learns how to shake hands and bow, does some music (not much). This may be his only experience of a mixed-sex school. In the country, Sloanes keep their children at home much longer. Mothers organise themselves into groups and take turns having the other children one morning for activities, thus the playroom/kitchen is covered with Red Indian headdresses, frieze alphabets and paper-plate clocks.

The nursery school is usually chosen geographically. These are London Sloane favourites:

London nursery schools and kindergartens

Amanda Hanbury's, 15 Kempson Road, SW6 (736 8377). Now twelve years old, expanded from twelve children to 60, spread over two terraced Fulham houses. A few 18-month-old babies (plus nannies) do a couple of mornings a week, but it's mainly $2\frac{1}{2}$ to 5-year-olds, and 5 to 8-year-olds. Strong on music, also swimming and gymnastics. Mornings only, £210 a term; full day, £385 a term.

Miss Morley's Nursery School, Fountain Court, Buckingham Palace Road, SW1 (730 5797). 30 tip-top junior Rangers. 2 to 5. Mornings only. From £120 a term.

Pooh Corner Montessori Nursery School, Christ Church Vestry, Victoria Road, W8 (937 1364). Nineteen children. Mornings only, £190 a term, afternoons £90 a term.

Ranelagh Kindergarten, St Barnabas Hall, Pimlico Road, SW1 (730 3596). Thomas's most junior branch—and oldest. A feed for the big Thomas's, though some boys go on to Eaton House. Fashionable with Chester Square diplomats. Montessori-based letter and number programme. 40 children on average. Mornings only. £160 a term.

Scarsdale Kindergarten School, 38 Scarsdale Villas, W8 (937 6496). Started in 1949 by Mrs Mais, the present principal. By five, the children are definitely doing addition and subtraction. Fashionable for Hammersmith and West London Sloany children. 75 children in the morning ($2\frac{1}{2}$ to 5 years), £175 a term; 35 children in the afternoons, £150 a term. Also holiday school, by the week £13 a week.

The School Room, 20 Gwendolen Avenue, SW15 (789 1916). Harriet Sykes and Montessori-trained Judy Alexander plus helpers run school in the Sykes house. Started in 1975 with twelve children, it now has 25, and has the 5-year-olds reading and writing. Mornings only, £100 a term.

The Willow School, St Barnabas Parish Hall, 2 Lavender Gardens, SW11 (228 6363). Modified Montessori, opened in September 1981 by Lisa Nickell-Lean (after seven years' experience at Ranelagh Kindergarten). 30 children (perfect for Clapham and Wandsworth parents). Mornings only, £150 a term.

Young England Kindergarten, St Saviour's Hall, St George's Square, SW1 (834 3171). Now known as the school where Lady Diana Spencer taught. 50 children in the morning (£200 a term), 25 in the afternoon (£110 a term). Montessori-based, and very good—swimming, dancing with Miss Ballantine. Run by Mrs Wilson and Mrs King. Feed for Thomas's, Kensington High and Eaton House.

The second rung of the ladder for boys

The pre-prep school introduces a boys-only world and is the school that comes before the school that comes before your public school. You mustn't be a weak link in the chain your father has forged for you, whether it leads to the heights of Eton, via Eaton House-Summer Fields, or tackles Wetherby's-Sunningdale-Winchester or assays another difficult and dangerous ascent. You're four-and-a-half, and you're already under pressure.

London pre-prep schools

Eaton House School, 3 & 5 Eaton Gate, SW1 (730 9343). Age: $4\frac{1}{4}$ to 8. Fees: £400 a term. 250 boys. Joint principals: Mr and Mrs Harper. Uniform: green plus scarlet, grey cap. A pressure-cooker for bright boys. Rupert put down at birth. Eaton House Sports Day one of the Sloanes' annual events. Delivery/pick-up queues disrupt Sloane Square traffic daily at 8.45 and 3.15. The Kent boys came here. Feed for top country preps, Summer Fields in particular, also Westminster Under and Colet Court.

The Vale, 4 The Vale, Chelsea, SW3 (730 9343). Age: $4\frac{1}{2}$ to $8\frac{1}{2}$. Fees: £360 a term. 90 boys and girls. Headmistress: Miss Terry O'Neill. Recently bought by the Harpers (of Eaton House) and revitalised. Up-and-coming since the takeover.

Wetherby School, 11 Pembridge Square, W2 (727 9581). Age: $4\frac{1}{2}$ to $8\frac{1}{2}$. Fees: £425 basic a term. 120 boys. Headmistress: Mrs Gerald Russell. Uniform: grey plus red. The only real alternative to Eaton House (and less of a pressure-cooker): academic, but relaxed, traditional. Feed: as Eaton House.

The third rung of the ladder for boys

You're seven or eight and, unless you're

one of the London few, you leave home to go to prep school. This is a wrench, and not only for your mother (but she has already trained you in the stiff upper). You enter the closed male society and soon absorb its special language and jokes and snobberies. At your preparatory school ('my private school', as your father called his), you aim yourself towards your public school.

London day prep schools (some include pre-prep)

Colet Court, Lonsdale Road, SW13 (748 3461). Age: 8 to 13. Fees: £546 a term. 380 boys, including 50 boarders. Headmaster: W. Howard. The hardest London prep to get into: *the* prep for St Paul's. More popular with non-Ranger intellectuals.

Dulwich College Preparatory School, 42 Alleyn Park, SE21 (670 3217). Age: 3 to 13. Fees: £300–800 a term. 750 boys (and a handful of girls in the nursery school). Headmaster: H. E. P. Woodcock. It's sink or swim, due to sheer size. Gamesy. The place for Clapham, Stockwell, Wandsworth—south-of-the-river Rangers. Majority of boys go on to Dulwich College, the Ranger minority to other public schools.

The Hall, 23 Crossfield Road, NW3 (722 1700). Age: 6 to 13. Fees: £555 a term. 330 boys. Headmaster: R. P. Heazell. Geographically Sloane believers are thin on the ground: this is arty, liberal Hampstead. Famous for lengthy (18-mile) Saturday history walks. Feed for London day schools, second XI public schools.

Hill House, 17 Hans Place, SW1 (584 1331). Age: $3\frac{1}{2}$ to 13. Fees: from £160 to £420 a term. 800 boys and girls. Headmaster: Col. Townend. Uniform: mustard tops and rust-coloured corduroy knickerbockers or shorts, and skirts for girls. You either like it or loathe it. Prince Charles's old school. Outdoorsy, musical, for energetic extroverts. Academic accent minimal, though they work hard in last years. Big boys ski, climb mountains, build characters in Swiss branch. 50 per cent foreigners, many American. School dictum: 'A boy's mind is a spark to be kindled, not a vessel to be filled.'

Sussex House Preparatory School, 68 Cadogan Square, SW1 (584 1741). Age: 8 to 13. Fees: £530 a term. 164 boys. Headmaster: J. H. E. Whittaker. Uniform: tweed jackets: grey and maroon. Its own tough entrance exam; boys go on to Westminster, St Paul's and all the top public schools, particularly Eton and Marlborough. Sound, thorough, disciplined—and fun.

Thomas's, co-ed. See *Girls' London pre-prep/prep*.

Westminster Under School, Adrian House, 27 Vincent Square, SW1 (821 5789). Age: 8 to 13. Fees: £575 a term. 180 boys. Headmaster R. W. W. Dawe. Uniform: grey and pink. Very academic, very difficult entrance exam. Feed for Westminster—and many

other top public schools. Great cross-section of pupils, hopefully heading for the Great School, from far-flung parts of London. Boys look scruffy.

Country boarding prep schools (boys and co-ed)

Ashdown House, Forest Row, East Sussex. (Forest Row 2574). Age: 8 to 14. Fees: £925 a term. 100 boys, 20 girls. Headmaster: M. V. C. Williams. Straight, traditional, lots of individual attention (because of size), feed for all the top schools.

Aysgarth School, Bedale, North Yorkshire (Bedale 50240). Age: 8 to 13. Fees: £875 a term. 150 boys. Headmaster: S. J. Reynolds. The best prep school in the North. Boys from Yorkshire, Northumberland, Cumbria, go on to Eton and the top public schools.

Cheam, Headley, Newbury, Berkshire (Newbury 23242). Age: 8 to 13. Fees: £950 a term. 140 boys. Headmaster: M. Wheeler. Solid straightforward prep, very strong on games, happy lads. Prince Charles was here.

Dragon School, Bardwell Road, Oxford (Oxford 55000). Age: 7 to 13. Fees: £950 a term. 615 pupils including girls, treated (ie referred to) as honorary boys. Headmaster: R. K. ('Inky') Ingram. Early (embryo on) registration. Impressively academic, individualistic and progressive. Sink or swim. Regularly get 20 or more scholarships or exhibitions a year to major public schools.

Farleigh House School, Farleigh Wallop, Basingstoke, Hampshire (Basingstoke 21640). Age: $7\frac{1}{2}$ to 13. Fees: £810 a term. 140 boys. Joint headmasters: Frank Macadam and Michael Needham. *The* smart Catholic prep. Inevitably, Ampleforth—or Eton—follows.

Hawtreys, Savernake Forest, Marlborough, Wiltshire (Marlborough 870331). Age: 8 to 13. Fees: £940 a term. 124 boys. Headmaster: G. E. Watts. Magnificent setting—this was the Marquess of Ailesbury's house. Up-and-coming into the first division, for smart Wiltshire boys heading on to Marlborough and other top public schools.

Horris Hill, Newtown, Newbury, Berkshire (Newbury 40594). Age: 8 to 13. Fees: £1,020 a term. 160 boys. Headmaster: M. J. Innes. Straightforward prep, not too much pressure: on to Eton, Harrow, Marlborough, Radley.

Ludgrove, Wokingham, Berkshire (Wokingham 789856). Age: 8 to 13. Fees: £900 a term. 180 boys. Headmaster: G. W. P. Barber. Very social school: London boys have come from Eaton House and Wetherby's. Hard work. Parents all know each other. Feed for Eton.

Maidwell Hall, Maidwell, Northampton (Maidwell 234). Age: 8 to 13. Fees: £950 a term. 80 boys. Headmaster: J. H. Paul. A sound boys' prep school where Sloane parents send sons who have failed the Summer Fields exam or not been put down for the smarter preps early enough. 65 per cent go on to Eton or Harrow.

Papplewick, Ascot, Berkshire (Ascot 21488). Age: $7\frac{1}{2}$ to $13\frac{1}{2}$. Fees: £1,005 a term (£720 for day pupils).

185 boys. Headmaster: J. S. M. Morris. School boasts 20 fully-qualified members of staff, 16 of whom are resident. The atmosphere of 'cheerful Christianity' emphasizes individual development.

Summer Fields, Summer Field, Oxford (Oxford 54433). Age: 8 to 13. Fees: £1,020 a term. 225 boys. Headmaster: Nigel Talbot Rice. Uniform: navy blue guernseys and dark trousers. The 'in' prep school. Pre-Eton (produces scholars). Headmaster organises bi-annual fund-raising ball. 'The best party I've been to in years,' said a parent, 'Full of old chums.'

Sunningdale School, Sunningdale, Berkshire (Ascot 20159). Age: 8 to 13. Fees: £740 a term. 120 boys. Headmaster: Nicholas Dawson (twin brother Tim is deputy head). Très snob: smart, rich, elite, very traditional. Mostly the sons of Old Etonians (friends of the Dawson twins). Boys from Scotland, East Anglia: put down early. Daddy was here. Feed for Eton, also Winchester. Good Common Entrance results.

Wellesley House, Broadstairs, Kent (Thanet 62991). Age: 8 to 13. Fees: £960 a term. 160 boys, 30 girls. Headmaster: W. F. Sale. Another smart prep, heading

not taken as seriously as their brothers'. But Caroline realises that things have changed since *her* mother chose her school for the right accent and nice friends and little else. Caroline knows it is difficult to get into good schools and that competition for jobs later is likely to be keen. She wants her daughter to be able to go to university if she wants to, though Caroline didn't.

London day pre-prep, prep and prep-to-public schools
City of London School for Girls, Barbican, EC2 (628 0841). Age: 7 to 18. Fees: £445–465 a term. 632 girls. Headmistress: Miss L. Mackie. Impressive, both architecturally and academically. The alternative for London day-girls to St Paul's and Godolphin and Latymer, but true Sloane Rangers find here a special ingredient: school is geographically and socially suited to City, Islington and Highgate pupils.

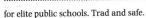

THIRD RUNG FUN

Prep school words: golly, gosh, whizzo, cor, wowee, crikey, super scoff. They are also used by older Sloanes as a joke language.

'Quis?' 'Ego' or 'Non ego' are the prep school equivalent of fains and bags. You can guess someone's age by whether they say 'Vaini, veedi, veechy' or 'Weeny, weedy, weaky' (a great prep school joke). Some preps kept the old pronunciation until 1973.

Other words: thicko, weed, wet, drip, idiot, nit,

spas(tic), fool, brill(iant), ex(cellent), twit, nitwit, snot rag, guff (fart).

Masters always have nicknames, usually based on some association with their name or on an animal they resemble, eg Badger. Girls divide their mistresses into silly old bags who are foul and always picking on them and really nice ones (usually younger, laxer, less endurance).

Everyone hates swots and teacher's pets and behaves like a dirty swine to them.

for elite public schools. Trad and safe.

Windlesham House, Washington, Pulborough, West Sussex (Findon 3207). Age: 8 to 13. Fees: £895 a term. 180 boys, 120 girls. Joint Principals: Charles and Elizabeth Ann Malden. In old family home. Many children go on to the co-eds—Bryanston, Bedales etc —and to a big variety of Sloane schools. Work hard, play hard.

Reserve
Elstree School, Woolhampton, Reading (Woolhampton 3302). Age: 7 to 13. Fees: £945 a term. 150 boys. Headmaster: T. R. McMullen. The boys go on to all sorts of public schools. This is where Henrys get slotted in at the last minute.

The second and third rung of the ladder for girls

Daughters are considered their mother's department; and their education is still

Falkner House, 19 Brechin Place, SW7 (373 4501). Age: 4 to 11. Fees: £275–435 a term. 130 girls. Headmistress: Miss E. Thomas. Uniform includes red jelly-bag hat, tie, cloak. No frills, sound, traditional. Three Rs. Non-giggly girls treat teachers as Mummie's friends (they probably are). Waiting list. On to St Paul's, Godolphin & Latymer, Tudor Hall, St Mary's Calne, St Mary's Ascot, Woldingham (past headmistresses have been RC, though the school is not).

Garden House, 53 Sloane Gardens, SW1 (730 1652). Age: 3 to 11. Fees: from £250 a term. 170 pupils, boys in kindergarten only. Principal: Mrs J. K. Oddy. Uniform: prettiest of all—blue Harris tweed coats and velvet berets. Started in 1951 with three pupils as ballet school: still strong on arts (fencing, drama, gallery visits). Recently expanded to Common Entrance age, with very good results. Happy and bright. On to Godolphin & Latymer, More House, Queen's Gate, Tudor Hall, Benenden, Stonar, Roedean.

Lady Eden's School, 39–41 Victoria Road, W8 (937 0583). Age: $3\frac{1}{2}$ to 11. Fees: from £265 a term.

170 girls. Headmistress: Miss Trevethan. Uniform: predominantly blue, jelly-bag hat. So Sloane it squeaks. Rich and social parents. Girls go on to a wide selection of London and country schools.

Lady Eleanor Holles, Hanworth Road, Hampton, Middlesex (979 1601). Age: 7 to 18. Fees: £475 a term. 752 girls. Headmistress: Miss E. M. Candy. Sound, traditional, large. Very OK for Twickenham, Richmond, Chiswick Rangers.

Thomas's London day schools, 17–19 Cottesmore Gardens, W8 (150 pupils) and 15 Cadogan Gardens, SW3 (90 pupils). For registration at either, telephone 938 1931. Age: 5 to 13. Fees: from £420 a term. Co-educational. Joint principals: Joanna and David Thomas. Uniform: boys (winter) polo necks; girls, pinafores and cloaks. They come on from the Thomases' own Ranelagh kindergarten. Includes all the frills—skating, dancing, gym (terrific), drama, etc. Heavy on homework. On to a big cross-section of top schools.

The fourth rung of the ladder for boys

The Etonian, the Wykehamist and the Harrovian are at a party. There are not enough chairs. The Etonian asks for a chair for his girlfriend. The Wykehamist fetches it. The Harrovian sits on it.

You are twelve or thirteen and only five years away from the Old School Tie. You have reached the goal your father planned, flattered and saved for you. If you're in one of the teams and a prefect, these could really be the best years of your life (another Sloane cliché). You may never command such respect again.

How Mummie Helps Henry And Caroline At Every Stage

0–8: Keeps notebook of when measles, mumps etc struck them, to tell matron. Also when tonsils and adenoids (Herr Adenoiden) taken out.

4 on: Buys Henry's and Caroline's uniform secondhand from the school's own bazaar or shop. Nothing infra dig about this. Also buys new school clothes from the school's outfitter: probably Billings & Edmonds, Harrods or Peter Jones.

4 on: Spends hours and pounds making chutney and buying bran-tub presents for school bazaar.

4–8: Orders a gross of Cash's name tapes saying H. SLOANE and a gross saying CAROLINE SLOANE from one of the school outfitters. And sews in 288 name tapes.

7 on: Makes appointment and takes Henry or Caroline to educational psychologist (no disgrace nowadays) about awkward progress on educational ladder. Shrink gives the child an hour and a half (tests and talk) and advises parents. He knows the schools, the type, the IQ, the emphasis. Session costs about £60. Mummie takes Caroline to James Stevenson, 20 Bloomsbury Square, WC1 (631 1209).

Before each term: Haircut. Up to 8, in Harrods, booked minimum four weeks ahead, with Mrs Baird. (Older haircuts at Mummie's place or Trumper's with Daddy.)
Dentist: Cavendish Square or Queen Anne Street. At about 12, bands dentist (orthodontist) is also engaged, to start the struggle against buck teeth. Mr Endicott is sadly dead. But there's Mr Alan Lynch, 31 Queen Anne Street and Mr Roy Sharland, 30 Wimpole Street. Peter Jones shoe department. Last moment, because feet grow so fast. Get ticket and wait and wait and wait . . .
W. H. Smith for pencil cases, rulers etc, Harrods for tuck (favourite source) and last-minute presents, eg posters for study, new hairbrush.

8 and after: Keeps first letters from boarding school. (A good school letter *is* something to treasure: more and more children now telephone.)

11–13: If Jamie has not mustered the necessary qualifications, he may be sent for a crash course to the junior department of Davies, Laing & Dick or Mander Portman Woodward (see page 82).

Try to control any crushes you may get on masters or other boys: you will soon fall for girls instead and be less likely to get yourself or someone else expelled. (Sloanes are *buggers*, not homosexuals.)

Whether you leave to go up to university or down into the City, you will find that the world is not run by Sloane rules. The behaviour that took you to the top at school will not take you to leadership in the jungle. But you are never *alone* as a Sloane. Not even 'Forty years on, when afar and asunder/Parted are those who are singing today'.... Sing up, Harrow!

Public schools: the First XI

Ampleforth College, York, North Yorkshire (Ampleforth 224). Age: 10 to 18. Fees: £1,130 a term. 740 boys. Headmaster: Rev D. L. Milroy (previously Basil Hume). Unquestionably the best Catholic school. Relaxed nice guys: lots of charmers. Tend to end up very pro- or very anti-monk.

Charterhouse, Godalming, Surrey (Godalming 6226). Age: 13 to 18. Fees: £1,520 a term. 720 boys, 50 sixth-form girls. Head: P. J. Attenborough. Hearties, local Surrey and Sussex lads: not very sophisticated. Because Charterhouse produced a pop group (Genesis) the school is considered a breeding ground for talent (by boys).

Eton College, Windsor, Berkshire (Windsor 69991). Age: 13 to 18. Fees: £1,260 a term. 1,250 boys. Headmaster: W. E. K. Anderson. Uniform: tailcoats etc apart, Etonians may wear what they want, and are fancy dressers. Hard work now, and very liberal compared to Daddy's day. Trendies, originals, self-confident, cocky, London-lovers: girls love them. Currently only 50 per cent are sons of Old Etonians. It's amazing how Eton towers above the rest in fame and glamour.

Fettes College, Carrington Road, Edinburgh (Edinburgh 332 2281). Age: 13 to 18. Fees: £1,300 a term. 445 boys, 60 girls (sixth form). Headmaster: A. J. C. Cochrane. Victorian Disneyland chateau exterior, Dickensian interior. Hardy (no heating), rugby emphasis, academically OK. Fettes boys have the faintest tinge of a Scots accent, perceptible only to the initiated.

Gordonstoun, Elgin, Moray, Scotland (Elgin 830445). Age: 13 to 18. Fees: £1,325 a term. 460 pupils (one-third girls, two-thirds boys). Headmaster: M. B. Mavor. One of the best of the northern schools. The Royal Princes went here. Hard work, supposedly tough and character-building. Good for difficult young Henrys.

Harrow School, Harrow on the Hill, Middlesex (422 2783). Age: 13 to 18. Fees: £1,400 a term, 740 boys. Headmaster: I. D. S. Beer. Uniform: strictly worn—own clothes off the Hill only. Contemporary

St. Andrew's Day Wall Game at Eton. No goals have been scored since the First World War, but Henry is always hoping.

and recent Harrovians are inclined to believe the school has been on the decline for the last fifteen years. Very disciplined: rebelling against the school system equals expulsion. Traditionally, Harrovians include the flashy, and money-lovers. Many Harrow boys are from the home counties, and grandparents pay the school fees. Good Sloane Ranger material; will not hesitate to wear the country gear in Sloane Square.

Marlborough College, Marlborough, Wiltshire (Marlborough 54173). Age: 13 to 18. Fees: £1,320 a term. 800 boys, 90 sixth-form girls. Headmaster: Roger Ellis. The Old Marlburian hard to recognise. At school, boys are cliquey; worried parents regret the liberalism. The first public school to take sixth-form girls: other schools look to Marlborough for the trends. (Rumour: will go co-ed all through.)

Milton Abbey School, Nr Blandford, Dorset (Blandford 880484). Age: 13 to 18. Fees: £1,140 a term. 290 boys. Headmaster: S. R. D. Hall. Oddballs. The joke among public school boys is that this is the place for boys who fail to get into the academic institutions. Nice guys.

Stowe School, Stowe, Buckingham, Buckinghamshire (Buckingham 3165). Age: 13 to 18. Fees: £1,400 a term. 670 pupils, including 40 sixth-form girls. Headmaster: C. G. Turner. Dark horses. Stoics have no recognisable traits, though a number end up in the art world (the influence of the Vanbrugh and Kent architecture?).

Wellington College, Crowthorne, Berkshire (Crowthorne 2261). Age: 13 to 18. Fees: £1,300 a term. 750 boys and 50 sixth-form girls. Headmaster: Dr D. H. Newsome. Fast losing its military, disciplined image. Produces bright boys (majority go on to some sort of university), very county, conceited.

Winchester College, College Street, Winchester, Hampshire (Winchester 4328). Age: 13 to 18. Fees: £1,400 a term. 620 boys. Headmaster: John Thorn. Has its own entrance exam. Academically excellent. Wykehamists are recognisably clever, witty, detached, precious, sometimes cynical (Treasury men etc).

The Second XI

Bradfield College, Bradfield, Reading, Berkshire (Bradfield 744203). Age: 13 to 18. Fees: £1,280 a term. 498 boys. Headmaster: A. O. H. Quick. Academically, good second division for Eton and Wellington failures. Convenient for fraternising with nearby Downe House Sloanes.

City of London School, Victoria Embankment, EC4 (353 0046). Age: 10 to 18. Fees: £606–620 a term. 850 boys. Headmaster: J. A. Boyes. Very good B stream day school. Gothic Victorian gloom, sports facilities acres away. Very musical, fashionable with City, North Londoners.

Clifton College, Bristol (Bristol 735945). Age: 7 to 18 (own prep school). Fees: £496–1,372 a term. 670 boys of public school age, some day boys. Headmaster: Stuart M. Andrews. One Jewish house. Good musical reputation. Not for London Sloanes.

Haileybury, Hertford, Hertfordshire (Hoddesdon 462 352). Age: 13 to 18. Fees: £1,150 a term. 600 boys and 55 sixth-form girls. Headmaster: D. Summerscale. Used to be imperial services college, producer of rugger-playing empire builders. Famous for its orchestra, since it opened its doors to the non-military and girls.

Loretto School, Musselburgh, East Lothian (Edinburgh 665 2567). Age: 8 to 18. Fees: £1,200 a term, seniors; £990 a term, juniors. 255 boys and 24 girls. Headmaster: D. B. McMurray. Sound and traditional. Socially undistinguished.

Oundle School, Peterborough, Northamptonshire (Oundle 73536). Age: 11 to 18. Fees: £1,420 a term. 780 boys. Headmaster: Barry Trapnell. Founded 1556, trad. 15 rugger teams, no soccer. The cane is held in reserve. Electronic workshop at the school, also foundry and machine shop. Arts recently emphasised—a civilising influence say the boys. Oundle boys go into professions and business. Nice lads. (School *almost* First XI material.)

Radley College, Abingdon, Oxfordshire (Abingdon 20294). Age: 13 to 18. Fees: £1,250 a term. 580 boys. Headmaster: D. R. W. Silk. Gowns worn in school. Harder to get in since Radley was made fashionable by series of BBC television films about the school. Old Boys do the Ranger things—go to the Admiral Codrington, work in the General Trading Company. Try to be cool but miss. Have complex that Radley is second-rate socially, though not academically. Mistaken—by the uninitiated—for Etonians.

Rugby, Warwickshire (Rugby 3465). Age: 13 to 18. Fees: £1,360 a term. 720 boys (50 girls in sixth-form). Headmaster: Brian Rees. Traditional. Socially a cross-section ('And the vowels have become wider,' lament some parents). The Rugby Sloane looks as though he was born in a trilby and tweed suit.

ENTERING A SON AT BIRTH: WHAT REALLY HAPPENS

The Sloane myth that if it's a boy, the father dashes off a letter to his old school the same day is almost accurate. Doing it immediately *does* help, even in these exam-ridden days. It shows the school that you have done and will do all you can.

What actually happens happens usually the day after. Henry goes to his club (more impressive paper) and writes several letters, starting with:

1 *A prospective housemaster at Eton or Harrow, or the headmaster of another school, or a connection at Henry's old school*

Henry has done his homework on the Old Boy network to find out who are the good *young* housemasters, and whether one should be in college or in a house at Marlborough. One does not want to be merely on the general waiting list: though that's better than nothing until you find out the exact form.

If Henry knows a master at the school, the latter will get a letter:

> TURF CLUB,
> 5 CARLTON HOUSE TERRACE,
> SW1
>
> Dear Tim,
> I am delighted to tell you Caroline gave birth to a son—our first!—yesterday. We are thinking of calling the brat James, and—I know it seems premature, but I've heard you can't do these things too early—we would of course love him to go to the old school. Could you please put his name down on a suitable list, and send me all the bumph in due course?
> Love to Charlotte and the boys: we look forward to seeing you over Christmas.
>
> Yours ever,
> Henry

2 *The headmaster of a prep school*

Again, Ludgrove, or whichever 'feeds' the public school Henry has chosen, or Henry's own prep school.

3 *Mrs Harper at Eaton House*

The first rungs of the ladder dictate the young Sloane's chance of getting into the Big League later.

It is mutually understood that Caroline will know best about nursery schools and will put the baby on the waiting list when he is 18 months old.

There is nothing to stop the Sloane father putting his son down for several schools, since it's harder, academically, to get into the one you want nowadays. The important point is that a correspondence is started between the school and the parent. Then Caroline and Henry can relax. They won't go and visit the boarding schools (discreetly dressed: Caroline in loden, lowish heels, a good skirt, pearls, nice scent; Henry in soft hat and tweeds) until much nearer the time.

But occasionally, while young Jamie is on the waiting list or on the ladder, Mummie and Daddy will nurture any contact they have among his future heads and teachers, inviting *them* to the theatre, *him* to shoot.

Daughters are considered Caroline's department: their education is not taken so seriously academically, nor need a girl be put down on any lists so early.

St Paul's, Lonsdale Road, Barnes, London SW13 (748 9162). Age: 8 to 18. Fees: from £546 a term (8–13), from £716 a term (13–18). 774 boys (120 boarders). High Master: J. W. Hele. Academically top-rate; like Westminster, very difficult to get in. Boys from Highgate and Hampstead. Not a priority for Sloanes.

Uppingham School, Uppingham, Rutland (Uppingham 2216). Age: 13 to 18. Fees: £1,420 a term. 674 pupils, 60 girls in sixth form. Headmaster: Col. Macdonald. Boys come from preps all over the country —Yorkshire, Oxford, Northamptonshire. Solid lads, serious, good social mixers.

Westminster School, 17 Dean's Yard, London SW1 (222 5516). Age: 8 to 18. Fees: £1,350 a term (boarders), £790 a term (day). 500 boys, 100 sixth-form girls. Headmaster: Dr John Rae. Highly academic, intellectually arrogant, cool.

The fourth rung of the ladder for girls

Sloanes find it far harder to choose a public school for a daughter than for a son. Should little Caroline go to a day or a boarding school? And should she go to a girls-only school at all? The traditionally co-ed schools are not Sloane, but some Sloane daughters now aim to enter the sixth-form minority in great Sloane schools such as Marlborough.

If Caroline is to be educated with girls only, the type of school must be decided upon. Girls' schools seem to go in fashions more than boys', and be more changed by a new headmistress or master. The schools can be London day (too sophisticated?), country (with horsy a subdivision), academic (too academic?), traditional (dreary?). It matters a lot to Sloanes who Caroline is meeting. But some of those grand country schools are very snobby to girls whose parents live in a town and haven't a country house. On the other hand, some of them are so cut off and mouldy Mummie fears that Caroline wouldn't meet anyone fun enough.

And there's a last consideration: with the Sixth-Form Switch so popular, a girl can go to a safe old-fashioned school and try to get good enough marks to switch to a racier place when she's ready. All in all,

Mummie finds it very difficult to decide between the following schools:

London girls' day public schools (some include pre-prep and prep)

Francis Holland School, 39 Graham Terrace, SW1 (730 2971). Age 5 to 18. Fees: from £465 a term. 310 pupils. Head: Miss R. E. Colvile. Sixth-form entry. Very safe, very traditional, very OK (practically in Sloane Square). Strenuous efforts made to be 'modern': thus sixth formers are uniformless and wear make-up, lots of it. Francis Holland in Clarence Gate, NW1 (350 11-to-18-year-olds) is envied academically by some SW1 parents. But they're very NW1 over there, and it's not much fun if all your friends live that side of the park, is it? (Westminster headmaster Dr Rae's four daughters went to SW1 Francis Holland.)

Godolphin & Latymer School, Iffley Road, Hammersmith, W6 (741 1936). Age: 11 to 18. Fees: £500 a term. 700 girls. Headmistress: Miss B. F. Dean. No uniform in sixth form. Government-assisted places for pupils from State schools. Very bright girls, extremely difficult to get in, most go on to university. Dress sense sane, not zany. Parents feel it is safe.

Kensington High School, 17 Upper Phillimore Gardens, W8 (937 0108). Age: 5 to 12. Fees: from £279 a term. 210 girls. Headmistress: Mrs J. Bayldon. Uniform: grey. Aptitude test at the age of four (the only school to do so). Bright intellectually and socially (snobby, say some): people drive miles to take their girls in. Feed for the most academic girls' schools— St Paul's, Godolphin & Latymer, Wycombe Abbey, Benenden, Cheltenham, Sherborne.

More House School, 22 Pont Street, SW1 (235 2855). Age: 11 to 18. Fees: £520 a term. 230 girls. Head: Miss P. M. Mathias. No uniform. Catholic. Lots of foreigners. Academically good.

Queen's College, 43–49 Harley Street, W1 (580 1533). Age: 11 to 18. Fees: £460 a term. 380 girls. Headmistress: Mrs Fierz. No uniform. Friendly rivals to Queen's Gate. Socially, more professionals and north-of-the-parks. Top forms full of fun, snappy dressers. Their hang-out, South Molton Street.

Queen's Gate School, 133 Queen's Gate, SW7 (589 3587). Age: 4 to 18. Fees: from £224 to £678 a term. 345 girls. Headmistress: Mrs C. M. Newnham. No uniform. Fun. Good-looking girls, noted for fancy dressing: the perfect place to mark time in London doing A-levels. Sixth-form entry. Their hang-out, Hereford Arms in Hereford Square, is Mecca for boys cramming in SW7.

St Paul's Girls' School, Brook Green, Hammersmith, W6 (603 2288). Age: 11 to 18. Fees: £620 a term. 570 girls. Headmistress: Mrs Heather Brigstocke. No uniform. Academically the top (it's extremely difficult to get in: most girls go on to Oxford or Cambridge). Elite, and they know it: arrogant, cold. Envious other girls say St Paul's girls are encouraged to be on the Pill at thirteen.

Girls' boarding schools

Girls' boarding schools are on the whole far more trad and schooly than boys' boarding schools. Gymslips have gone, but ties still exist as part of some uniforms. The shift at Sixth Form to boys' schools is ever more popular—to the fury of the heads of the bereft girls' schools. Sloane mothers are caught between fear of exposing their daughters to early make-up and sexual promiscuity, and of burying them in safer, duller institutions. And what boys' schools does the girls' school have to its dances?

The first XV

Benenden, Cranbrook, Kent (Benenden 592). Age: 11 to 18. Fees: £1,200 a term. 345 girls. Headmistress: Miss J. R. Allen. Jeans may be worn beneath the uniform, a curious compromise. Cloaks. Snobby and smart (Princess Anne's old school). Academically competitive. Sixth-form shifters.

Convent of the Sacred Heart, Marden Park, Woldingham, Surrey (Caterham 49431). Generally called Woldingham. Age: 11 to 18. Fees: £990 a term. 400 girls. Headmistress: Sister M. Hinde. Nuns (RC) mostly out of habits. Popular school—girls stay for A-levels—envied by many for freedom and fun. Snappy dressers.

Cranborne Chase School, Wardour Castle, Tisbury, Wiltshire (Tisbury 870464). Age: 11 to 18. Fees: £1,220 a term. 130 girls. A few boys in sixth form. Headmaster: M. D. Neal. Wonderfully beautiful place where academic learning is not stressed. Back in the Sixties, it seemed miraculously enlightened and liberated. Good musically, and good art.

Downe House, Cold Ash, Newbury, Berkshire (Hermitage 201151). Age: 11 to 18. Fees: £1,175 a term (boarders), £745 a term (day). 310 girls. Headmistress: Miss S. E. Farr. Bright girls, work-minded (Miss Farr is *very* against the sixth-form shift); straight girls, sweet girls, *nice* girls.

Heathfield, Ascot, Berkshire (Winkfield Row 2955). Age: 11 to 18. Fees: £1,075 a term. 180 girls. Headmistress: Mrs R. H. Parry. Uniform includes ties. Rich spoilt girls, say some. They mix with nearby Etonians.

North Foreland Lodge School, Sherfield-on-Loddon, Nr Basingstoke, Hampshire (Basingstoke 882 431). Age: 11 to 18. Fees: £975 a term. 160 girls. Headmistress: Miss R. Irvine. Lodgers are zappy and fun. Often do A-levels at Queen's Gate.

Roedean, Brighton, Sussex (Brighton 680 791). Age: 9½ to 18. Fees: £1,050–1,197 a term. 445 girls. Headmaster: John Hunt. The first girls' school to take on a headmaster (from Stowe), ten years ago. Now has ten assistant masters. Produces clever career girls. The only girls' school with individual bedrooms, no dorms. Fashionable with rich grand Asians.

St Mary's Convent, St Mary's Road, South Ascot, Berkshire (Ascot 23721). Age 10 to 18. Fees £950 a term. 270 girls. Headmistress: Sister Emmanuel Orchard. *The* Catholic girls' school; très snob, high academic claims, foreign Sloanes (ambassadors' daughters, Princess Caroline). RC mothers ring up from St Teresa's to put two-hours-old Caroline down for Ascot. Girls emerge innocent—or decidedly zappy.

St Mary's School, Curzon Street, Calne, Wiltshire (Calne 815 899). Age: 5 to 18. Fees: £1,100 a term. 289 girls. Headmistress: Mrs J. D. Walters. Academic, currently very fashionable. County and country Sloanes. Social girls.

St Mary's School, Wantage, Oxfordshire (Wantage 3571). Age: 11 to 18. Fees: £985 a term. 275 girls. Headmistress: Mrs Johns. Nuns until 1974, lay teachers now—and distinctly less academic. Girls are social-minded—weakness for double-barrels.

Sherborne School for Girls, Sherborne, Dorset (Sherborne 2245). Age: 12 to 18. Fees: £1,140 a term. 450 girls. Headmistress: Miss E. M. Coulter. Clever, quiet girls from the West Country. Good musically.

Stonar School, Cottles Park, Atworth, Melksham, Wiltshire (Melksham 702 309). Age: 5 to 18 (boarding 8 to 18). Fees: from £995 a term (boarding), from £318 a term (day). 390 girls, including prep pupils. Headmistress: Miss F. D. Denmark. Smart, monied, very horsy, country-house atmosphere: the nearest thing to home. For non-academic county Sloanes.

Tudor Hall School, Banbury, Oxfordshire (Banbury 3434). Age: 11 to 18. Fees: £1,050 a term. 227 girls. Headmistress: Mrs Blyth. Tudors are bubbly girls, man-chasers, 'always talking about boys' according to other schools. New flats for older girls. Dance with boys at Bloxham ('yobbos').

West Heath School, Ashgrove Road, Sevenoaks, Kent (Sevenoaks 52541). Age: 11½ to 17½. Fees: £1,125 a term (boarders), £825 a term (day). 140 girls. Headmistress: Miss R. M. Rudge. Princess Diana's old school. Not very academic, but hard-working and sound. Traditional—old school does not mix with young school; instant expulsion for smoking. After games, into 'evening wear': home shirts, skirts.

Wycombe Abbey School, High Wycombe, Buckinghamshire (High Wycombe 20381). Age: 11 to 18. Fees: £1,220 a term. 470 girls. Headmistress: Miss P. M. Lancaster. For really clever girls (swots get up at 5.30 to keep ahead), hearty and jolly, often career girls.

Reserves

Cheltenham Ladies College, Cheltenham, Gloucestershire (Cheltenham 20691). Age: 11 to 18. Fees: £1,120 a term (boarders), £725 a term (day). 820 girls. Headmistress: Miss Joan Sadler.

Cobham Hall, Cobham, Nr Gravesend, Kent (Gravesend 823 376). Age: 11 to 18. Fees: £1,226 a term (boarders), £752 a term (day). 245 boarders, 45 day girls. Headmaster: Christopher Dixon.

Oxenfoord Castle School, Pathhead, Midlothian, Scotland (Ford 320 241). Age: 10 to 18. Fees: £950 a term (junior), £1,150 a term (senior). 100 girls. Headmistress: Miss Carmichael.

Option I: Caroline is finished off

Sloane education still has more layers than other people's, though finishing schools have had their three score years and ten. They are rather old-fashioned in the age of The Course. But to be finished is still undeniably smart, since it implies the last stage before Society. Finishing schools are like geisha school; you are supposed to emerge adept at mystic social graces which fit you to spend evenings with the highest in the land, a haven of calm and a chaste solace after their days spent wielding power. You then marry one and are able to do the flowers, direct the cook in French and run a large house. Like so much in Sloane life, this picture belongs to the past, but Sloanes conscientiously perpetuate the past.

Eastbourne College of Domestic Economy, 1 Silverdale Road, Eastbourne (Eastbourne 30851). Fees: £2,400 (residential), £1,500 (non-residential) for one-year course in cookery, dressmaking and tailoring, housecraft, laundry, flower-arranging, child care, and typing. Strong emphasis on cooking—you can specialise in Cordon Bleu or catering in your third term.
Eggleton Hall, Barnard Castle, Co. Durham (Teesdale 50378). Fees: £4,140 (fully residential). One year course with cooking, floristry, dressmaking and typing (see also p 84). Foreign Sloanes (Australian and South African) as well as British.
Evendine Court, Colwall, Malvern (Colwall 40428). Fees: approximately £1,200 a term. Cordon Bleu Diploma cookery, needlework, typing, child care, plus an opportunity to retake O-levels and take A-levels 'if the student is sufficiently keen'. Second-league Sloanes.
Lucie Clayton College, 168 Brompton Road, SW3 (581 0024). Where Mummie learned how to get into Daddy's sports car. The four-week *Young Londoner* course teaches grooming—deportment, make-up etc, and can be combined with the *Young Idea* course in the afternoons, which includes lectures and visits to galleries etc. For the Sloane who wants to be a model. The secretarial students (see p 84) have access to the grooming classes, as do the fashion design students. There are two fashion courses—the *Testimonial* of two twelve-week terms (£1,035) and the *Diploma* of four terms (£2,070).
Winkfield Place, Winkfield, Windsor, Berkshire (Winkfield Row 2031). Founded in 1946 by Constance Spry and Rosemary Hume and still going strong. One-year diploma course in cookery, dressmaking, laundry, home furnishing, flower-arranging and typing. Twelve students a year stay on a term to get their Cordon Bleu diploma. £1,163 non-residential, or £2,061 fully residential in this country house (see also p 84).

Abroad

Parents think of a year abroad as 'improving your languages' and introducing you to smart foreign girls to supplement the unsmart girls you seem to have chosen from the whole of your expensive school. And it keeps you out of London. A Swiss finishing school is traditional, and Caroline likes it because of the skiing.

Caroline measures up: finishing at Lucie Clayton.

Option II: A-level Caroline

Sloanes are not stupid, they merely operate in a different convention. When they 'put their thinking caps on', as they call it, they are certainly able to think. If Caroline wants to do A-levels and go to university, there are four alternatives to staying on at boarding school. She can move to:

1) a London day school

Queen's Gate is the most popular—the girls are not very academic, but bright and 'super fun', and so snappily dressed Caroline wonders if she dare copy them. The sixth form has a great influx from schools like St Mary's Ascot who 'go wild—they're so pleased to get away from the nuns'. Caroline can lunch in the Hereford Arms with her friends who are doing typing at Queen's and St James's; but so could she if she went to

2) a London crammer

Here she will find herself working alongside boys from Harrow etc who broke out early (it's costing Daddy £1,000 per subject). Crammers teach more minority subjects than schools, so this might be another reason for a move into London:

Davies, Laing & Dick, 10 Pembridge Square, W2 (229 9591) and 7 Holland Park, W11 (727 7437). O- and A-level and Oxbridge tuition in the 15-to-21 age group. Normally a one-year course with a maximum of six students to a group. Six hours tuition per A-level each week; £2,300 a year for three.
Mander Portman Woodward, 5 Wetherby Place, SW7 (370 3544). 15-to-19 age group. Os, As and Oxbridge. Fees: One-year course, £1,012 per A-level (retakes £441). 350 students, maximum of seven to a group.
The Westminster Tutors, 2 Westminster Palace Gardens, SW1 (222 2976). Age group: 17 to 18. One-year course, £795+VAT per A-level. About 100 students. A-levels and Oxbridge tuition, with three or four students per group.

3) an Oxford crammer

Oxford is *safe*—it's full of other, secretarial Sloanes or undergraduate Sloanes who may outwardly look cool and trendy, but underneath have the same values and are only temporarily in disguise. As

Granny used to say, 'You don't have to *look* for money . . . just mix where money is'—and the same applies to Sloanes.

Beechlawn Tutorial College, 1 Park Town (Oxford 57805). Mostly girls (just starting to take boys), 16 to 19. Usually two-year courses leading to three A-levels (also extra or retake O-levels, Oxbridge), taught in groups of one to four pupils. 80 students. Fees range from £500 to £1,000 a term for three A-levels (sciences cost more). Arranged accommodation, £25 to £40 (with breakfast and dinner) a week.
St Clare's Hall, 139 Banbury Road (Oxford 52031). Mixed, though girls outnumber boys. 16 to 19. Two-year course leading to three A-levels and, increasingly the International Baccalauréat; also a one-year US University exchange. 180 students doing As, 15 in a class. Fully residential, all meals, now about £4,200 a year.

But the most popular choice with girl Sloanes at the moment is

4) a boys' boarding school

The girls are keen on being in the first years of mixed sixth forms in male bastions like Marlborough, Wellington, Rugby, Stowe, Bryanston, Charterhouse. Daughters announce they want to go to Daddy's old school, or where their brother is (as the rhyme says, 'The Bible says to love my brother/but I so good have grown/that I love other people's brothers/better than my own'). The drawback is that you need excellent academic qualifications.

The Sixth-Form Switch takes Caroline to Lancing and other boys' schools.

Option III: The Course

You're brave—you're the *first generation* of female Sloanes to face years of earning your own living. (Mummie went to St James's and worked on and off until she met Daddy, Granny and Great-Granny were presented and never worked.) But even you don't want to be a *career girl*, to carry the stigma that word implies. To repeat, the *word* career is unSloane: it implies that you won't marry anyone decent.

You got the Grown-up Sloane Cert on the stroke of seventeen: now you're 'Have driving licence will do anything'. When considering what that anything might be, you apply five criteria.

SOFAS   Suitable Occupation For a Sloane
MEET   Mix with Educated Eligible Types
TOFF   Time Off For Fun
JET   Job Equals Travel
WEDS   Will Enable Devoted Sloanes (to work after marriage).

Mummie and Daddy want to keep you out of the Sloane capital until you are Old Enough to Cope. You meanwhile are trying to get *into* London to grab a head start on the social scene. You know instinctively that boys can better withstand exile from the capital. They are always a scarce commodity.

You probably don't want to go to university (or can't). The Sloane alternative to A-levels and university is The Course. Here you meet other Sloane girls and go to their parties even if you're not doing the season yourself (ie Mummie and Daddy are saving £3,000 on your dance). Courses accommodate TOFF: students always seem to be struck down by sudden illness the day before balls in Scotland or Ireland.

Sloanes train for things that are definitely not serious, things other people call leisure or hobbies. Subjects that are crackpot (china-mending), ladylike (flower-arranging), and obvious (cooking) are *taught* to Sloanes, they don't ask Mummie or read a book. The Course itself is the point.

Tap, tap, tap at the Ox & Cow.

In the game of Sloanopoly, you will often throw 'Go on a course'. Sloanes at crossroads (bored, divorced or widowed) check in at a course to find fresh pals and directions new. This lasts until they are 45 or 50, after which they decide to become educated, which they do by taking holidays in far-away cultural places.

One's first courses divide into three categories: Cookery, Secretarial and Other. Expense is a factor, or that-which-cannot-be-named. A residential course will provide discipline and protection from men. You are then returned home, washed, brushed and reasonably civilised, at 18 to 20; and you immediately go off and live in a flat.

Sloane Rangers' contempt for university and professional qualifications seemed to make them a doomed species in the Fifties, the age of the meritocrat. But along came Sixties doubts about the whole capitalist and consumerist system, and old-fashioned country-squire aspirations fitted in surprisingly. Then came the Eighties, and tax relief for the better-off, which includes Sloanes, and the rise of little service and knick-knack businesses, Sloanes again. So Caroline has never been forced to pay for not getting a proper training. The amateur is through to the next heat.

The secretarial course

One must be able to type. It's like driving a car. Sloanes are people who can *do* things. It's only a pity it's bad form to type personal letters,

Many kinds of girl train as secretaries, so what is Sloane about it? Two things:
1) Sloanes go to *Sloane* colleges (MEET), in (in order of preference):
Oxford
Cambridge
London
All the rest.
2) Sloanes learn the right way to set out a letter (eg that the person writes in ink the 'My dear Binkie' and 'Yours ever,

Alistair' with only the message in the middle typed. And you put Binkie's name and address at the *bottom* on the left).

You hate nine to four, of course. But the social life redeems the purgatory. Every Sloane secretarial college has a nimbus of girls with their shorthand books or red speedwriting books sitting in the Sloane cafés being chatted up by Sloane boys or unenthusiastically swotting. Oxbridge trainee secs are rushed off their feet in the first weeks before the Sloane men students discover there are girl students. The girl students, although they provide stern competition, do not possess the money or the sheer numbers to even up all the parties.

Sloane secretarial colleges

All courses are split into three terms of approximately twelve weeks: fees given are for this unless otherwise stated.

London

Lucie Clayton College, 168 Brompton Road, SW3 (581 0024). Fees: £1,552.50. More Sloanes and less trainee Mayfair Mercs than one might imagine (the modelling school's at the same address). Cookery, deportment and visits included, good fun and convenient for Harrods.

Queen's Secretarial College, 20 Queensberry Place, SW7 (589 8583). Fees: £1,380. A natural Sloane habitat; South Ken home of the Baby Legs variety and a great hit with Sandhurst.

St James's Secretarial College, 4 Wetherby Gardens, SW5 (373 3852). Fees: £1,440. Old-fashioned, disciplined and very trad Sloane: you have to wear a skirt of some sort. Many of the girls are doing the Season but they are not as trendy as those at Queen's.

Speedwriting, 59 South Molton Street, W1 (493 3401). Fees: Intensive twelve-week course £532.20 or part-time typing course (six weeks, two hours a day) £143 for Sloanes attempting a triangle (see p 105) or for post-university students itching to get a job in the art world. Many Sloanes won't learn at the 'intensive' speed: who wants to leave South Molton Street?

Country courses

Hartwell House, Hartwell, Aylesbury, Bucks (Aylesbury 748 355). Fees: £3,300. 18-month residential course, hot on worldwide current affairs, with lectures and exams. Convenient for Cirencester, Oxford, Sandhurst and London.

Camden Secretarial College, Nelson House, 2 Pierrepont Street, Bath, (Bath 63573). Fees: One-year course, £1,020, or intensive one-term course, £340. Accommodation in student flats or in families. Sloanes love historic and majestic cities like Bath, and Nelson lived in the building that houses the college.

St James's Secretarial College, Bradpole, Bridport, Dorset (Bridport 22447). Fees: £1,650 or residential, £3,405. Affiliated to the London college. Conscientious Rangers get good results as there is little distraction.

Cambridge Marlborough Secretarial College, Bateman Street, Cambridge (Cambridge 67016). Fees: £1,610.25. More provincial than its Oxford counterpart, but there's not much difference in student entertainment, which is based around undergraduate activities and local horsy events. Most Sloanes live at 'The Bevanry', a hostel owned by Dr Bevan.

Eggleston Hall, Barnard Castle, Nr Darlington, Durham (Teesdale 50378). Fees: £3,600 plus VAT with full board. Residential courses including cookery and dressmaking. Wonderful for hearty Rangers—lots of riding, fishing, long walks and legitimate use of Huskys and green wellies. (And not far from Durham, if your brother's there.)

Dugdale-McAdam's Secretarial College, 23 Abercromby Place, Edinburgh (Edinburgh 556 7698). Fees: general course £1,207.50, with option of extra academic subjects (£100 each); bi-lingual course, £1,092.50 plus a month in France at approximately £400 extra. Oxbridge equivalent for Scottish Sloanes.

Marlborough Secretarial College, 110a High Street, Oxford (Oxford 49484). Fees: £1,200 plus VAT. Girls are slightly brighter and trendier than at the other Oxford colleges, but also lots of jolly county beaglers and point-to-pointers.

Oxford & County Secretarial College, 34 St Giles, Oxford (Oxford 511404). Fees: £1,680 or including self-catering flats, £2,475. The 'Ox & Cow' has a similar intake to the Marlborough and there is mild competition between the two (in social rather than working life).

Mrs Thomsett's Secretarial College, 1 Ewert Place, Summertown, Oxford (Oxford 514 718). Fees: Two-term, two-hours-a-day course or one-term, four-hours-a-day course—both £790 plus VAT. For Sloanes who want a part-time job or more time for other activities.

Miss Sprules' Secretarial College, North Gate Chambers, St Peter Street, Winchester (Winchester 3393). Fees: £1,163. Another of the St James's group. Strict and hard-working, with a local Sloaneshire intake.

Winkfield Place, Winkfield, Windsor, Berkshire (Winkfield Row 2031). Fees: Residential £2,061 per term, non-residential £1,163. One of the Sloanest establishments, where girls are finished (see p 81) in addition to their secretarial (or cooking) course.

The quick brown forx jumped over the lazy dog

The quick brown fox jumped oer the lay dog

The quickl brown fox jumped over the lazy god

The cookery course

Cooking is an obvious Sloane choice, a hangover from the finishing school approach. It is a passport to the City, to Scotland, to the Alps and to the Med. Cookery schools (generally non-residential) abound, and most finishing schools include cooking as a major subject (see p 81). You have to arm yourself with an apron, a set of Sabatier knives and a recipe book; half the day you cook (ingredients all-inclusive in the fees), the other half you have demonstrations and lectures. At first you tend to mark everything out of ten in restaurants, while your Keen Stage lasts.

London cookery courses

Cordon Bleu Cookery School, 114 Marylebone Lane, W1 (935 3503). Not related to the original Parisian Cordon Bleu school; in fact it was founded by former pupil Rosemary Hume in 1933. Highly disciplined; written and practical work with exams and a diploma at the end of the year course (£2,764). Also a three-month certificate course for £1,537. Full of Carolines who want to be pros.

Leith's School of Food & Wine, 36a Notting Hill Gate W11 (229 0177). Their diploma course is split into three terms—beginners (£1,020), intermediate

Country cooking courses

The Grange, Beckington, Nr Bath (Frome 830 607). Four-week general course for four to six students in pretty house, part of a medieval abbey. Residential £400 (weekends are £5 a night extra); non-residential £300. Also four-day course from £65.

Halwill Park, Halwill Town, Beaworthy, Devon (Beaworthy 201). Four-day residential courses in this pri-

PARIS COOKERY SCHOOLS

French cookery courses are *obviously dotty* unless you are going to earn your living as a chef—and are therefore highly suitable for Sloanes. They are a sort of finishing school too.

Le Cordon Bleu de Paris, 24 rue de Champ de Mars, 75007 Paris (555 0277) and 40 avenue Bosquet, 75007 Paris (705 7980). Courses can be followed from six weeks to four twelve-week terms. Cooking (FF9.100 a term) and pastry (FF8.070 a term) courses lead to a certificate after one or two terms, a diploma after three terms and the Grand Diplôme after four terms (also available to students from the Ecole de Cuisine Française in Sussex). Advanced course, FF10.060 a term. Short summer courses too.

La Varenne Ecole de Cuisine, 34 rue St Dominique, 75007 Paris (705 1016). Courses in six-week units (usually FF15.540 a unit), divided into Orientation, Intermediate (twelve weeks), Advanced (twelve weeks), and Graduate (FF18.650 a unit)—or reduced fees for longer-term students. Condensed summer programmes also available from FF14.580 for five weeks. Visiting master chefs do demonstrations, instruction is in English. Run by Englishwoman Anne Willans.

(£1,090) and advanced (£1,160)—the complete course is taken by girls who want to become professional and costs £2,865. Lots of Sloanes emerge ready for the directors' dining-rooms.

The Jane Mann School of Cookery, 10 Tyrawley Road, SW6 (736 5108) runs three-month diploma courses in cooking and wine, including a day-trip to France. Private house with 12 students; £1,058.

La Petite Cuisine, 54 Hill Rise, Richmond, Surrey (940 7583). Three-month intensive diploma course, £1,487.50, for beginners who plan to make cooking their job. Five-week courses, beginners' certificate or higher certificate, £609.50.

Elizabeth Pomeroy, 51 Hornton Street, W8 (937 4297). Three-month certificate course, £546.25, and refresher/advanced course, two mornings a week for six weeks, £97.75.

Mrs Elizabeth Russell, 5/18 The Grange, SW19 (947 2144). Ten-week course, £700. About six pupils on personal recommendation only. Lady Diana was one.

vate hotel, £85. Cookery demonstrations (tuition kitchen ready soon); also needlework and dressmaking courses. Good for bored-housewife Sloanes.

Ecole de Cuisine Française, Clapham House, Litlington, Sussex (Alfriston 870 047). One-year course run by Sabine de Mirbeck. Her chef, Christophe Buey, goes to Paris regularly to keep up, and exceptional students may do an additional six-week residential Grand Diploma course in Paris. Up to 30 students, £2,580; one-term certificate course, £920.

Ewert Place School of Cookery, 1 Ewert Place, Oxford (Oxford 514 719). Eleven-week certificate course or Cook's professional NCHEE course, £1,185 plus VAT. 32 students. Under same ownership as *Mrs Thomsett's* secretarial college. Similar young trendy Sloanes.

Tante Marie School of Cookery, Woodham House, Carlton Road, Woking, Surrey (Woking 4050). One-year diploma course, with some flower arrangement, dressmaking and upholstery included, £1,065 a term. One-term certificate course, £990. 84 students. Lumley's agency are keen on Tante Marie girls.

The art course

Made for Sloanes—so civilised, so about the things you like anyway—The Good Stuff. You aren't stuck in one place all week (you're in galleries, museums and country houses) and it looks so nice on your CV. And an art course means you know what's what when you visit a grand house.

Art courses are popular later, too, at the bored-wife stage.

London

Christie's Fine Arts Course, 63 Old Brompton Road, SW7 (581 3933). 20 places to do this year's course part-time, four mornings a week plus all 'field trips' (five a term), £1,550 plus VAT. 60 places full-time, £2,500 plus VAT. Part academic, part practical training, with visits, lectures etc, and it *is* an entrée into Christie's itself for a few Rangers who are dedicated to becoming Brides of Art (see p 107).

The Inchbald School of Design, Fine and Decorative Arts Course, 7 Eaton Gate, SW1 (730 5508). One-year course covering the history of Western European Art from 1500 to the present day, £2,856.38, with optional trip abroad at an extra £632.50. Students can attend one term (ten weeks) only, covering part of the set period: £1,064.30. The school is most loved by Sloanes for its one-year Interior Design Course (see p 137), including history of design, technical skills, design projects, etc, £4,237.75. Also a Design and Decoration Intensive Course, £1,064.30 and a Garden Design Course, £1,076, both ten weeks. The dreaded scumbler, dragger, marbliser Sloane has learned it all at Inchbald's (if not in the workroom at Colefax & Fowler or another of the decorators).

Modern Art Studies Diploma Course, held at the Institute of Contemporary Arts, Nash House, The Mall, SW1 (write to 140 Sloane Street, SW1, 730 5608). The only London course concentrating on modern (1850 to the present day). Run by Diana Weir (now Johnson). Three eight-week terms, with three lectures and one seminar a week, leaving lots of time free for thought, visiting galleries, etc (some organised visits). Non-

Christie's gives Caroline her first taste of culture.

diploma students can do just one term (£145) or the whole course with no exams; diploma course, £440. Also eight-week special interest courses, £50 a term. (Popular with married Sloanes at a crossroads—the King and Queen of Greece took it.)

The New Academy for Art Studies Diploma Course, 3 Albion Street, W2 (262 5462). One-year course covering early Renaissance to modern times, with a wide focus on all the arts. Visiting lecturers from the National Gallery, Tate, etc; practical work on galleries, auction houses, restoration, publishing art books, etc, in order to widen job opportunities. 30 places, £1,610, plus trips abroad in vacations.

Sotheby's Styles in Art Course, held at 19 South End, St Albans Grove, W8 (937 2554). (Write to Sotheby's, 34/35 New Bond Street, W1.) 13-week course, held three times a year. A good background to fine and decorative arts; 30 places, £800 plus VAT, but no foot in the door of Sotheby's or of the *Works of Art Course*, held at 6 James Street, Oxford Street, W1 (408 1100). This one-year course is intended for ages 20 to 23 and is a vocational training only for Sloanes ambitious to make it in the field of art and antique auctioneering. Some students are taken on to the staff. The commercial side and the working side of the auction house are taught. 50 places, £2,600 plus VAT.

Study Centre for the Fine and Decorative Arts, write to 16 Barton Road, W14 (794 1243). History of the Decorative Arts. Ten-week course held three times a year. 20 places, £330 plus VAT. Held in the Holy Trinity Church-house (behind the Brompton Oratory) and the V & A amongst other places (it is thus wrongly described by Mummie as 'the V & A course', which *incenses* the V & A). Perhaps the most popular Sloane course, along with the one-year Diploma Course (30 places, £1,350 plus VAT). The oldest and most academic course in the decorative arts outside the universities. But this does not discourage Sloanes —its reputation, tradition, and association with their favourite museum elevate it above all others.

There is also Abroad. Italy—Florence, Venice and Cortona—is ultimo on the Ranger list:

The British Institute of Florence, Palazzo Lanfredini, Lungarno Guicciardini 9, 50100 Florence (055 284 031).

Pre-University Course, run by John Hall. Secretary: Mrs Augarde, 18 Carlton Road, Oxford (Oxford 56952 after 6 pm). Course based in Venice.

St Clare's Hall, 139 Banbury Road, Oxford (Oxford 52031). Summer course based in Cortona.

A course in flower-arranging

Most Sloanes take a course in flower-arranging, an essential that looks frankly Marie Antoinette. But consider the logic; Sloanes have formal events and every Sloane event *must* have flowers, and florists do not know how to do them: 'florist's flowers' means 'common'. 'Nice flowers' are the ones in Sloane arrangements. The bunch has an imposing but slightly shaggy outline, and is naturalistic (no crosses or wreaths of flowers at funerals). Sloane species are ruffled, as though they're flying through the air— peonies, sweet peas, anemones, flowering branches, Regale lilies, scabious, narcissi, tulips, hyacinths, cyclamen. If a flower looks like a propeller or a wheel it's Sloane. Gladioli, ball chrysanthemums, arum lilies and tight red roses are *not* Sloane. Carnations are just acceptable because they are always available—but Sloanes try for the 'cottage pink' look rather than the more usual synthetic puffs. When Sloanes send flowers to their cleaning woman in hospital or to her funeral, the relations purse their lips at the meanness—no cellophane, no bow, a rather small bunch (it costs pounds more than the bow-tied bunch but not everybody can read Sloane).

A hostess must speak Sloane with her flowers, so a Sloane with a training can always get work doing weddings, a hospital or a hotel. Nine Elms has a group of young Sloanes around seven every weekday morning. A hostess who doesn't know a freelance Sloane trusts Pulbrook & Gould because 1) Lady Pulbrook's a Lady, 2) she sells 'flowers from country gardens' (country Sloanes deliver them on Monday, the back of the Volvo full of shed petals).

Constance Spry Flower School, 53–57 Marylebone Lane, London W1 (486 6441). Various four-week introductory courses, £260; certificate course of three months, £806; six-month diploma course, most popular with school-leaver Sloanes, £960. You are taught how to handle flowers, arranging, making bouquets, headdresses and wreaths, etc.

A dressmaking course

Sewing is not essential to a Sloane, because it's useful and the other classes do it: *embroidery* is the Sloane needle skill.

But some Sloanes do learn dressmaking and save/make masses of money.

Katinka, 178 King Street, W6 (748 3700). Moved from Knightsbridge, but still the prime Sloane college of dressmaking. One-year course in pattern-cutting, dressmaking, tailoring etc. 28 students, £900 plus VAT.

China restoration courses
(*Not as crackpot as it sounds*)

You might be able to learn as an unpaid skivvy via a friend of Daddy's who is an antique dealer/auctioneer. Or some china-mender Sloanes teach others, at a price they may be unwilling to disclose: 'It's savola tavola—d'you know what I mean?'

China Restore Studio, 25 Acfold Road, SW6 (731 2809). Shirley Paul and Tania Buck-Keene run courses of two mornings a week for five weeks. The interval between lessons is intended for practice at home. Five or six students: £120.

The Studio, 18 Norland Square, W11 (229 8503). Suzy Bellow and Marion Norton run china-restoration courses twice a year for just two students. The four-week intensive course costs £1,000 (£600 for training, £400 for equipment). (The V & A recommend Misses Bellow and Norton.)

The child-proof course
(*For the rare Sloanes who don't prefer dogs*)

Sloanes tend to be nervously bossy with children (their own overdisciplined upbringing), but the Princess of Wales has given encouragement to warmer ways and also (one hopes) killed the old bugbear of social stigma—that non-U employers wouldn't treat you as a lady.

The name in teacher training (always nursery or possibly primary, never O- or A-level) is Montessori.

Montessori St Nicholas' Training Centre, 22 Prince's Gate, SW7 (584 9232) runs one-year courses with a new intake every term, £900. There are 25 Montessori schools within a seven-mile radius of the training centre, at which students do practical work in their last term.

Where Nanny Ranger goes to college

There are three Sloane schools running two-year NNEB (Nursery Nursing Examination Board) courses, leading to work with private families, in nursery schools, maternity nursing, and work abroad:

Chiltern Nursery Training College, 20 Peppard Road, Caversham, Reading (Reading 471847). Founded 50 years ago; 85 students; navy-blue uniform with white aprons. Residential, £2,301 a year; non-residential, £1,425.

Norland Nursery Training College, Denford Park, near Hungerford, Berkshire (Hungerford 2252). Founded in 1892, the most renowned of the three colleges. 130 students; fawn uniform with brown velour hat and leather gloves from Harrods. Own day nursery. Most Rangers cast off their uniform as soon as they leave college. Probationary first job organised by Norland for nine months, after which you get your diploma and badge. Residential, £1,050 a term (sixth term is spent at a hospital and is non-fee-paying).

Princess Christian College, 26 Wilbraham Road, Fallowfield, Manchester (Manchester 224 4560). Established in 1902; 50 students; brown uniform. Playgroup and children in residence (in the care of the local authority). Three months spent each in a primary and a nursery school. Residential only, £2,000 a year.

After the Course, Caroline hopes to get a job at Chinamend in Walton Street.

Training for a gentleman's occupation

Henry's whole training is for the best things, the high Cs:
My Country
Country pursuits
Country-house culture
the Carriage trade
the City
(the Colonies, where Henry used to toil, do not take as many Sloanes now).

Henry's academies for the smallish range that Sloanes describe as 'a gentleman's occupation' are far less diverse than Caroline's: the Army, Cirencester, university or law school (some Sloanes get their university career paid for by the Army, in which they serve for five years in return). Or Henry might be a trainee in some Sloane business such as a chartered surveyor or accountant.

Henry doesn't normally do a sixth-form switch, because sixth form is the year he makes his mark on the school, under important SR titles like member of the First XI and Prefect. It is probably the last time he *will* make a mark. If he isn't making a mark at school, he may enrol at a crammer (see p 82), and make an inverse, *conversational* mark by 'never ever' going there. *Warning*: one of the fastest routes out of Sloanedom ('We don't see much of Bloggs any more') is to take up some unrecognised profession (Bloggs tries to defend it: 'It's hardly a gentleman's occupation, but my office is only half an hour from the best stretch on the Test, so...'. His Sloane hearers are unconvinced).

The Sloane Ranger in the Army
The fount of style
The Army is the Sloane service (Navy: a bit common since the War. Air Force: very common since the War. Airmen

In Wolfenbuttel with the Queen's Royal Lancers.

never never never shall be Sloanes). Because all Sloane children are drilled, disciplined, uniformed, herded in squads, and forced to eat spuds, Sloane style is exactly the same as Army style and sometimes as inappropriate to the 1980s. The despatch telling the Sloane regiments that the horse has been superseded failed to get through. Consequently, the modern Army as advertised doesn't appeal to Sloanes.

The part-time Army—TA—*does* appeal to them, particularly the HAC and Sherwood Rangers.

Sloane regiments

Grenadiers; Coldstream; any other Guards regiment (all 'solid'. The Micks—the Irish Guards—don't get sent to Northern Ireland in case they get suborned by native Micks); Household Cavalry (the Tins: the Life Guards, and the Blues & Royals); Scots Dragoon Guards (the Carabiniers saved by the Greys...); Black Watch; Queen's Own Highlanders; other traditional Scottish regiments, if there is a family connection with them, eg the Argylls (One of the 'best' regiments of all is the Atholl Highlanders which has the added advantage that it never goes to war—like the Shrewsbury Hunt Club which doesn't hunt. The basis for membership of either is feudal); Royal Hussars (the Shiny 10th merged with the Cherry-pickers of the 11th, but they still have the cherry trousers); 14th/20th and 15th/9th Hussars; 16th/5th, 9th/12th and 17th/21st Lancers (the Death or Glory boys, also called the 17th twenty worst dancers); QDGs (Queen's Dragoon Guards); Skins (5th Royal Inniskilling Dragoon Guards); Royal Welch Fusiliers; Royal Greenjackets (utterly typical); Gurkhas (soldiers super, though officers rather better in battle than in Mess).

Getting in

The academic requirement is five O-levels, not very taxing. But in addition to this you must be found suitable for the Army. This is more difficult; only 34 per cent get in, and background counts ('Private income', they tell you, 'is helpful'). Henry always tries for Daddy's regiment—that should help. One nineteen-year-old OE comments, 'I had an interview at school with the CO of my father's old regiment. I said I came from Leicestershire, we talked about hunting for ten minutes and he said "Right, I'll take you".'

If bright, Henry applies for a *cadetship* (about 40 annually in whole Army; commission before university, full 2nd Lieutenant's pay through it, five years' service after). If less bright, a *bursary* (£1,000 a year at university, commission afterwards, then three years' service after Sandhurst; easier to get, and easier to buy your way out of).

The three-year *short service commission* is very popular among school-leavers keen to fill The Gap and have no strings

★ **Two golden rules**
Don't grumble about anything till afterwards.

Never let your picture be taken at parties by a glossy magazine (fines in some regiments for this, plus great ribbing in Mess if your face is in *H & Q* or *Tatler*).

SANDHURST

'Sand'st' (the Queen says that, so it must be right). Often called RMA (Royal Military Academy, Sandhurst) by the students.
Horrible experiences, RMA students for the disciplining of
● The haircut. Shortly after your mother in her Ascot hat leaves you and all the others at New College, a large and antiquated lawnmower is run over your head by a careless driver who cuts and recuts until the very scalp is exposed.
● Green string underpants. Look like armchair covers with moth. Feel horrid.
● The sa'nt-major's voice. You had heard about this but you are awed to see that the windows in Camberley are taped up.
● Ironing everything all the time, including PE shorts (Henry likes the feel of ironed underpants throughout life, but he often does it himself).
● Sarcasm. The NCOs may have to call you Mr but they have ways like the Marquis de Sade's to roast officer cadets.

attached afterwards.

Three-month 'suck-it-and-see' commission before you go up to university is to tempt you to join properly afterwards.

Army-as-a-career still goes on, though rather mocked by university types. At Oxbridge, people on cadetships don't advertise their military rank.

SRmy talk

solid: what 'sound' is to the over-30s. 'They're all solid chaps' (dependable because they're our sort of people).

fish 'n' chip mob: non-U regiments, and by extension all hoi polloi.

good/bad news: registering approval or otherwise, especially of girlfriends (always referred to as 'women' as though prostitutes: 'Charles's woman').

grockly: common, tacky, shoddy, grotty (word also favoured by Sloane girls of fifteen or sixteen). A grockle is a mixture of an oik and an incompetent.

extraordinary: used in every conceivable context and of the most ordinary things, eg, on opening *The Sunday Times* at weekend house party: 'Let's see what's in this extraordinary paper.'

super: favourite word, still going strong. '*Super* to see you' is said at least a thousand times in Hyde Park on the first Sunday in May (the Cavalry Memorial Parade).

CO, NCO, RHQ, RSM etc: they bandy initials, but so do the BBC.

YOs (young officers) say 'sir' every two seconds to older men, every half second to girlfriend's father, and always call Mrs Blank Mrs Blank rather more often than necessary. They thank hosts incessantly and talk like machine guns, never starting their sentences, eg 'delighted, delighted. Just go up and change. With you in a tick.' Have perfect manners.

Dress

A smooth 'Sandhurst' or hairy 'Burghley' soft hat from Herbert Johnson.

Black bowler hat from Lock's teamed with Swaine, Adeney umbrella, for Cavalry Memorial Parade, etc.

Suit whenever in doubt—in front of elders and betters, and in London.

Stripy shirt, spotted, striped or paisley tie, lambswool V-neck in navy/yellow/maroon from New & Lingwood.

A blue polka dot handkerchief.

Regimental blazer/tie OK if worn occasionally.

A stable belt—webbing with two leather buckles (grooms wore them and cavalry officers still do, with grey flannel trousers).

Guccis or imitation Gucci loafers.

Either brothel creepers from Poulsen Skone or lightweight brogues. Guardsmen 'bull' their brogues like boots: 'Once you know the trick of it you just can't stop, you bull everything in sight' —Grenadier.

Point-to-point and country clothes: same as civilian Sloanes.

The Sloane Ranger at Cirencester

Farmer Sloane making hay

The Royal Agricultural College at Cirencester, Gloucestershire, is proper *people*, none of the fish 'n' chip mob. 'Ciren' is easier to get into than university or Sandhurst. Over 90 per cent of English land is run by ex Royal Agricultural College people...because it's their fathers who own the land. Great chunks of ex-Imperial foreign parts are also run by RAC graduates, in Africa particularly. Sixty or seventy of the 720 students are from overseas. The course is one, two or three years, at £1,281 a year. A sprinkling of mature students in their thirties and forties adds variety.

You're never alone as an RAC student —you go round in groups (and you *hate* being called a student). You all have nicknames. Henry's is Hotsie. Mark Phillips' was, as we all know, Fog. Sadly, Fog provided few anecdotes for his fellow Cirencester men. He wore chaps and was frequently late because of chores at home. The hero of recent times was Robin Naylor-Leyland. He was there on and off for years and was a real name to conjure with, 'seriously' wild. The students who arrive by helicopter are fun—Agusta 109s whirring in to roost. At Cirencester, the talk is of Performance—cars', girls', horses', helicopters', combine harvesters', friends'.

The nearest you get to solitude is in your Lancia or Alfa, in which you come into Cirencester from your shared cottage, or speed the 90 or so miles to London for the evening. In the back are green wellingtons, a Barbour, walking stick and gun dog, all of which remain in the car during a visit to Tokyo Joe's or whatever. You likewise always carry your London *A to Z* and Swaine, Adeney umbrella. You're ready for either of the Cirencester high-risk sports—car-crashing or gatecrashing.

You call your indispensables 'a real friend'. Anything you like is called that. For example, on seeing a Wemyss pig: 'Oh look, it's a real friend.' Affirmative: 'Oh yes, isn't it a real friend,' etc.

Your studies: through a glass darkly

Classes begin at nine, two 45-minute lectures then coffee and a comparison of hangover states and causes. Confessions of 'seriously drunk', 'hog whimpering' and 'paddled'.

Two more lectures, then break for lunch at 12.30, and out you all rush for more drinking. You go to the Bathurst Arms, North Cerney (top of the pubs); Corinium Court and the Nelson in Cirencester (the Nelson's barmaid is a Quaker, pretty and virtuous, the despair of Cirencester men). You go to the Wild Duck, Ewen; Crown, Ampney Crucis; Spotted Cow, Marston Meysey; Highwayman, near Birdlip; Trouble House, Tetbury; Trout, Lechlade. You drink beer, whisky macs, cherry brandy, sloe gin—or neat whisky. Lectures begin again at two, the insensible students being conveyed in the back of someone's estate among the hay

Closet Hoorays: Thames Valley police are charmed by Henry.

bales (always carried, in case of a sudden point-to-point).

Your evenings: nubiles and Newbury

More lectures until four, then the students wake up. Cirencester is the centre of a web of good things: Oxford (girls at the Marlborough, the Ox & Cow, Brown's), Hartwell House finishing school, reeling parties at Chedworth village hall, and the more social counties with their house parties. Cheltenham and Kemble are served by trains which connect with famous SR trains like the 16.52 on Friday, Paddington to Newbury. Orf steps Caroline, shooting stick in left hand. (Orn she steps again at 6.30 Monday morning, with her small sausage bag and a very large hangover.) And the wrinklies come by train from Badminton.

With no Caroline to distract him, Henry may spend a happy hour on Saturday in the Tetbury Joke Shop, searching out the most sophisticated of whoopee cushions and most lethal of stink bombs to use on friends from rural cottages.

My weekend for the horse

Cirencester men populate point-to-points from November to April. More often than not there's also a rugger international, big race etc on at the same time, so wirelesses beside the course are turned on full blast and crowds gather round the Range Rover with a portable TV. One or two RAC students are riding in the p-to-p races—but seldom winning.

Many RAC people join the TA for the duration of their course: the Wessex Yeomanry. They are on duty at Badminton, doing wireless relay and taking messages round the course in Land-Rovers. They love the dash they cut with their smart khaki uniform and red hat.

While good Americans must die before going to Paris, the lucky Sloane may only need to fail his As before getting to Cirencester, Sloane for heaven.

The Sloane at University

Studying social life

The Sloane university *is* Oxford and Cambridge. But if you can't get in you go to one of the other British Sloan*ish* universities, or abroad. You used to go to TCD, Trinity College Dublin, which was the most fun of the lot, a leisurely four-year course instead of three and surrounded by country houses and packs of hounds. But the Irish government de-Sloaned Trinity in 1968, stipulating Irish blood. Even now, with the education rat-race, Sloanes think it is better not to go than make the wrong (ie non-Sloane) choice.

There are only ten universities in Britain with many Sloanes, because to become Sloane, a university must pass a strict exam in three parts: smartness, age, subjects.

1) *Smartness*. Social rather than academic. The Sixties vogue for York, Sussex and radicalism is *very* dead. They have now become quite outré.

To get into a Sloane place you need influence and a good educational history. Men have the advantage over women with Sloane Oxbridge colleges, since they are more traditional than their unsmart counterparts, and the dons are male and pro-male. In addition, being an excellent bow-side oar, full back or opening batsman is as likely to help as good A-levels at some colleges.

2) *Age*. Sloanes like to live in stone houses—at school, at university and at home. If it has to be brick, let it be Tudor or Queen Anne brick.

3) *Subjects*. The Sloane subject now is History of Art: research in country houses, France and Italy in a civilised atmosphere (a 'civilised atmosphere' means the cedar-pencil smell of a fine old vintage). The Courtauld Institute has been always with us, but the move by non-bent Sloanes into History of Art followed the setting up at Cambridge in 1961 of a Fine Art department by Old Etonians and Kings-men Michael Jaffé and Francis Haskell. It was an instant success, but neither Cambridge nor Oxford let you devote your three years to it: it's allowed two years at Cambridge and only a term at Oxford (under Haskell, who moved there). The first choice is still the Courtauld, then Cambridge, then East Anglia.

Other Sloane subjects are the Arts in general (especially History) and Agriculture. There are very few Sloanes doing Experimental Psychology or Cybernetics (whatever that is).

The Sloane Ranger at Oxford

No. of Sloanes at Oxford: about 200

Colleges for men

Christ Church: ('the House'): home of the beagle pack (every girl wants to know the Master), the college which captures best the SR mixture of heartiness and refinement; public-school atmosphere now slightly diluted. Wonderful lawn for weddings.

Magdalen: similar but less conspicuous.

Oriel: slightly too hearty, in the sporting sense; too many rowers with nothing else to recommend them—the last bastion of male supremacy.

Trinity, University, Merton, Worcester: quiet but not boring, though a strong contingent of academics. Admit people on the basis of overall contribution to college life. Sloane Ranger men who fail to get into these will go anywhere, even *Keble*, if Daddy has a string to pull or their tutor at school advises one of the less fashionable colleges. Their friends will be all over Oxford anyway.

Colleges for girls

Bright girls try for *Christ Church, New College, Worcester, Trinity, St Catz. St Hilda's* if pushed. *Somerville* is the best all-girl college. *Wadham* probably the best of the rest (brilliant English tutor).

Behaviour

Exhibitionism is indulged and frequent

Cutting a dash at Eights Week.

The Oxford 'bulldog' hates Sloanes. Everyone celebrates after exams.

The bicycle on the left is not Sloane. The wheels are too weedy.

torious point-to-point at Kingston Blount in February); or the Piers Gaveston (bigger, artier, marginally more meritocratic; excessive in its drinking, parties—open to girls—and appearance: make-up the rule, drag the norm. Its infamous debauched Christmas ball is banned from almost every venue). Trendy go-ahead girls and, since 1981, an esoteric selection of men get into the George.

Sports

Beagling (the Christ Church and Farley Hill), hunting, rugger, rowing (Torpids and blissful Eights Week), skiing at Easter (the Alps but *not* Italy), real tennis to get coveted Blue.

Work

Most SRs read History, PPE, Law or English; perhaps Modern Languages or one of the sciences. They do the minimum required to get a second, most of it just before finals; they are at Oxford to have fun, and any effort made is social, aimed at election to the Buller or Gavey. They are not careerists and have no ambition to edit *Isis*, run the OUDS, etc; they may run for the Union (which is going through a relatively right-wing phase and recently elected OE Rupert Soames and Amplefordian Chris Wortley to its coveted presidency). But mainly the SRM likes to carry on what he did at school—rowing, cricket, football, spot of acting. Since he/she has no great ambition, Sloanes think it rather vulgar to cultivate a real CV. Their extravagance—on clothes, meals out, travel at home and abroad, drink, cigarettes, records—leads them to look for holiday jobs. They go, not for an interesting one (tutoring, freelance writing), but for a well-paid dull one (shop assistant in the sales, temp, helping with the harvest at home). All the same they maintain modest overdrafts (c £500).

Pubs

The Bear is Oxford's Hereford Arms only more so: not a non-U accent in the place.

drunkenness expected (in the men)/tolerated (in the girls). Thus wherever he is and whatever the occasion the SRM will Get Pretty Pissed. He'll swear a good deal and flirt less than subtly with his girl friends, and not inconceivably with other men as well. Both sexes call each other by their surnames. After an Oxford drinks party (small, frequent and lasting until about ten) he and his chums stage a mixed doubles wheelbarrow/piggy-back/supermarket trolley race down the High/the Broad/the Cornmarket. Silly stunts prove you're The Goods.

Clubs

The SRM's college has its own U and long-established dining club; he joins it soon after coming up, and hopes from that platform to make the step up to the Grid (big club with own rooms that boasts 100 leading male socialites); the Bullingdon (small, rich, square, introspective; excessive in its drinking and the vandalising of new members' houses/rooms. No-

Marlborough girls flood in at lunchtime but most SRs, being snobbish but not insensitive, prefer the King's Arms, the Roebuck, the White Horse, the Turf, the Duke of Cambridge, the Trout near Woodstock, the White Hart.

Oxford Sloane girls

Most SRs are not undergraduates. They're doing a secretarial, or a cooking course (though Leith's Notting Hill seems to be gaining on Oxford), or A-levels (at the High School or St Clare's or Beechlawn), or they're at the Poly (often in preference to a second-division university), or they've finished a secretarial and love Oxford so much they've found a job.

Sex

No longer taboo. Oxford SRs are terribly confident with the opposite sex and assert the fact by kissing everyone on both cheeks, putting their arms round each other at parties, and talking freely about pretty well everything (usually about too much). Since all is public, quality of partner is paramount; for undergrad men, sex with secs is too easy. Ditto with fast college girls—the SRM may well come back from supper at Browns to find one especially impressed with his class and charm sitting up in his bed. He turns her down politely, rather pleased with himself.

Clothes

Men: At Oxford the SRM develops the habits that will see him through his twenties. His day-to-day wear looks more like young Army types (see p 92) than anything remotely undergraduate. Cords, plus one suit in blue/grey pinstripe, two-piece, to cope with heavy use; the jacket is also worn with cords/jeans. One tweed jacket.

NEVER: college scarves or funny sweatshirts, duffle-coats, training shoes. One loud touch is permissible—bright green sweat-shirt, scarlet or yellow socks; but *not* red trousers (too young). Club tie and cricket sweater, if owned, are worn frequently.

Girls: as young London SR.

P.S.

The cocktail party train is the 5.15 to Paddington.

The Sloane Ranger at Cambridge

No. of Sloanes at Cambridge: about 200

Colleges for men

Magdalene: the most public-school intake, lowest admission requirements (interview decides it); amenable to sportsmen.

Trinity: large, rich, and if Daddy didn't go to Magdalene he would have come here; the prestige of inviting girls to tea in Great Court is difficult to surpass.

Pembroke: most in fashion at the moment.

Peterhouse: rather a barrel-scrape, divided distinctly between the academic and the indulgent; age, tradition and clubs are for it, position away from town centre, strident Catholic and homosexual minorities are against it.

Fitzwilliam: the last resort: they take anyone; Fitz SRs few but good, to set foot in college is taboooooo!

The King's Parade, Cambridge is one of the great Sloane streets of the world. You might meet Magdalene Man there.

Colleges for girls

Only *Newnham* remains, with *Trinity* and *Girton* as second choices (the latter is now mixed and rather hearty). Failing that, Cambridge College of Arts and Technology (Tech).

It used to be that 'varsity girls were all ugly, hence the tech girl and sec student syndrome. Recently, however, Uni girls have improved. Tech and sec girls, being thick, go for even thicker Magdalene Man. There is an absolute rush in the first few weeks before Uni girls are noticed.

Some Sloanes are actually clever.

Subjects

First year: Architecture & Anthropology. Second year: History of Art (very trendy faculty).

Sloanes swotting for Tripos.

Fun and clubs

Drinks parties in the Pitt Club—otherwise in one's rooms. House-warmings (all the best people live out). Hunt dinner. Rock 'n rolling. Balls: Pitt, Hunt, the May balls in June—Magdalene (best), Trinity (biggest) —and Girton at Christmas.

Club membership is by election: Muckleflugga, the exclusive Scottish dancing club; Isherwood (Fitzwilliam's dining/drinking club); Wylie (Magdalene's infamous club); Vile Bodies: Wandering Pythons (mixed; summer party at the university bathing place—guests arrive by punt); and Beaufort (Christ's—an invitation to their cocktail party in May is highly coveted). The 30 male members of the Wylie club call themselves the 'executors of (the fictitious) Sir Joshua Wylie' and hold a vodka and grapefruit juice party in May; it lasts for two hours and glasses have to be constantly drained and refilled. The result is about ten people in hospital with stomach pumps each year.

The secs have made their move into Magdalene by the second week.

Couples meet at bops or know each other from London, or meet at those trendy lunch parties. He then takes her to Don Pasquale.

Sports

Real tennis, beagling (Trinity foot beagles), the Drag hunt, rugger as training for sex, or vice versa (probably versa). Lawn meets at Longstays are the *best*. Rowing in Isherwood or college boat (Lents and heavenly Mays). Skiing at Verbier or Val d'Isère at Easter.

Pubs

Pickerel (pre-beagling tinctures), Crusts (7 to 9 pm), Eagle, Rose and Crown, Spade and Bucket, Tickell Arms (eccentric Mr Tickell throws out people he dislikes—girls in trousers, men without hats —and plays Wagner loudly). Queen's Head or Chequers at Fowlmere. Green Man or Red Lion at Grantchester. The Anchor or Mill in summer.

Sex

See Oxford.

Clothes

Not really bought in Cambridge. Shirts from New & Lingwood in Jermyn Street; Welsh & Jeff in Eton. Culottes, thick blue tights, baby legs, skiing jerseys. The Wardrobe for balls etc. Otherwise Oxfam.

P.S.

The cocktail party train is the 5.00 to Liverpool Street.

Other universities where you will find Sloanes

These places are solid

You steer clear of the union and other University buildings and social events. You move out of residential halls after a term or sooner, like some Etonians at Exeter who pay their way out after a week. Social life revolves around your clique—Sloanes always stick together— and dinner at each other's houses, weekends bombing off somewhere together in your young Sloane motors (see p 120), and local country pursuits.

You all know the time of the Friday afternoon train to London.

Bristol

You live in Clifton—Victoria Square, Royal York Crescent, Cornwallis Crescent —or in cottages on the other side of the suspension bridge—Bower Ashton is a favourite village. Men read History and English, girls English, or History of Art with a language.

Drinking: the Plume and Feather (especially OTC), the Greyhound.

Eating: at lunchtime, you gather at the Wills Memorial Building. Eat at Bumbles.

Scottish dancing gatherings at friends' houses—some men wear kilts. Beagling. The Pig Society is full of SRMs who meet once a month and perform the Dance of the Flaming Arseholes; they have a pig stencil which they playfully spray on people's cars.

Exeter

First term in the Duryard Halls—Moberly House (women) and Murray House (men), then move to 'the cottage' (anything from rooms to a large house, as long as it's off the campus).

Ex-public scholars—lots of Carthusians and Wellingtonians—are called Wellies (after their boots not their school). Some are in the OTC.

Drinking: Cowley Bridge Inn, Double Locks, the Passage at Topsham. Crediton Wine Bar. Mostly G&Ts. Many Sloanes join the exclusive Wine Society. Parties: $2\frac{1}{2}$ hours away by 125 to Paddington, and you do your shopping in London.

Durham

Durham is the only university apart from Oxbridge run on a collegiate system. You live in all-male University College—housed in the castle itself—or the more modern, mixed Van Mildert and Collingwood colleges. You move out to west Durham or a village—Bowburn, Sherburn or Gilesgate.

Students do English or Sociology or, best of all, a general degree, studying a variety of subjects. Lots from the home counties. Campus wear consists of traditional tweeds or tight jeans and bright jumpers.

Very little nightlife—you have to go to Newcastle; a good club is Tuxedo Junction.

Beagling with the Northumberland beagles.

London

Excellent for History of Art—the Courtauld, University and Westfield. King's and Bedford are also Sloane. You live out, and social life is as for the rest of young London Sloanes (see p 101).

Reading

Good for agriculture as an alternative to Cirencester and the other colleges. Close to London and Oxford for socialising.

St Andrews

Preferential admission to Scottish students gives rise to a Scottish landowning contingent. Heavy drinkers. Skiing and beach weekends in season for the English, as it's too far away to go home.

East Anglia

Only for History of Art students—lots of Sloane girls and Army men.

Drinking at the Ferry Boat or Adam & Eve in Norwich.

Racing at Fakenham and Newmarket and point-to-points.

Edinburgh

The other Scottish university, with a larger number of English students. Training corps for all the services.

Abroad

It isn't ultra-Sloane to go to university abroad. You do consider the colleges of your American cousins, the preppies, however. They understand Sloanespeak, and standards are lower than in British universities.

The 'Ivy League' schools used to represent the young elite, but they are too large and diverse to be utterly preppy. You still go to Harvard and Yale though (often for a post-graduate course or to the Harvard Business School), also Princeton and Amherst. Stanford in California has been a Sloane refuge for decades. The popular girls' colleges, in the 'Seven Sisters' group, are Smith, Wellesley and Vassar.

If you don't know how to arrange entry, visa etc to an American college, the US–UK Educational Commission. 6 Porter Street, Baker Street, W1 (486 7697) (open 11–4.30) will help; or Marcia Evans of ERDT, 52 Gloucester Crescent, NW1 (485 2832) counsels (£40 plus VAT for interview and advice) and fits you in somewhere you like (£114 extra for a guaranteed place). Anthony White, Flat 12, 4 Cranley Place, SW7 (584 6053) runs a well-known service for placing Etonians and pupils of other top public schools. (£20 for interview, £80 follow-up services.)

THE
SLOANE RANGER
AT LARGE

Heaven SW7

The flat-sharing years

You always live in the city, once. Every Sloane has to try the assault course, a few years between The Parents and marriage. And it's always London; you've got to do London, really know it. Knowing London means meeting people who know someone you know (better still, their parents know yours). Your address will be SW1, 3, 5, 6, 7, 10 or 11—for about three years. You don't take scholar's trips to Ilford.

The city means flat-sharing. Sloanes always share; whoever heard of a Sloane in a bedsitter, Sloane solitaire? Sloanes *know* people, so a gathering of them is a *shriek* of Sloanes. Your parents—the first flat-sharing generation themselves—feel you're running absolutely *wild*. But you never do. You're wonderfully hermetically sealed-in with other Sloanes, like Russians on a conducted tour of Disneyland.

You share with people you know, often people you've shared with before at your tutorial, or school or somewhere; ideally one of you actually buys the flat with the *tiny capital*. You're all trying to buy now —estate agent friends keep saying 'it's a buyer's market'. Even if that falls down, there are understanding agencies who deal with tenancies on whole flats, or who match people for sharing—ie vet them for Sloaneness. *The Times* isn't what it used to be (when you're looking for a flat-mate 'you get such *ghastly* people') so now, some ads say, unabashedly, 'Sloane Ranger seeks same for flat in SW7'.

London becomes your base for meeting people, for The Work Experience. You Get to Know London Like the Back of Your Hand (the bike route from Fulham to Bond Street). As for Learning About Life, you meet all walks of it (Gloucester Road Friday evening, Fulham Road Saturday morning). In the Europa Supermarket in Old Brompton Road, or strap-hanging in the tube from Gloucester Road, astonish-ingly, you meet *more* people you know. *Extraordinary.*

The teeming slum

The first flat is wonderful; desperately untidy; for the first and last time you can be untidy; you can pile your clothes around so they look like the bed at a party. You can be *schizo*—your idea of seriously bad behaviour one night, your own first dinner party the next. You go out of that flat—which is your idea of Chelsea Set épater-les-bourgeois-Bohemia 1956, or *Vile Bodies*—dressed for Kit Inspection as a City Trainee (stripes) or as a Bond Street receptionist (navy blue pleats).

Take three girls. Or four men (or latterly, *mixed* flat-sharing). But *one's own room*. Three sets of parents give cast-offs and secondary furniture, supplemented by a bit of Habitat and the Furniture Cave. This means despite the intended Bohemia, something between school and the miniature eighteenth-century mansionette emerges. However seedy, battered, or dusty, there'll usually be some reminders of things the Parents have, a proper mantelpiece or a drinks tray. Some little shrine will remind you of WRM—an eighteenth-century print, a Peter Jones repro table with a huge scratch mark and horsy table mats on it. There's got to be somewhere for the dinner parties.

Sloane sharing produces a definite Look, a combination of anyone-for-tennis and fast food.

1) *Parental overflow* The Parents have donated a cretonne-covered sofa, four heavily repaired Regency repro chairs (you make up the dinner party numbers with kitchen ones). Some chintz curtains. Things that say Rectory/Mill House.

2) *The holiday/sportif touches* Fixture lists, sports equipment (skis in the hall). The stool covered in African fabric from the Kenyan cousins, a Super-travel memento.

3) *The modern world intrudes* (you're only

Did Henry say something funny?

Hi-ya!

THE PARTIES

☆ ☆ ☆ ☆ ☆ ☆ ☆ ☆ ☆ ☆ ☆

Sloanes are fanatical party-givers. It's *always* time for another party. The key pretexts are:

Flat-warming
Bring-a-bottle, informal, dips and quiches provided, 8 or 9 till late, held on Friday.

Christmas
Glühwein and mince pies, bring-a-bottle-of-red-wine, mistletoe and tinsel. 7.30 to 9 or 10, then on for meals at Tootsies or Luba's (where you take the left-over bottles). Midweek.

May
At the first sign of summer, Pimm's or Buck's Fizz (using Veuve du Vernay—'V du V'—or méthode champenoise sparkling wine), booze provided, French windows open on to patio/garden until it gets too cold. Starts 7-ish, then on for a meal. Midweek (Wednesday or Thursday).

Birthdays
Drinks, 7.30-ish, select group either to dinner or out for a meal afterwards.

21sts
Either at flat, drinks and smart dinner afterwards with parents and a few friends, or drinks (Buck's Fizz and chewy eats) at Daddy's club—the Army and Navy, Cavalry and Guards, Royal Thames Yacht Club (not so popular now it shares with the Anglo-Belgian) etc. Then smart dinner.

Celebratory
Including national events, especially *royal*. Royal Wedding parties sprang up everywhere, like the ones where you had to come as Charles or Di, or the Patriotic Pimm's Party, dress red, white and blue. Impromptu gatherings with champagne—like when the royal baby was born; also for getting exams or a driving test, new job, etc.

Sloanes in Sloane mood in Sloane Square, the Centre of the Known World.

young once). A Robert Redford/Sting poster in the kitchen (Blondie, Kate Bush or Dolly Parton for boys). Ethnic fast food containers. The Habitat blinds.

4) *Dispatches from Headquarters* Stiffies on the mantelpiece, a yellowing dog pic stuck in the looking-glass frame. Team photographs.

The atmosphere will be unmistakably reminiscent of *school*—the same sort of dormitorial chumminess and jokiness.

Behaviour's fairly school too. Sloanes will lie about each other's whereabouts, support each other in mutual penury; girls lend stockings and washing powder. As they've been brought up in exactly the same way, they almost certainly share fundamental feelings about men and morals, and what to do with both. The same code that assesses suitable guests monitors behaviour, which makes Sloanes very easy to live with. (For example, you know when to leave, even when pressed to stay.) Men know the importance of drinking, have the same tastes in girls and cars (aesthetes, whatever their backgrounds, do not).

Meeting nice people

You live in London to promote your social life. There are more jobs and lots of courses available, but you choose the kind that most enhance your real (ie social) life. You almost always stop for a drink with pin-striped colleagues after work.

Young and hopeful, new to London, Caroline makes a tremendous effort to invite assorted OK friends, acquaintances and friends of acquaintances to dinner. She shrieks 'Drop round for a drink', 'Stay for dinner', 'A crowd of us are going out for a meal, come too'. Of course, her social circle consists entirely of her own kind, so there is no danger of a non-SR turning up. The invitations snowball. Every night should be booked up.

Other people's *serious* dinner parties,

drinks parties, dances, balls and house-parties are four- and five-star events, and warrant a fair amount of anticipation; you might meet Him (or Her). Meanwhile, there's reeling parties at a friend's house, roller-skating, groups for Ascot, Badminton, Henley, Wimbledon, point-to-points, racing and many other Sloane events.

YOUNG SLOANE'S GUIDE TO LONDON

Restaurants/Cafés
You are hardly a mainstay of *The Good Food Guide*. You don't go by the *food* but by the location and people: Sloanes Café (of course); Pizza on the Park; Bistro Vinos everywhere; Peppermint Park; Olivers; Pizza Express, Fulham and Gloucester Road; Parsons; Ambrosiana: King's Road Jam; Foxtrot Oscar; Foxtrot Qango; Hard Rock Café; Luba's Bistro; Nineteen Mossop Street (next to the Admiral Cod); Twin Brothers; Porters; Monkeys; Tootsies; La Brasserie in the Fulham Road for breakfast; Richoux for tea.

Drinking
L'Escapade; Corks; Draycott's; Beachcomber in the Mayfair Hotel; Bas & Annie's Pheasantry; Feelings.

Key pubs
Admiral Codrington; Marquess of Anglesey; Antelope; Australian; Scarsdale Arms; Hereford Arms; Surprise; Windsor Castle; Grenadier.

Nightlife
Witchity; Roxanne; Soul Furnace—sometimes Tokyo Joe's; Annabel's; Raffles.

Also
Roller-skating at the Cornet of Horse, Battersea ice-skating at Queen's, Queensway; Ceroc at Porchester Hall, Bayswater.

Balls
Feathers, Blizzard, Rose, Cinderella, White Nights, Bluebird, Le Ball, Rollerball, Masked, Silent Movie, Thirties, Mayfair, Berkeley Square, Royal Caledonian, St Andrew's, Boat Race, Varsity, Northern Meeting, Perth, Oban and Skye, May and Commem Balls, hunt balls in the Shires. And the Belgrave Square 'Beano'—*the* Sloane funfair.

Discos
Gibson's, Juliana's, A Touch of Class, Rough Silk, Bentley's, Joffin's.

Bands
Chance, Dark Blues.

Two's company—so's three

The Sloane girl doesn't come out any more, she worms her way back in. With all the groundwork done, all she has to do is to capitalise on the contacts that she has made through family, school and school holidays. There'll have been rows at home over the set-up: 'Who are you sharing with?' But Mummie should relax. It's 'independence', but the group won't let you down. They're there to monitor, chaperone and make sure you don't go off the rails.

well, *character* of any man you meet. No one entirely unsuitable would be there in the first place. It's one of the most subtle vetting systems in the world.

Dinner and house parties are the most popular places to meet and pair off (though drinks may mean more chances), since they mean an opportunity to know a new entry on neutral ground. The SR is careful; two or three casual meetings at drinks parties equal one dinner. House parties pre dances are the most popular. You can assess a newcomer before, during and after in an ideal mixture of privacy and company, so any embarrassing silences—lack of basic knowledge—can be avoided on the crucial first date. Balls aren't quite so good, save for the large London charity occasions SRs go to en masse. You feel a certain sporting loyalty to your partner, even if he is a bore.

A meeting over a weekend in the country (dinner, dancing, prolonged lunch and a walk) can be followed by a dinner party at the SR's flat; again more chance to observe on neutral ground (with other people present). An independent assessment's *so* important.

Flat agencies

Malverns Estate Agents, Malvern Court, Onslow Square, SW7 (581 2337) manage flats, and you can take out a tenancy on a whole flat. They charge the landlord 15 per cent on full management and 10 per cent for collecting the rent, but you just pay the normal rent plus one month's rent as a deposit.

Beauchamp Estates, 24 Curzon Street, W1 (499 7722) do the same. They charge the landlord $12\frac{1}{2}$ per cent on full management and 10 per cent for rent collection; you pay the normal rent plus one month's as a deposit.

The following agencies charge one week's rent plus VAT on finding you a flat:

Flatmates Unlimited, 313 Brompton Road, SW3 (589 5491). The Sloanest agency. £2.50 registration fee (if they think they'll be able to find you something).

Flat-Share, 213 Piccadilly, W1 (734 0318). £2.50 registration fee.

Share-a-Flat, 175 Piccadilly, W1 (493 5941). £2 registration fee.

Markham Accommodation Bureau, 70 Old Brompton Road, SW7 (584 7315). No registration fee.

Lunch outside at the Admiral Cod.

Jolly good fun in Redcliffe Gardens.

The Sloane's social system has its own hidden formality. Sloanes don't like over-familiarity from strangers, particularly attempted pick-ups. It's insulting. Young Caroline meets new men—gorgeous, surprising, extraordinary (ie totally familiar) —at point-to-points, balls, drinks parties and dinners (not at work) and always through a third party. Even at a small drinks party you prefer to be introduced rather than to 'get chatting'. This means you can make automatic assumptions about the background, behaviour, and,

The Dinner Party

Who's there

Sloane dinner parties are usually 8 to 12 people. A dinner party usually contains one of each of the following men (so you know where you are):

A Guards or acceptable other regiment officer (the Guards are based in or near London and can easily zoom over for the evening).

A Cirencester man: adds a sense of 'country' to the evening—can be relied upon to wear his tweeds instead of dark flannels or cords and the lambs-wool V-neck. (Estate agent or surveyor is a possible substitute.)

A City Sloane; any one of stockbroker/Lloyds/accountant set and...

A lawyer: probably both these last still pin-striped.

NB *At least three will already know each other*, or at least have mutual friends.

Girls: the two giving the party will be flatmates (one is a 'City' secretary, the other works in a Fulham Road shop). One will invite a friend who 'does' directors' lunches, another will be something slightly wild—in Sloane terms (maybe still a student, doing something *arty*, looking baby-legsish)—but somebody knows her brother. She will add a touch of mystique and cosmopolitanism to the evening.

Typical menu

If a Cordon Bleu trainee/graduate (very likely):
Smoked salmon mousse
Duck with honey
Gratin dauphinoise
Mange-tout
Carrots vichy
Chocolate roulade

If not:
Green pea soup/gazpacho/jellied consommé—all
　served with cream
Quiches and salads or chicken and rice
Mousse or cheesecake
Garlic bread

GAMES YOU PLAY

Sloane dinner parties *degenerate* into *riotous* affairs —meaning games and tricks and jokes. More School.

Eggs

You say 'Give you £10 if I can crack two eggs over your head' and then you crack one and keep the money.

You ask people if they can put an egg in their mouth and then push their jaw so it breaks. You try and crack an egg by squeezing it in one hand (impossible). It ends up with the egg being thrown and the pudding follows.

Moriarty

Two people lie on the floor, face down, blindfolded, holding hands. With the other hand they each have a rolled up magazine (hardened players use *Country Life, Harpers*; sissies use a Sunday supplement); one says, 'Are you there Moriarty?', the other answers 'Yah' and the first has to hit him over the head. Can be dangerous. Col Sir Mike Ansell was lethal because he was blind.

Trains

The leader picks a member of the opposite sex to join on the train and they go chuff-chuffing out of the room. The first slaps the second on the cheek and they return and pick up another. Off the three go, the first then passionately kisses the second, who in turn slaps the last on the cheek. And so on. Fights to be next to the person you fancy; fights not to be last (no kisses at all).

Charades

A variation: one person is told he has to act 'duck-billed platypus', but everyone else is told the answer. So he tries desperately to act it out, while the others put forward ridiculous suggestions and never guess it. Real charades is *the* ideal putdown for anyone who doesn't speak Sloane.

Dreams

Someone says he's thought of a dream and the others have to guess it. In fact he just answers 'yes' to questions ending in a vowel and 'no' to those ending in a consonant. You get situations like 'Was it something to do with bondage?'—yes—'Was Rupert in it?'—no—'What about me?'—yes—'With you?'—yes—etc.

Botticelli

For intellectual Sloanes only—a complicated word game too difficult to explain.

The job as means to an end

A Sloane's job is just a job, not a career. It's not as important as the Things that Really Matter. Excessive enthusiasm about a career is essentially unSloane.

This doesn't mean a lack of willingness to work. Sloanes are always lending a hand—though they are inclined to ask for it back. They are always Doing. Lying around eating grapes is for the non-U and foreigners. It's because *everything* is a job that the job can't be everything.

Five motives lie behind the why and where of Sloane employment:

Why Sloanes work

1 *Keeping busy*—the Devil finds work etc (. . . for the idle hands of rich London debs and Café Society).
2 *Bride of Art*. The Sloane scholar/vestal virgin. Do not imagine that Sloane Rangers *never* immolate themselves on the altar of some high purpose.
3 *Social work, Sloane style*. ie meeting more people.
4 *Lots of walkies*. Sloanes like to get ite and abite; they are like dogs, always jumping up and rushing off somewhere. They hate to be tied to one desk or counter or stove for more than two hours. Because of this, Sloanes are natural temps, natural travellers on well-defined Sloane routes. They bring the open air in on their clothes.
5 *Making money to help Henry* (if married). Though Sloanes don't get paid that well. But the odd thousand seems little to give up for the advantages of working in a firm where you can do number 3, and where, with luck, there is a kindred spirit of the same age to chat to, with whom you can carry on where you left off at secretarial college.

So where exactly should one lend a hand? Well, there are twelve obvious probabilities—jobs where Sloane is spoken:

Where Sloanes work
Travel/Secretarial/Publishing world/Art world/Looking after children/Looking after animals/Estate agents/Shops/Own businesses/'Handicrafts' and 'creative design'/Flowers/Cooking.

The secretarial Sloane

The secretarial Sloane helps 'Top-Job Men' in a non-specific way. Secretarial skills are one passport to travel (cooking is the other). Or you can work in Britain if the social life is simmering nicely at the moment.

You are on the PA or receptionist level; never in the pool. You're not very good at typing—speeds about 90/45—and not a natural speller, but you've got common sense and a jolly good telephone manner (you're not that good at taking the messages, but still). You are rather stylish, fairly conscientious and project a good image for the firm: the right sort of girl.

On the debit side, you cannot immerse yourself in the job because you have Higher Obligations. It is one's *duty* to go to the year's events, not optional fun. You expect two or three days or at least afternoons off for whatever part of the Victorian Season your parents have taught you to observe (say, Wimbledon, the Royal Academy private view, Glyndebourne, Ascot, the Derby), and two or three more for weddings. It would be *appallingly* wrong to miss a friend's wedding for any reason but serious illness. Nor do you approve of the modern habit of skipping the church and going to the reception afterwards.

On days without important public ceremonies, you have your own small round to keep up. You spend idle moments making lists of people to telephone, shopping to buy, and dinner party guests. Your mind is always recalculating the moment when you will arrive home in Fulham, and the real day can begin.

This brings us to two questions.
1 *Why is Caroline valued at work despite her clock-watching?*

THE SLOANE TRIANGLE

Some Sloanes have been to the Inchbald School of Design *and* Constance Spry's Winkfield Place *and* the Cordon Bleu, so can make their living any one of three ways: or, like one overtrained Sloane cook, can ride to do the lunch *and* the flowers on a bicycle she painted to look like bamboo.

2 *Why does reliable Caroline not go higher at work?*

The answer is: 1) integrity; 2) trains.

Caroline's value to her boss, apart from her pleasantness and classiness, is that she works to help him in the hierarchy. She will not lend her support to any ambitious young thruster or leak the firm's secrets to a rival. Slyness is literally foreign to her (she often doesn't notice it in a well-bred Briton. If she does, she says 'He could hide behind a *corkscrew!*').

She identifies completely with the management because they are the officers, but in reality she isn't like them. She *isn't* trying to win in a competitive world.

Trains remind you of what really matters. The hour or so on Friday evening a Sloane spends in the train ticketytocking through the landscape to some Old Rectory is what sets the office in perspective. One can't *imagine* why the boss was so upset about that contract we missed—we'll catch another at the trade fair, it stands to reason...and now for the weekend...

So, when it comes to promotion, the boss chooses the involved, sly Merle the Knife, who takes the game seriously. The Knife will never see the rat-race in perspective and keeps its head down reading reports if it goes in a train.

Sloane secretarial job agencies

The Golden Rule is: go to an agency which will know what suits you and not try to harness you to the accounts department of Blogg's Pharmaceuticals in Brentford. All the Sloane agencies pay a moderately good rate and their clients for temps are the same as for permanent jobs (temping is almost a Sloane verb), so you are sent to *nice* companies.

Secretarial job agencies in London
Bernadette of Bond Street, 55 New Bond Street, W1 (629 1204)—art world jobs; *Curzon Bureau*, 30 Brook Street, W1 (629 3258); *Grosvenor Bureau*, 43 South Molton Street, W1 (499 6566)—publishing and the arts; *Joyce Guinness Staff Bureau*, 21 Brompton Arcade, SW3 (589 8807); *Winifred Johnson*, 118 New Bond Street, W1 (493 3005); *Angela Mortimer*, 166 Piccadilly, W1 (629 9686)—art world, estate agents; *Senior Secretaries*, 173 New Bond Street, W1 (499 0092)—more high-powered, but send you for jobs with good pay; *Gordon Yates*, 35 Old Bond Street, W1 (493 5787)—art world, estate agents.

The Sloane in the publishing world

Publishing is deeply Sloane; jobs here merit a congenial corner with your own desk and own *telephone*; therefore proper publishing—books, newspapers and magazines (not microfilm, technical papers) —is a natural habitat for the Sloane Ranger. There are two Sloane types in publishing:

Caroline A
left school after O-levels, or after the first year of A-levels, and took a secretarial course. Book publishing appeals as you can enliven parties by describing what a famous author said to you on the telephone or did to you in the lift.

Caroline B
read English or History at university, then did a speedwriting course. Unlike Caroline A, she is eager to read scripts in her spare time, makes fewer telephone calls and is a member of the Society of Young Publishers. She could be a Bride of Art. (This is one of the few jobs at which she could become a real pro.)

Book publishers Sloanes work for
Mostly literary houses, pillars of Bloomsbury—never trade or scientific.

Jonathan Cape (books with class—and a managing director with a gift for publicity); *William Collins* (Scotch and solid, home of the Bible and David Attenborough); *Debrett's* (Fulham local, complete record of people who matter); *Faber & Faber* (a delicious managing director); *Hamish Hamilton* (wonderful parties and a list that solves Christmas agonies); *Heinemann* (not as trendy as it was, but convenient for the Curzon); *Hodder &*

Sloanes spend hours on the telephone in search of 'a man for Tuesday'.

Caroline chains her bike—well-built and sensible—outside Hodder and Stoughton.

Stoughton (Stoaton, *not* Stouton); *Michael Joseph* (home of the middle-brow best-seller; Herriot and Edwardian Ladies); *Oxford University Press* (in Oxford—ex-Ox & Cow/Marlborough intake); *Quartet* (solidly Sloane); *Weidenfeld* (convenient if you're a rare South of the River Sloane, but such a bore at lunchtime).

Other publishing options

The literary agencies can be livelier and better paid than actual book publishing, and it *feels* so high-powered. And now Sloanes are back in newspapers in a big way (in the ghastly Sixties there was said to be a sole Etonian in Fleet Street). The Sloanes' perennial eagerness to get on to magazines, preferably a glossy, has been fed by seeing the pictures of untapped parties in the *Tatler* and the give-away magazines. They also like (and are needed by) certain advertising agencies and public relations firms: Sloanes add tone. In fact, most of the Sloanes working for the newspapers and glossies are in the advertising section, not editorial. Intellectual journal-ists despise the advertising people, but Sloanes are after *class* status. They would rather be secretary to the amusing advertising manager, if he's a civilised person (public schoolboy), than to the literary editor, a dreary little lecher in spectacles. After all, the newspaper's name is what counts.

The Sloane in the art world
The auction houses

The London auction rooms have nice people—and other nice people's things on the block. The great auction rooms are part of What Really Matters. Your family are keen for you to exploit that friend/relation on the board of Sotheby's, so after a short arts course and a few weeks at speedwriting (see p 84), armed with the difference between walnut and mahogany, you approach the Contact. You soon start work on the front counter. You are horrified to find you must be there when the doors open at 9, but at least you can leave at 4.30 when the doors shut. You are told never to wear trousers ('You are always on view') and to be gentle with old ladies ('You never know what they may have hidden in those brown paper parcels'). You soon learn to avoid eye contact and thus keep clients waiting without apparently realis-ing. You enjoy being an art world receptionist (at dinner parties you simply say 'I'm at Sotheby's'). The only bore is not being able to use the telephone often enough.

Christie's is similar. Full of Sloanes paid a pittance but aiming for the picture or furniture departments and saying they want to get 'out of the secretarial rut' and become, perhaps, a technical assistant. But openings often actually scare Caroline and she neatly forgets to put in her application in time.

The only danger is that you'll stay there forever—a Bride of Art, a spinster in the world. This was the fate of several of the Sotheby's Sloanes in the early

On the Works of Art counter at Sotheby's.

sixties. There is little husband material in the London auction-houses—some of the young men, though nice, being...bachelors.

Sloany sale-rooms in London

Bonham's, Montpelier Street, SW7 (584 9161), and Knightsbridge and Chelsea. The most relaxed, smallest one of the top four. Very Sloane.

Christie's, 8 King Street, SW1 (839 9060), and South Ken (and New York, Paris, Geneva, etc—*never* forget that). Similar to rival Sotheby's. Cosy from the inside, and you might *get* in, as there is a quick turnover (low wages, marriage).

Phillips Son & Neale, 7 Blenheim Street, W1 (629 6602), and NW1 and W2 (Phillips West). Has even more sale-rooms in Britain outside London than the Big Two. Professional but not so social.

Sotheby's, 34 New Bond Street, W1 (493 8080), and Belgravia. Plus Parke Bernet in New York and branches all over the world and the country.

Art galleries and museums

Art galleries have their pluses too—some of them. Prints, antiquities, coins and jewels all count for something. The Tate and V & A have *racks* of Sloanes. You want to work with old things, or new things where you can tell what they are, but not those ridiculous abstracts. You're a natural for water-colour galleries since, unlike oils, they are unchangeable and

assert all that is best in British landscape and architecture. You love helping to organise private views when all your skills are used.

Estate agents

If you have the gift of the gab and a shade more ambition than most SRs, an estate agent opens exactly the right door for you: you can become a negotiator, selling houses, and get your own secretary, all without being qualified. Young firms are brimming with self-confident, self-made salesperson Sloanes, all telephoning and seeing clients noisily at once. They sweep clients along with their OK certainty. Estate agentry is Caroline's equivalent of the City Money Game.

Timider Sloanes can play safe as estate agent secretaries, mixing with the *gorgeous* young men (this is one field of work where men actually outnumber women). For London estate agents manned by Caroline see Henry working as an estate agent, p 115.

The institutional options

Certain institutions are at the heart of Itness, What Really Matters—like the National Trust; stately homes. The most stately of course is Buckingham Palace (known as BP, which confuses non-Sloanes). You have to be ultra discreet but you might get called in for Big Occasions. Sometimes Buck House puts on a do for its staff—like the one to celebrate PC's engagement. Lovely to type in those big letters on that grey paper with the red heading: 'I am commanded by Her Majesty...'

MI5 and MI6 have the Sloane as secret weapon. Below the middle levels, the security services are 100 per cent staffed by Sloanes.

Or you can glimpse the life of the famous by working for a Conservative MP (other parties unheard of—even SDP). 'Dear Mrs Creepe, Thank you so much for writing to Mr McNair-Wilson about badgers with TB. Although he is not in London at present he has asked me to write and tell. you how much he appreciates your views. Yours sincerely, Arabella Sloane'. From obvious motives, you could also work in one of the men's professional worlds such as Lloyds, ICI, the Stock Exchange.

The Sloane cook

Sloanes have taken over cooking: 'Sloane' and 'cook' are practically the same thing. There Caroline is, grating carrots for the directors' lunch beside the East End cleaning lady (even Sloanes are beginning to drop 'char') and feeling proud to have the job. Mummie's thrilled too. Why? Because

A WORKING SLOANE DOES NOT LUNCH ALONE

Lunch is the highlight of the working day: almost two hours of fun. You always take it at 12.30 or 1, never later. You book up four days of the week with friends, one or two or even three a day (you need one lunch hour to shop for a dinner party or have your hair done). The night before simply hasn't happened until it has been discussed, analysed or shown off to a girlfriend the following day—girls seen *lunching* with men are in all probability Mayfair Mercenaries.

You order a glass of vino and lasagne (hence the Sloane figure) and get down to news from home, dispatches, consolation for defeat in skirmishes: all offered with hoots of laughter. You discuss the boss: he is *'totally* unreasonable' when he is not being *'so sweet'*. You swap news of friends.

Your own revelations are conducted in double-talk unless the friend is the very best and closest variety and the crisis very serious. Normally, 'I am about to be sacked' is rendered: 'I am thinking about taking a job as a chalet girl'. 'My boyfriend has taken up with another girl' becomes 'I haven't seen Charlie for yonks, I've been too busy.' And later, with feeling, 'Sarah P-W is very attractive, isn't she?'

Parting involves the full ritual. 'You *must* come to dinner'/'We *must* meet for lunch more often'/'I really *will* telephone you—it's been lovely to see you—bye.'

You briefly window-shop and buy a *Standard* before returning to work at 2.25.

Travel agents

These appeal to sophisticated Rangers, the ones who wear more make-up and who take Mr Hovis to work in a shopping basket. Being the usual mad keen traveller, you like the perks ('We can get you cheap flights over to Palma') and enjoy spending a lot of time on the telephone ('You can paint your nails at the same time').

The ones to fly to

John Morgan Travel, 35 Albemarle Street, London W1 (499 1911); *Small World*, Russell Chambers, WC2 (240 3233); *Supertravel*, 22 Hans Place, SW1 (584 5060).

Other travel jobs with the same agencies include couriers, cleaners, cooks, receptionists, secretaries in the office abroad. 'You've got to be good at languages, good in a crisis—the loos in the villa seize up and you've got to lay your hands on the local plumber pronto.'

cooking was an Empty Quarter and you've colonised it and now administer it. Granny didn't cook, of course, but the working class has now moved out ('Kathleen *could* boil an egg—if it came frozen in a packet'). Mummie is an *amateur* follower of Elizabeth David and Robert and Claudia and Anton M., Caroline has gone *professional* and joined a cooking service whose officers will go anywhere in the world to ensure that a skier or villa person or hunting-house-party guest gets proper leek and potato soup and boeuf en croûte and lemon soufflé.

Hundreds of Sloane cooks operate on their own, getting jobs by social contacts or a Personal Column ad in *The Times*, the *Telegraph* or the local paper, but some work through Sloane agencies.

Sloane cooking agencies

All these work in London and the rest of the country.

Blues Agence de Cuisine, 19 Oxberry Ave,

THE CORDON BLUES

Caroline gets tired of her round of Leadenhall Market (like a club for young Sloanes), followed by the feeding of the 5,000 (well, twelve) directors, all of whom are married or worse. She gets Lumley's to book her for a shooting party in Scotland.

But the castle is freezing cold and the hours virtually solid from 7 am—making porridge, bacon and eggs and real coffee for fifteen people—to 2 am next morning, when the last of the dinner crocks are washed up. And she has to make a picnic lunch for the men and ends up having to trek up the hills with it.

She has had enough. Back she goes to her agency, who send her to 'a really super job doing a little cooking for a film star in the South of France'. This turns out to be looking after three illegitimate spoilt children (nanny left the day before Caroline arrived), giving his current wife's incontinent mother blanket baths, cycling miles to the nearest village at 6 every morning because wife likes *fresh* bread for breakfast, cleaning all the rooms and looking after a constant stream of famous guests, who treat her as if she wasn't there. Caroline goes home whiter than she arrived, her nerves in shreds. She should have known. Theatricals are a nightmare.

But a Cordon Bleu doesn't stay blue. She contacts John Morgan Travel, who pack her off to cook in a villa in Greece, where the heat goes completely to her head. She has an affair with semi-literate, devastatingly handsome Spiro from the village, gets brown (Sloane word for tanned) and thin and makes *thousands* of wonderful friends. At the end of the season she comes back to England and realises that apart from 3 to 5 with Spiro, she was working like a slave. 'Never again,' she resolves. Next summer she rushes back; Spiro is marrying his village bride this year, having broken fifteen villa Sloanes' hearts.

So, picking up the pieces of her own shattered thumper, she defects to Small World and becomes a Muribird. It turns out to be a *very* small world, full of libidinous guests and crews, who all know each other and are *bent* on sharing the Good Life. For the winter it is off to Méribel as a chalet girl. Piste day and night.

Back in England, after all this Broadening, Caroline becomes tremendously fat and emotionally unbalanced. With half her heart in the Med and the other half in the Alps, she is well and truly off the rails: a *fermented boozy* Sloane. Whether she meets a nice Sloane Ranger man and gets back on the track for his sake is crucial now. Other Sloanes can be cruel if someone's 'a bit of a mess'.

London SW6 (731 4353); *The Lumley Employment Co*, 17 Walton Street, SW3 (581 2241); *Lucie Morton*, 16 Star Street, W2 (402 7339); *Party Planners*, 56 Ladbroke Grove, W11 (220 9666), run by Lady Elizabeth Shakerley, who is the Queen's cousin ...

A *must* for professional pot-bangers is *Cooking for Profit* by Sloanes Sukie Hemming and Rosamund Wallinger, published in '82 (Jill Norman & Hobhouse).

Cooking can enable you to see the world, and see Life.

The Sloane as shopgirl

As with cooking, so with shopgirling; it's moved upmarket. 'You look just like a shopgirl' used to be the Sloane father's insult. But the original shopgirls are moving up and out and the Sloane finds it fun to serve, though only in Sloane shops.

I know we haven't been introduced but may I buy this saucepan?

Proprietors were having difficulty getting salespeople to be deferential, but the more socially secure of the Sloanes positively enjoy saying 'Sir' or 'Madam' in stores—it rubs in one's sense of superiority.

In the boutiques and present-shops patronised by Sloanes, of course it's invaluable to be served by a Sloane, who will have an unerring instinct as to what is right and acceptable, without embarrassing explanations.

Shops with Sloane staff
Asprey's (a few); the General Trading Co (100 per cent); Harrods (have a training scheme leading to becoming a buyer if you're lucky, but hundreds of Sloanes, male and female, work there at Christmas); Harvey Nichols; Hatchard's; Jones; Justin de Blank; Liberty's; Night Owls; Parrots; Presents; any ski shop or department.

The Sloane as entrepreneuse
A few Carolines use their initiative and start 'little businesses' or shops to make money from other Sloanes. They don't look 'down the market', or plan to go commercial. They set up plant-sitting or flower-watering businesses; they do interior decorating (see pp 136/137); mind houses and forward letters; feed cats and walk dogs; arrange other people's parties; make sandwiches and sell them to City businessmen; do shopping and ferry children: Universal Aunts love them.

A Sloane might set up a business in which Henry was more than a sleeping partner. See p. 116.

The Sloane as flower-arranger
Many Sloanes do the flowers for hospitals, big firms, weddings etc, going to market like the cook Sloanes but earlier. For them it's to Nine Elms market, and then arranging the unfortunate chrysanthemums, gypsophila, pittosporum etc into those pretentious shapes Sloanes like, perhaps because they resemble a three-dimensional chintz. British upper-class aesthetes arrange flowers with unparalleled naturalness and beauty, but Sloanes believe in disciplining them firmly.

The Sloane as craftswoman
'I do special painting'. The freelance dragger, stippler, marbler, trompe l'oeiler and all the other things Sloanes have learned to do to walls in recent years makes up the third side of the Sloane triangle. Other creative Sloanes tie-dye fabric, knit 'specials', do patchwork and dressmaking, make lingerie, mend china. They like sil-

versmithing ('It's so relaxing in a funny sort of way, hammering and making a dreadful noise'), and make silver jewellery, pillboxes and sets of teaspoons. They flog their handiworks to their friends, above all the friends (older entrepreneurial Sloanes) with shops. There has to be an easy outlet for what they make, because Rangers find it very demoralising tramping round shops trying to do a *saleswoman* act (although brash when pushing other people's things, they have been trained not to be able to sell themselves or their own work).

Looking after children

Some Sloanes are terrific disciplinarians —natural *fathers*. (Most relax only with their animals.) The Sloanes who work with children (like the Princess of Wales) because they like them are the rare Sloanes who are not too nervy to show warmth. But Sloane nannies *can* be the dread any-where-as-long-as-it's-abroad Sloanes.

Caroline as nanny runs into problems with nouveau-riche families who do not understand that they have a *lady* working for them. Some even put the nanny on a semi-servant footing with young men who are guests of the house! When this happens to Caroline, Mummie and Daddy try to give her employers a hint as to her true standing, such as getting the local bigwig to invite her to something.

The nice nanny

Trained at Norland or Princess Christian or the Chiltern College, armed with her NNEB (see p 88), Caroline copes admirably with the bawling baby, and could make its clothes and wash its cotton nappies, but she usually finds she learned these skills for nothing. She becomes terribly attached to gorgeous little Charlie Bubbles and can't understand his parents: 'Why don't they hug him more?'

Sloane au pairs/mother's helps

Not a natural Sloane job, because of the housework. Also, Sloanes are not tactful enough to fit easily into a foreign family. However, as you do want to work in France, Switzerland and America (most; and a string of countries after that), you decide to have a go.

Posts in America are usually with the Army or diplomatic families. 'I got paid extra for cooking formal dinners.' Of course, looking after American children is a bit of a strain. You have to teach them table manners, and that television is not essential to life.

Sloane babysitting

Hard work for the parents. When Caroline sits, she likes the children to be in bed when she arrives and the fridge and the drinks cabinet to be full. Nothing can make up for this intrusion into her social calendar—but the party-going Mummie and Daddy must certainly *try*.

Caroline as teacher or matron

With your nursery nursing course, you can work in a kindergarten, or you can do the Montessori course like the Princess of Wales and work somewhere like the Young England school in Pimlico. The hours are short but it's very hard work, though rewarding. You are quite ready to go home by 2.30. The pay is appalling; you can't live on it, and if your parents are going through a financial crisis you may have to work in the evenings, say, as a waitress. Bistro Vinos are bursting with Sloanes.

Or what about assistant matron at a prep or public school? If you become an assistant matron at a boys' public school, you will be pursued by the Sixth Form but will probably marry a master (Sloanes are in demand to help young masters qualify for their own House). Your motto should be *ave care, Caro*.

The myth of the bone-idle Sloane

The Sloane man's approved job circuit is still pretty narrow. Girls can go into nice parts of unSloane businesses sometimes. Men can't. You go into what you were trained for or it's a *tragedy*. How many Sloanes has anyone met in, say, plastic moulding manufacture, ladies' dress wholesaling or library work?

Sloanes usually don't go into the mainstream of commercial and industrial middle management—the modern world —either, because Sloaneness hasn't got any particular edge there. And being a marketing manager for something that fills a shelf in Tesco won't get you far with a girl from Supertravel at a cocktail party.

The exceptions are those huge international businesses which are city states in themselves and have gentleman ambassadors—BP, Shell and so on.

As a Sloane you're also cut off from the jobs the trendy middle-class find exciting —most media; some academia; intellectual and arty stuff—which Sloanes consider only suitable for swots or buggers. Sloanes don't have a word for NW1, but they know it when they see it.

The ideal Sloane job is one you could imagine in a set of engravings of eighteenth-century characters: the Lawyer, the Farmer, the Wine Merchant, etc. If Sloanes work for a company they like it to be old: ideally a family business. Hard-selling businesses and hard(ware)-making businesses are unSloane, because they don't have room for your particular intangible skills. Anyway the people there have the wrong shoes and those furnishing fabric ties.

Which leaves the country, the Law,

'I'm in the City, for my sins.' After work, Sloanes accumulate more sins at their favourite watering hole.

the City and the Services (Civil and Military). Sloanes aren't the only men there but they're the dashing men there. There's no special way to sift them out ('Carriage for country member Sir John!' brought half the members of White's into the hall when England was a White's man's country. You might get a few Sloanes if you Tannoyed 'Will the gentleman who's left his car number XXX 000 on a double yellow line in charge of a dog...' or 'Important announcement concerning the 4.52 to Newbury' or 'the 3.30 at Sandown', or 'Will the person who owns the very ripe cheese please...' or 'Will the gentleman who placed a call to Lucie Clayton's please . . .').

Apart from diversions, Henry works away: never rising to the top, because he despises the scramble of ambition and anyway doesn't know how to win on the corporate battlefield. Henry is a serving animal, a horse or dog. Any attempts to turn himself into a shark only lead to disaster (or prison). Henry talks about office politics as though it was germ warfare and *naturally* he's hopeless at it ('I'm no good at office politics,' he will say in a tone both cheerful and relieved). He feels he's *entitled* to respect from the lower orders, as he gives respect to his superiors. But the calculated gaining and manipulating of power is not Sloane; perhaps because the Sloane hierarchy is fixed.

Jobs for the (Sloane) boys

Something in the City

Henry is a stockbroker (in Cazenove's—the Sloanest —Rowe & Pitman, Grieveson Grant, Capel-Cure Myers) or he is in the commodity markets or insurance. Many SRMs are members of Lloyd's. At the Stock Exchange they carry on those schoolboy pranks of throwing bits of paper at each other (sometimes alight) and trading jokes. Unfortunately the heyday of Stock Exchange wit is past, as the members get more professional and more like boring other people.

Banking attracts Sloanes. Investment wanking is particularly popular, so is merchant wanking (merchant wankers are coveted by Caroline for dinner parties: she loves securing a Hoare—or someone from Warbugger's). Henry travels to the States, Middle East, Far East (catch up with Hong Kong Sloane contingent, get clothes copied by Sam). It's just the ticket at Guinness Mahon, Kleinwort Benson, Lazard's, Warburg's, Hambro's, Baring's, Schroder Wagg, Morgan Grenfell, Hill Samuel, Rothschild's.

The Law

'The Bar' is the ultimate in Sloane legal WRM. The world of solicitors is more mixed. Dealing with important matters in archaic clothes (Sloanes wear the wig and gown with the dash of the top-hat classes), in important archaic buildings like your old school: all very suitable. Old social chestnuts promulgate the gentlemen's club aspect—when two barristers are introduced they never shake hands (both being men of honour, they traditionally have no need to demonstrate they are unarmed). Shy SRMs who have not shaken off the mantle of public school are relieved there are so few women at the Bar (just enough to load the family work on to—SRMs dislike Divorce). Prime SR solicitors are Slaughter & May, Freshfields, (Sir) Charles Russell, Clifford-Turner, Theodore Goddard, Allen & Overy, Farrer's, Frere Cholmeley, Withers (divorce), Linklaters & Paines.

The gentlemanly voice used to be an asset to a barrister, but these juries nowadays...Sloanes proliferate in all four Temples, though they used to congregate in the Middle—like an Oxbridge college. The old rhyme has some truth:

> Inner for the rich,
> Middle for the poor,
> Lincoln's for the scholar,
> Gray's for the bore.

Gray's Inn has the best wine cellar, Middle

the best food and the nicest Hall. Inner is probably the most reserved; Lincoln gets the bulk of Chancery work. All the Sloanes affect very dirty *old* wigs—they think it's chic. Meanwhile the jury are longing to slip them a packet of Persil.

Chartered accountancy
Full of SRMs, who know this is the modern gentleman's qualification and have slogged to get it. You like going out on

go-ahead company led by the dashing Langton brothers), Chestertons (the Church of England people, lots of luxury lets in London but country houses department attracts Sloanes), Cluttons (handle the Queen's land), John German Ralph Pay, Hampton's (started as an upmarket movers, now a residential agent in London and Surrey), Humberts (who achieved the double coup of selling both Highgrove to Prince Charles—and Land's

---

THE BOOKS HENRY REWRITES

PARKINSON'S LAW
C. Northcote Parkinson
Henry's job doesn't expand to fill the time available. He finishes it at the double and goes out for an hour or works on his form book or writes to his sister.
THE PETER PRINCIPLE
Laurence J. Peter and Raymond Hall
Why shouldn't a person be promoted above their ceiling of competence? Dr Peter's got it wrong too. The top men *are* often gaga, but it's only fair. They've worked for it.
UP THE ORGANIZATION
Robert Townsend
The organization as an all-absorbing life style— that's *self-evidently* ridiculous.

POWER (IN THE OFFICE)
Michael Korda
Getting a corner desk—surely one wants the desk near the window? Anyway one takes what one's given—for a time. And behavior in the lift—Henry is only interested in misbehavior in the lift.
THE PRINCE
Niccolo Machiavelli
Those bloody Iago types. The office has too many of them already. Othello was a rough, black-diamond Sloane.
WINNING THROUGH INTIMIDATION
Robert J. Ringer
Henry refused to open this one. But he says his boss knows it by heart.

---

audits—fresh pubs and shepherd's pie new, and the possibility of blasts from the past. You claim to be the men from Peat Marwick Mitchell, Price Waterhouse, Saffery's or Arthur Andersen. You might learn a bit *too* much about the books here.

Estate agents
Sloanes like houses and land, and customers like Sloanes. Estate agenting appeals to the slicker SRM: deals and property talk. You could set up on your own later, having worked for one of the top firms: or move out to country branch (covered in scars). Sloanes with no estate agent connections in the family will tell you that they are all a shower of sharks. Top firms include: Aylesford's (a young

End), Jackson-Stops & Staff ('Jackson Stop-Start'), Knight Frank & Rutley (king of the residential agents. Grand offices in Hanover Square with Sloane receptionist), Savills, Winkworth and John D. Wood.

The arts
Henrys are relatively rare in the art world —frankly, it's often too poofy and/or intellectual for you (this is *very* sad for all of the greenery-yallery, Grosvenor Gallery Carolines). You understand land, money, property, horses far better than the arts. Still, occasionally a Sloane will be found in the sale-rooms—perhaps working for a country branch of Phillips Son & Neale— or even in a gallery for a spell. A few hide in Sotheby's, Christie's, and Bonham's.

The Army

A natural. Being a leader, being of service, being regimented, come easily to you. Any regiment that sounds as though it is still in the saddle or carrying weapons obsolete by the seventeenth century. See page 90 for what your mobs are called. A lot of City Rangers train with the Honourable Artillery Company in the evenings.

Medicine

Medsun. Some Sloanes become doctors (*none* dentists), and they're very re-assuring at the bedside. For instance, Sir John Hunt's practice in Sloane Street (he's the Queen's physician).

Business

Covers a multitude of unSloane outfits, but OK if it's a family one—import/export, say, or manufacturing paper.

The wine trade

Very Sloane. Wine merchant is a Sloane word like merchant banker. Country estates. Very Special Old Pale families, and alcohol. Lots of chums in it too. Justerini & Brooks, Christopher's (masses of Christophers and Henrys), Morgan Furze, Peter Dominic, Berry Bros & Rudd. Also the OK brewers, the beerage and grouse-moorage: Vaux, Courage, Guinness, Bass Charrington, Whitbread.

Own little business

Sloanes often start up on their own. You don't try to sell to the masses, you go for things you like yourself. Sloanes were the fire behind various smoked-fish and smoked-poultry businesses in recent years, such as Mostly Smoked.

You particularly like telephone-and-we'll-bike-it-over businesses. Duff & Trotter, the high-class grocery firm started by two young London Sloanes, combines the two.

Sloanes liked the days when London telephone exchanges had letters on the dials and were called things like PARk, FITzroy, KNIghtsbridge, FLAxman, FRO-

I'm a pop star, ha-ha!

bisher, because they could try to get appropriate numbers and call their businesses PARtyfd, FIToeat, KNIts4u, FLAtshr, FROgwyn and other such Sloane ideas. All-figures haven't the same flavour.

When they have moved to the Old Rec, Henry and Caroline may start up in mail order, selling such Sloane essentials as printed dishcloths or tapestry kits.

Country jobs

The country SRM is the one who adores his work and talks of little else—limiting the field of friends thereby. Henry makes an excellent *land agent*, after Cirencester and a couple of years on the estate of a landed family friend. SRM are extremely good *farmers*, engrossed and bossy: Caroline mayn't produce anywhere near lambing time because she has to help. On the White's Club principle (see p 114), a loud shout of 'Henry! The animals are out on the road,' anywhere in Cheshire, Shropshire, Northumberland, Herefordshire, Hampshire or Berkshire should produce at least two Sloanes.

Henry might be a *solicitor* with local top firm, something in the *bloodstock industry*, an agricultural *salesman*—rural repping. He knows his life looks stodgy viewed from the rat race, but he values living in the country and having time to do What Really Matters more than the opinion of City slickers.

Public relations

Firms who represent important things like merchant banks and foreign governments still need you, with your good seat on a bully, calming voice and light hand on the old-boy net. People have to be taken out to lunch. PRs known for SRs are Dewe Rogerson, Forman House, Charles Barker Lyons, Welbeck, Shandwick, Neilson-McCarthy.

Advertising

Not as many OEs as when Bernard Gutteridge wrote *The Agency Game* about them, but J. Walter Thompson still shelters many Sloanes, as do Charles Barker and Vernon Stratton (OE, O. Cherrypicker, O. Olympic yachtsman).

New fields that have opened in the last ten years

Acting didn't use to be a Sloane profession, but now public-school boys are working like navvies to people all the television dramas of high life (Christopher Cazenove, Anthony Andrews, Nigel Havers, etc). Smart *journalism* is aspired to by young Sloanes who have seen Nicholas Coleridge, Tim de Lisle, Bobby Butler-Sloss leap into glossies straight from the *Eton Chronicle* and thence into newspapers without a break in studying or party-going. *Waiter or barman* is all right at a restaurant or bar run by other Sloanes. SR *builders* are becoming thick on the ground: Alistair Dickson of Treliganus, Nick Jenkins, Dominic O'Halloran, Simon de Haan—all public-school builders operating in London.

──HENRY'S DAY──

Getting to work in London

About half an hour before the army of female Sloanes, Henry leaves the flat he shares with a couple of friends in Chelsea, Earl's Court, SW7 or W11, feeds his trousers into his bicycle clips—relished because they're charlie—and heads for the City on his bike. Or he might mount his motorbike; he greatly enjoys the effect he makes, helmeted, begauntleted, padded, on early-bird Ranger girls, who tell him he looks 'a scream', 'an oik', 'a messenger boy', 'a moon man'.

If he goes by tube, he goes via one of the Sloane stations—which are *rather* grim and silent at this unearthly hour, 8.30, before the dawn chorus of Carolines—and gets his head into the *FT*, always standing up for the old and ladies, often finding a mate on the train with whom he can discuss his 'senior hangover'. His friend is also 'feeling a bit silly'. Since the sky is grey, they might have their rolled umbrellas and galoshes (loafer type, from Harrods). One has Sloane brief-case A, purposely old and battered, the other has Sloane brief-case B, a smart black leather number with his initials and a gold lock. The brief-cases both contain the Sloane bible cum joke book, *Private Eye*. Henry also has *Punch*, to augment his joke intake. He gets off at Temple, Mansion House, Monument, Chancery Lane or Bank.

Now for the unfun bit.

Propping up the lads

Four hours later, Henry lunches with the lads, in a restaurant, pub or a specially treasured working-class caff ('greasy spoon'). They have a bit of a giggle, discuss form, recount the jokes they read in the *Eye* or heard on the car radio or in the office, build (not buy) each other a drink and pay for it with greenies, crispies, lottery tickets, drinking vouchers. The Sloanes provide a background of noizak wherever they are. The lucky places they do the noizak for at lunchtime are: R. M. BIRLEY'S SANDWICH BAR (son of Mark Birley who owns Annabel's), 9 Fenchurch Street, EC3 ● BOW WINE VAULTS, 10 Bow Churchyard, EC4 ● THE CITY BOOT, 7 Moorfields Highwalk, EC2 ● THE CITY FOB by Tower Bridge (have special beer, their own brew) ● FINO'S WINE CELLAR, 123 Mount Street, W1 (all the estate agents go) ● GEORGE AND VULTURE CHOPHOUSE, 3 Castle Court, EC3 ● THE GRENADIER, Wilton Row, SW1 ● JAMAICA WINE HOUSE ('Jampot'), Jamaica Court, off Cornhill, EC3 ● LOOSE BOX, 7 Cheval Place, SW7 ● MOTCOMBS, 6 Motcomb Street, SW1 ● MYTTONS ('Gloves') CLUB, 25 Lime Street, EC3 ● OLDE WINE SHADES, 6 Martin Lane, EC4 ● ORMOND'S, Ormond Yard, SW1 ● SIMPSON'S, 38½ Cornhill, EC3 ● SWEETINGS, 39 Queen Victoria Street, EC4

Now for the unfun bit again.

Home by way of Australia

At last it's time for the really fun bit. Henry may stop off at a stand-up-and-shout (cocktail party) or be going out to dins. Otherwise he will head straight for the young SRM's HQ, the Admiral Cod in Mossop Street, or the Australian in Milner Street. There the barman builds him several drinks—snorts and wets are what Rangers call them. Whisky is nutbrown, gin and tonic Ranger's Delight or or gee and tee. Other SRM pubs: the Windsor Castle in Campden Hill Road, the Hereford Arms in Gloucester Road, Finch's in Fulham Road, the Duke of Wellington and the Antelope, both in Eaton Terrace, the Denmark in Old Brompton Road. The noizak is turned up full blast at them all. Eventually, Henry has enough alcohol, jokes and gossip in his bloodstream for one day. Bachelor SRM head home, pissed, to cod-in-a-bag, Ambrosia creamed rice, toast and the telly. After telly shuts down he builds himself a chutney sandwich. The married squadron go back to their Carolines, and cutlets and candlelight if it's still the early days.

Hooray Henry

The noisiest part of the Sloane world

Hooray Henrys are the tip of the Sloane iceberg, visible and audible for miles. They are the *only* male Sloane Rangers as far as the ignorant world is concerned. 'Those yahoos in Gucci shoes who make a lot of noise and throw bread rolls.' In fact a Hooray Henry is well-behaved when on his own, but when a Sloane with HH inclinations gets together with a few others of his kind (about 10 per cent of the SRM population) they turn into the dreaded Hooray Henry pack.

Hooray Henrys are aged between 18 and 30; main interest, getting drunk together; ambition if ambitious: to get drunk enough to do some crazy thing which will go down in the Hooray annals as a Historic Act of Hilarity. The existence of these annals (it's an oral culture), means that Hooray Henrys don't *necessarily* need an audience—they can be very happy at a stag do in a private room with only the waiters to shock. But they do like to have an array of not-like-us's to tease; though HHs never turn nasty and end up killing, maiming or raping like men's groups in American films.

Any Hooray Henry has breathed into more breathalyser bags than you and I have had hot dinners (as Sloanes say). The telephone call from the police station is a feature of an HH dwelling. They love being sick *on things* and leaving their mark by peeing and having a crap in places other than the lavatory (the telegram ALL IS FORGIVEN BUT FOR GOD'S SAKE WHERE DID YOU DO IT made the annals).

Disaster for a Hooray Henry would be battling your way through a blizzard to a dinner party and finding yourself the only man who got through. Then having to sit around all evening with six strange girls, making conversation. Isolated from their muckers, Hooray Henrys fall rapidly to pieces and become desperately awkward with women, especially when they have not met them before and their own Hooray reputation hasn't gone before them. That is why Hooray Henrys very rarely have girlfriends. This does not mean that they do not have sex. Sloane Ranger girls are frequently attracted to Hooray Henrys as a pack—their drunkenness, their complete absence of introspection, their manliness—and suddenly find themselves promoted to unofficial girlfriend of one of the boys.

A girl does not, however, have candlelit dinners with a Hooray *à deux* as you would with a standard SR man. Rather you hang about on the edge of the group, occasionally being addressed by your surname, watching your man getting totally slaughtered, until it is time to take him upstairs to bed. Not that the Sloane Ranger has much prospect of sex there and then. The Hooray is much too pissed for that at night. That is why Hooray Henrys associate sex exclusively with the morning.

In Oxford and Cambridge (qv), Hooray Henrys have a useful forum for their tomfoolery in the Oxford Bullingdon Club and at the True Blue and Beefsteak clubs in Cambridge. Here pure HH activities— such as pilfering beacons from roadworks and wearing them on your head, or removing gnomes from the garden of a neighbouring council estate and arranging them in the Fellows' Garden, or (at Cambridge) kidnapping live sheep from King's Meadow and being stopped by the police with them on the back seat—are performed on sanctioned evenings after official society meetings. University HHs also have the advantage of being indisputably intelligent, because they are *at* the university while their girls are only at typing colleges—so they can do whatever they like without fear of being dubbed intellectually immature.

It is a feature of Oxford Hooray Henryism that if an outsider makes some disparaging remark about Bilbo Berkeley, implying that he is an upper-class half-

Hooray for the Admiral Cod!

wit, he is immediately informed that 'in fact he is *really* clever. He got an exhibition to Christ Church and has an amazing collection of First Edition Ezra Pound.' Not that he will have *them* for long. The least attractive face of university Hoorayism is the charge en masse into a peer's room, after a particularly heavy dinner, and 'chundering' (being sick) all over the bookcase, having missed the basin by a short head.

Raids on each other's property are a distinct feature of Hooray Henryism, found most conspicuously at Cirencester (qv). Three or four HHs live in each cottage and after dinner, with no prospect of getting a clear picture on their old black and white television, they all leap into ancient Morris Travellers held together with baling twine, or new Alfas, and blitz neighbouring cottages with fire extinguishers ('red boys'). Girlfriends, never taken along on these punitive expeditions, must wait at base camp until the boys return triumphant or the telephone rings from Stroud police station.

Army Hooray ('Bore-ay') Henrys are a race apart in that they can be twenty, or even thirty, years older than HHs elsewhere. Regimental dinners are still red-letter days in the HH calendar. But City Hooray Henrys are a sorry crowd (see p 117). They are deeply aware that their midweek hooraying is less intense than elsewhere, since they cannot lie in bed until lunchtime after binges.

On any midweek evening, a dozen or so HHs can be found in the Admiral Cod, surrounded by other Sloane Ranger men. They are clearly discernible, however, by the desperate, dogged expression of men yearning to get pissed and steal a yellow beacon, but starkly aware that trading in financial futures starts at 8.30 am.

Sloane Transport

RAC spells car backwards

Rangers, despite their instincts, have been buying foreign for years, but never Japs.

The Young Ranger's nippy town car

Simple, basic small cars treated lightly (full of toffee papers, squashed Marlboro packets, old Christie's catalogues, cassettes, or other key detritus).

(a) Cheap, jaunty, colourful foreign cars: Renault 4 (van for men), Citroen 2CV or Dyane, Fiat 126.

(b) Girls' safe but smart cars: Renault 5, Mini Metro, Fiesta, Fiat 127.

(c) Men's old bangers: Morris Minor, Morris Oxford, Wolseley, Mini Van.

(d) Faster, especially army, men's cars: Volkswagen Golf GTI (black), Alfasud, Lancia (today's Mini Coopers), Range Rover, Volvo saloon, BMW, slightly bashed sports convertibles.

The Young Marrieds' car

Volvo or a smarter BMW sum it up between them: nippy for parking, but good for the country too and for the journey to and fro. Volvo is worthy, low-profile, lasts

BMW is reverse flash. You know it looks plain ('not much for the money') to lots of oiks. You know it'll accelerate their tin heaps into the ground. You know you can talk about the 'practical design' and quality engineering. Everyone who knows anything knows why one buys a BMW. It's for the Ranger who's making it at 30.

Peugeots and Audis are acceptable substitutes.

The Country Ranger family wagon

Here your car *declares* your affiliations with the country, animals, the Army and all that. The Land-Rover and big estate cars all echo the true dream car, the stout half-timbered brakes they don't make now. This kind of car is piled high with children/dogs/dead animals/sporting equipment, like a troop carrier. The Ford Granada estate—in the right colour— and the Rover 3500 hatchback are perfectly OK. The Volvo estate, of course, with bars for the Labrador. The Range Rover is a bit millionaire and countryesque for most Sloanes.

THE GREAT DEBATE

Porsches, like Mercs, are difficult. Some rather odd tradespeople have them—they're a Fulham Road favourite with restaurateurs and advertising men. And there's something a bit square-cut and over-chromed about a Merc. You have to be brave.

COLOUR PREJUDICE

Navy (of course), silver, bright pillar-box red, British Racing Green. Never turquoise or kitsch kandy kolors, except for jaunty foreign cheapos: bright green, bright yellow.

Nil decoration, but *mud* is good and a tow-hitch (horse-box) too. Stickers declaring membership of various societies and charities (RNLI 'It's great having you behind us', ISIS, etc) and advertising the local horse show can be discreetly displayed in the rear window; Members Car Park tickets in the front.

Young cars have jolly stickers: Snoopy slogans, 'My second car is a Porsche', etc.

for ever, hardly changes its design—never any excess chrome-work, flashy wheel-trims, etc—and they just seem to be made in the right Ranger colours. Built like a shire horse. Green wellies on the floor in a Harrods bag and a Billy Joel cassette in the deck.

Pedal Power Sloanes

A bicycle is the young Sloane girl's method of transport in London, for four reasons:

- It is archaic.
- It has a basket.
- It is a horse you don't have to feed or groom.
- It is dangerous.

Bicycling in towns is one of those slightly, mad, rather jaunty things Sloanes do.

It's a point of conversation at parties —comparing routes and horror stories with other cyclists or explaining to non-cyclists why you aren't scared. The reason why you aren't is similar to why Sloanes shouldn't be scared out hunting. It's outdoors; you love the feel of wind in your face, the element of risk and the superiority.

En route, you bump into at least two friends (often when going the wrong way down a one-way street) and stop for a quick chat. If you're late you shout to each other whilst cycling in daredevil formation across Hyde Park Corner; or race them at the underpass—one under, one over.

Biking gear

You always bike in the same clothes you wear in the office—you cut your time-table too fine to allow for a change. Court shoes just have to get scuffed—you don't wear a special pair of plimsolls.

In summer, girls wear flowing Monsoon skirts which get caught in the back wheel —to stop this, they gather up the hem in one hand and steer with the other, or make up an ingenious device with string or elastic bands. Men roll up their sleeves, discard their tie and roll up their jacket under the spring clip on the back of their bike.

In winter, you put on extra jumpers or a sleeveless Puffa (men—Husky waist-coat) as it gets so hot in a coat. Sloanes tend to be fair-weather cyclists when it comes to rain—or they might don a huge cape which covers half the bike as well. A

scarf or two wrapped round in the cold, and woolly gloves—but no hat: it gets in the way of your boogie-pack. Girls wear trousers if it's allowed at work, but you don't like bicycle clips. Men wear them, or tuck their trousers into their socks.

You're not very hot on safety gear, and helmets and goggles are for fanatics. But you don't mind a Sam Browne reflective belt—it reflects your military bearing.

Your kind of bike

Sloane women always have large-wheeled old bicycles ('No idea what make') with huge wicker baskets in front. Top of the class are the sit-up-and-beg or smart black old-fashioned lady's bikes, but unless inherited, these are quite hard to come by. You never have drop handlebars or more than three speeds.

The bike is usually dirty, beginning to rust and in need of an oil; it has a characteristic tick-tick-tick when in motion. Sometimes it is home-painted —pillar-box red, black, stripy or bamboo.

Sloane men have a rickety old machine like yours or maybe a new Stowaway. But these tiny-wheeled jobs are somewhat pretentious, try-it-once-and-stash-it-in-the-back stockbrokerish; it's difficult to appear cool and in command when your legs are flying about in a 6-inch circle.

The Sea 'n Ski Sloane

Down the slippery slope

Skiing is the single Sloanest sport. The voice sounds so good in the clear air—one can drink and FLY. There's 200 beautiful Sloane girls/men wherever you look, and beyond them a range of mountains that are as crisp and silken as a Hermès scarf.

Since the Seventies, almost all Sloanes have skied 'out of' chalets, as they say of long-distance lorry drivers: chalets staffed by pairs of young Sloane chalet girls.

Sloane Rangers are not usually expert skiers, but they are at least competent. At whatever grade, they are fearless ('Be weedy in front of the wops?'). They think they don't need ski school, but might attend in a group, or the girls might take lessons from a ski bum—especially if he's tall and tanned with a West Coast drawl or a Melbourne millionaire father.

The Sloane skier and the opposite sex

A season (December to April) as a chalet girl is more or less statutory for a Sloane Ranger. You apply in September, aged 18 to 22, to Supertravel etc with your *qualifications* (Winkfield, Cordon Bleu, Leith's, or lesser-known training grounds). You have *experience* (City dining-rooms, wine bars like Myttons, or, at a pinch, cooking for 'Mummie's friends').

Sloanes know that the Alps are *the* hunting-ground for SRM husbands. A quarter of your married friends met each other skiing. And if they bust up, they book a skiing holiday on the rebound. (Caroline beware! The rebounders await you.) A new influx of eligible men arrives every week. Skis give you an option: you can get into conversation ('Isn't the K-factor suffocating today?') or you can literally whizz away.

Sloane Ranger girls never holiday alone. That is thoroughly out of character. Caroline gets up a party and books a whole chalet for their ten—preferably one where a vague friend is working as a chalet girl. The newer chalet size is 30 or 40—the chalet operators are taking over small hotels. All Sloane parties fly from Gatwick to Geneva on Saturdays, on one of about ten charter flights.

There is a slight trend to self-catering holidays—booked through the same companies. Sloanes drive out in the latest registration Renault 5 or Volkswagen Golf with a smart new ski rack but no chains. The car is packed with tins of spaghetti sauce and a surrogate chalet girl: someone who prefers schnitzel-bashing to piste-bashing. An experienced SRM who wants to seduce a chalet girl brings with him Marmite, gelatin and Lyle's golden syrup—essentials of SR cooking unobtainable in the Alps.

Occasionally a chalet girl will fall for a ski bum and go and live with him in his Dormobile, returning to her chalet to cook the breakfast. This is bad, but not as bad for her ski company as an affair with a married ski instructor, which puts all the locals against her employer. (This is the first and last time a Sloane challenges the community.)

Sloanes on the slopes

Skiing brings out the Hoorayness in Henry. He does a lot of whooping and carries two hip flasks (both have cherry brandy and whisky mixed—chisky: the cheerer-up of deer stalkers). Sloane parties are noisy and obstreperous in lift queues—usually complaining about the K-factor and how noisy, numerous and GLUM they are.

Lunches on the terrace are long, in the sun if possible. Many bottles of Fendant (Switzerland) or Apremont (France) are drunk, plus large bottles of Kronenbourg for SRMs. The punters pay for the chalet girls, who get nominal wages and are permanently broke ('I had to sell my hunter to do this job'). There are numerous 'pit stops' or 'grog stops' throughout the day. Caroline loves glühwein and likes to give glühwein parties in Britain.

The clown of the party has *British pigs*

Whatever you do, don't shout 'Dead Ant'!

are best stickers on his skis and has props in his bum bag: one rubber mask you can talk through, one water pistol, one tin of that stuff that sprays out and hardens into coloured spag, two silk scarves—opera or similar. You knot the silk scarves round your wrists so they stream out like flags as you come down. There's no Sloaner sight than a Hooray Henry whooping down the hill in a warty mask with scarves flying. At the bottom, he stops neatly at the lift queue, asks some pretty girl 'What does a Frenchman do first thing in the morning?' and sticks his tongue in her ear.

As well as these little games (another is pushing each other off the T-bar), Sloanes have three group games which make the Ks frown:

Dead Ant is the most versatile. It can also be played on lawns, beaches and ballrooms and any number can join in. When the call goes out, all the Sloanes on the hill or in a queue fall on their backs and waggle their skis and arms (probably ripping their trouser shins).

The Snake Game is erotic. Maximum ten players. You fit close behind each other, girl-boy-girl-boy, the skis in Vs like a chevron, and snowplough down the hill. You end in a heap after ten yards, collapsed in hysterical laughter.

Hotdogging. For two players. (This is not what people generally mean by hot-dogging: ski acrobatics.) You slip two ski-stick straps through each other and each player holds one end. Then you take it in turns to be pivot while the other skier swings round you and down the hill as far as the two poles will allow. And so on down the slope (like dancing Strip the Willow).

Where Sloanes resort

Depending on age, Caroline would like to

go where the Eton party/the Oxford and Cambridge teams/the Lords and Commons ski team are booked. (Oxford and Cambridge and their hangers-on are so Hooray they are usually told to take their custom to a new place each year.) But since that's not always possible to arrange, there's never a dull day at Verbier.

Verbier in Switzerland is the peak Sloane resort—Chelsea am Alp. Almost every chalet company is there: in high season there are over 200 chalet girls. Sloane meeting places: La Luge, Le Phenix (sic), Le Pub. For dancing, The Farm Club.

Méribel in France (SRs pronounce it Maybelle) is the second highest peak. Night-out life is limited, but not night life. There is much to-ing and fro-ing between chalets, and obligatory weekly Supertravel and John Morgan drinks parties.

Courchevel, just over the mountain from Méribel, is also popular. Après ski: La Mangeoire, La Grange, the Club St Nicholas.

Val d'Isère (Val) is a favourite with real skiers. It gets a blizzard of Sloanettes at Easter and Peter Jones plastic bags are carried at mountain restaurants 10,000 feet above sea-level. Dick's T-Bar is the main rendezvous point, though the poorer know to leave at 10.30 when the disco starts and the prices go up.

Sloane ski clothes

Husky and Puffa jackets and green Hunter wellies take over Geneva airport on Saturday mornings, but the chic atmosphere of the resorts (a blast from the pederast) persuades SRs to invest in Lothar or Ted Lapidus jackets and Killy trousers—and, of course, moonboots.

In spring, jeans are de rigueur on the piste, with stripy leggings and gilets. The Sloane girls wear bright red lipstick and full office eye make-up. Foreign girls ski in sporty make-up, but Sloanes do not go native.

SRMs often wear Barbour jackets and plus-fours, occasionally finished off with a deerstalker. Some even wear dinner-jackets—anyone in fancy dress is British. The Fancy Dress Afternoon is a highlight of the chalet holiday. The Sloanes go up together in their kilts or whatever and come down whooping.

Après ski wear is fairly casual; but pearls—string or earrings—worn at all times, even on the slopes. Wise girls take out extra insurance with Michael Pettifer (Kent SRM and skier, the Sloane ski insurance man at Douglas, Cox, Tyrie). Sony Walkman (worn with ear-muffs) is also insured. You listen to Dire Straits as you come down, don't hear the 'Vorsicht!' and get run into.

Sloane ski shops

Sloanes pay a Saturday morning visit to Alpine Sports in High Street, Kensington. Occasionally SRMs nip up to the Holborn branch from the City during their lunch break.

Many Sloanes have their own equipment. The most popular skis are Dynaster Omesofts; boots and bindings by Salomon. SRs avalanche the Ski Show (Earl's Court, mid-November), especially on the weekday evenings when there are dry-slope races between Commons, Lords and Lloyd's teams.

Number one Sloane shop in the Alps is Ski Service in Verbier.

Ski words and phrases

ad hocer: skier who arrives at a chalet on spec with no booking

bash the bumps: ski down a field of moguls; also mogul-bashing

birdsnesting: skiing among trees

blood wagon: stretcher

bubble, egg: telecabin

K-factor: number of Germans (Kraut factor)

motorway: broad easy piste

pit stop: call at mountain restaurant for drinks

punter: chalet party guest

wipe out: spectacular fall

Sloane London travel agencies

Bladon Lines, 309 Brompton Road, SW3 (581 4861)

John Morgan Travel, 35 Albemarle Street, W1 (499 1911)

Ski Mac G, 29 Wrights Lane, W8 (937 9362)

Skival, 30 Salmon Street, NW9 (200 6080)

Supertravel, 22 Hans Place, SW1 (584 5060)

The Sloane sailor

You can't afford a decent boat, now they start at £30,000. Your grandfather had one with a hired hand, but you have fun as an unpaid hand. Your boss changes his boat every other year and you and five or six other young accountants and merchant wankers crew for him every weekend, April to September. You all drive down to the Hamble together on Friday evening, stopping at West Meon Hut pub on the way, and find 'your' boat in the marina. It cost £150,000 to £200,000, and you dress smartly for working on it—white trousers, blue T-shirts (the Sloanes on Edward Heath's boat wear red T-shirts). Getting in those big headsails is hard work—no wonder they call you a foredeck gorilla. When you're not racing (Cowes week; and you love the Fastnet or the Americas Cup) you like to put into Yarmouth or somewhere by ten, just in time for the Royal Solent yacht club or at least the pub. You whizz to shore in the rubber dinghy while your boss is pouring his first gin and tonic on board. You belong to the Royal Southern at Hamble and the Royal Ocean Racing Club or the Royal Thames in London. During Cowes week, most clubs open their doors to other yacht club members. You go to the Royal Corinthian and the Royal London and Island Sailing Club—but not the Royal Yacht Squadron. Too select for tycoons like your boss.

If you get any more time off, you go on a 'flotilla holiday' in Greece—these are the chalet parties of sailing, advertised in *The Times*, the *Yachting Monthly* and *Yachting World*. There's someone in charge of the fleet of little boats but he sees that you four or five Sloanes know what you're doing (you've got girls with you this time), so you sail away from the amateur sailors from Tooting and potter around the Aegean on your own, having a silly boozy Sloany time.

THE SLOANE
HATCHED, MATCHED,
DESPATCHED

The path to the altar

Meeting people is fine; it's the point. After a time, however, you have to meet someone in particular. Sloanes marry, how else can you be a 'we'? Sloanes have children, they don't go for long-term *official* living together—short-term is fine. So after a time of modest wild-oating (hereafter embroidered as incredible loucheness) you have to move towards a sensible arrangement. If you haven't met the Catch, you think of Duty.

The Parents are hinting away like mad. 'That terrible flat isn't amusing at 28, you need to get organised' (ie a wife). 'Aren't you bored with those twenty-one year-olds you're sharing with—you've nothing in common' (ie is there something you haven't told us?).

But nature is wonderful. Someone who's just always been there—Rachel's sweet sister (the braces are off for good) or Tim's solid brother (much more amusing after nine months in Hong Kong) reappears and turns out to be wholly brickish. Walking home from the ABC Fulham Road you *just know.*

The ideal is a slow-burn glow. You've got so much in common.

Henry and Caroline tie the knot

Aisle be saying yes
Yew'll be outside the church
White for me I'm coming
Bridesmaid an awful mistake
The pages are thick and thtick together
Usher hope this'll soon be over

In pious preservation of Victorian ways, a Sloane wedding occupies a year and three months: three months of frantic preparation by the bride's mother and the bride, three months after the wedding changing the presents and converting the cheques into knick-knacks, six months showing the friends and relations the nest beautified by their table-mats, silver pheasants and Pastamatic ('We couldn't *live* without your Pastamatic'), and to the end of the first married year going on appro to the more social relations, who have you over ('You're on Rupert's right, because it's not a year yet, is it?') to see if you fit in as a couple.

Sloanes like the actual wedding to be so conventional it's blatant. You believe in the rituals: the slate (a few scribbles) wiped clean with the white dress. Your father gives you away into another's protection. The bond (permanent) sworn in the presence of God and of this congregation (large). Your virginal (well, fresh and young) attendants, his dashing fanciable ushers. Sloanes don't believe that the men present could wear other than morning dress or that the wedding is for the *bride and groom. This* is the most dangerous modern heresy. The bride and groom are two specks in the Sloane galaxy that the engagement has suddenly enabled everyone to see lit up; but it is the two families of the *alliance* who are the real purpose of the occasion.

A wedding is the second most important occasion, after Ascot. But it's not about love: it's about pride of family. What Really Matters is where it is and who comes.

As soon as the announcement appears in *The Times* and the *Daily Telegraph*, pale blue letters fly in for the couple and their parents from well-wishers from Alaska to Zaire. Many of these have never met the affianced and some have never met the parents—but this is Sloanedom, where blood is thicker than water and letters maintain bonds in Einsteinian defiance of time and distance.

Who you marry

The mothers answer the good wishes with a formula in which the intended is '*such* a nice young (man or girl). They seem well suited and even the dogs like (him or her). They are going to start off in a charming little flat in _____ Gardens, quite near the Victoria & Albert

Museum' (where they have been living together for six months, but the mother doesn't mention that).

The mother gives the new member of the family a pedigree if she has to go miles to find it. 'His step-grandfather was a Bloggs of Bloggs cotton'; 'Her sister's husband is Sir Francis Sloane, who farms 5,000 acres in Blankshire'; 'He is the head singer, I think they call it, in one of the most famous pop groups here, the Orang-Outangs; their records are really very catchy.'

Letters from caterers and photographers have also been arriving; though not as many as twenty years ago, when Henry's father received a contraceptive leaflet among the useful information. But the best people still send—Asprey, Boucheron, Hermès, Dunhill, Lobb's. (You do love a glossy catalogue.) The choice of who to engage is not difficult. There are only one or two top names in each category. Of course you can't afford them so you just decide where to cut the corners. Mrs Kenward prints a list in 'Jennifer's Diary' in March every year where you can see the whole range.

How you marry

It's traditional, and cheaper (despite the marquee and the disco later on), to be married in the village church, but what if people won't come all that way? Many

brides go for Sloane London churches: St Michael's, Chester Square; St Margaret's, Westminster; St James's, Piccadilly; St George's, Hanover Square; Holy Trinity, Brompton; Chelsea Old Church; The Grosvenor Chapel; the Guards' Chapel; Farm Street or the Brompton Oratory; and the few more which regularly feature in *The Times*. The vicar won't have you unless you're 'of this parish', so you ask a local friend if you may leave a suitcase with her and give her address.

Meanwhile the bride has to buy a dress (Bellville Sassoon, Emanuel, Harrods) and coax a dressmaker (a Little Woman or a girlfriend, sights set on Beauchamp Place) to translate her scribble or page torn from a magazine into modest long frocks that will suit all the bridesmaids (two to six) of various sizes. Sloane pages wear kilts or velvet shorts, not miniature archaic uniforms like the rich.

The bride has chosen her Wedding List from the General Trading Co and Peter Jones, a minute's walk apart. This is the third dowry in her life, the real and vital dowry that starts a Sloane off on Life. Grotty flatland is left behind. Caroline chooses those key, token, expensive things a Sloane family needs (eg decanter—£52) and her family and friends buy them for her, or even *half* of something, chipping in together. Peter Jones irritates by expecting you to traipse all over the shop choosing your own things and noting down the stock number and details: the GTC makes it a pleasure by sending a *very nice girl* (Sloane) round with you. (The Princess of Wales had her list at the GTC.) They don't do sheets, though, so those are on your PJ list (linen doesn't *have* to be monogrammed any more—with your *maiden* initials. Sloanes go to Eximious in West Halkin Street for monogrammed everything else).

Blue remains the favourite colour for kitchen ware. Blue colludes with the strip lighting, and goes with the blue and white china Sloanes have: 'Denmark'

Here comes the Mumm
For me and my chum
Daddy will faint
When the bill for this has come.

is the usual pattern. You have Herend 'Rothschild Bird' for best—not realising it comes from behind the Iron Curtain. Herend is the Hermès scarf of porcelain.

Polite guests send their presents to the bride in time for her to write all her letters before the wedding, but nowadays a lot of people bring parcels to the reception.

Many Sloanes have not kept up with inflation when it comes to wedding presents, and think £10 is plenty. Meanwhile the bride's parents are paying roughly £15 a head to wherever the reception is held. Sloane wedding guests drink

9/10 of a bottle of champagne each, for every man, teetotaller and toddler (or the caterers will tell you they did).

Stag parties are usually held before the eve of the wedding—Prince Charles's was a week before. They are drunken Hooray affairs so it's just as well.

On the day, the families bury all their hatchets and pretend to the world that the match is perfect. Divorced couples are reunited and 'steps' trip into the church by the pewful. Those whom God has joined together have been easily put asunder. Mummie is in her Harvey Nicks outfit (or Hardy Amies or Jaeger), Henry's mother in pastel from PJ.

Flowers have arrived in huge boxes on roof racks and been arranged all over the place by talented girls, armed with secateurs in case the foliage runs out. Another group is beavering away making up goodies for the reception. Somewhere amid all this activity a young man and a younger woman are hidden, almost irrelevant to the proceedings, until the appointed hour.

Down the aisle into the sunset

The wedding day is terrible for the bride. Having had your hair done the day before, you wash it yourself neurotically on the morning, and it's too soft and shiny to hold the tiara, already attached to the veil by the dressmaker. Much hair-gripping and shrieks of pain and impatience. Daddy is nervous and the hired car takes the wrong route to the church —thank goodness, because otherwise he would have got there early as usual. You see your unfavourite cousins scuttling in as you arrive, looking drab. How *could* they? But the bridesmaids have done you proud—Lucy and Rupert look *scrumptious* —and so have most of your relations and friends—furs and feathers and veils and moth-balls and Miss Dior. *Your* side seems more splendid—but it may be family pride again. The bride totters down the *terribly* long aisle *gripping* Daddy to the Trumpet

Voluntary (not 'Here Comes the Bride'—short, fat and wide). What happens next you barely take in—it's like being a human sacrifice—but then you're sweeping quickly down the aisle again with Henry to Mendelssohn meeting the photographer's flash.

In the line-up at the reception it's hard to remember who everyone is without a shouter-outer of names (pity you told Mummie and Daddy that's pompous). Next, cutting the cake and the speeches. These let the Hoorays in. They've been waiting with their coarse sentiments, lewd, crude and Sloane all over. People talk all through the speeches. (Most frequent and unimaginative remark made in the best man's speech: 'We were a little late at the church—we had to stop at a chemist's.' Most outrageous: 'Caroline's a modest girl. She even eats bananas sideways.')

You *can* go away twice. Once you disappear in Jean Muir or Joseph, in a car trailing balloons and shoes, wreathed in squirts of synthetic day-glo spaghetti (the new confetti). You try your best to throw your bouquet to the bridesmaid who's almost engaged. You may reappear at the post-wedding party—a drunken orgy—at around 10 and go away a second time. You go back to your secret hotel, where the fire alarm goes off in the middle of the night but not much else happens.

A Sloane wedding is exhausting and any energetic celebrations are anticipatory—or postponed until the honeymoon. If anyone's scaling sexual heights it will be one of the few sober guests. What people saw at Lady Elizabeth Shakerley's party after the royal wedding, three Queens sitting on a sofa eating scrambled eggs and watching television, is about it.

Honour is saved and the consummation devoutly to be wished is achieved by a 'Hooray Henry speedy' in the morning, before you take to the seas or skies on your way to Kenya, Sri Lanka or the Loire Valley.

YOUR HONEYMOON

It's not the first time you make love, but you do make an effort. You always have a honeymoon because it's tradition and also because you're exhausted after the wedding. Caroline 'goes away' in a silk outfit and hat chosen as suitable for her first married Ascot.

Next day you fly to
Fisherman's Cove in the Seychelles.
The Cipriani in Venice. (You call your first dog Cippy in remembrance of the Bellinis at Harry's Bar and the luxurious siestas thereafter.)
Sri Lanka (you call it Ceylon), Kenya or Nepal ('I was at Eton with the King').
La Reserve at Beaulieu, with Mimosas (champagne and orange juice).
The Carlton at Cannes. You go to great lengths to nick the monogrammed towelling dressing-gowns; £50 on the bill automatically if caught.
Greece: Skiathos, Paxos and Crete if well-informed, Mykonos if young and foolish.

Clothes
You take your guernseys, Burb and Barbour just in case, and Caroline has new clothes from Fiorucci, Laura Ashley and Jasper Conran. Henry has bought yellow socks from Harrods as a concession to the Continent, Caroline a bikini from Harvey Nichols. They'll never be so smart again.

The portrait photographs
London
Patrick Lichfield, 20 Aubrey Walk, W8 (727 4468)
  (The Earl, of course . . .)
Country
Bridget Astor (Countess Tarnowska), Kirklands of Coull, Aboyne, Aberdeenshire (Tarland 345 and 01-788 1409)
John Bell, Leighton House, Goodmanham, York (Market Weighton 3405)
Tom Hustler, 9 Chiltern Road, Caversham, Reading, Berkshire (Reading 475804)

The wedding photographs
All these submit pictures to those glossy social pages in which Sloanes like to appear:
London and Country
Belgrave Press, 7 West Halkin Street, SW1 (235 3227)
Charles Fennell, Rossinver, 3 Churchtown Drive, Dublin 14 (Dublin 983 079)
Moira Leggat, 18 Clarendon Crescent, Edinburgh (Edinburgh 343 2531)
London & County Press, 16 Jacob's Well Mews, W1 (449 1782)
Desmond O'Neill, Wychwood, Leatherhead Road, Oxshott, Surrey (970 2998)
Portman Press, 3 Portman Road, SW1 (235 2566)
Barry Swaebe, 16 Southwood Lane, London N6 (348 6010)
Van Hallan, 16 Blenheim Road, Basing, Hampshire (Basingstoke 65217)

No holds barred

The Sloane Ranger is not taught about sex by Mummie or Daddy, and public schools are not like these state schools, with diagrams on the blackboard and 'meaningful' relationships and social worker talk. The public schools are heavy on naming of parts and light on how everything's normal between consenting adults. The young Sloane, if it asks its parent, is told 'It's the same as animals.' One Sloane virgin bride was astonished that the approach was not from the rear.

A person who has been taught *how to do* everything is at sea when there aren't rules. Most Sloane parents are too shy even to tell their children not to do it, with the result that Sloanes often spend a very randy sixteen to twenty-five. Nowadays, Sandhurst cadets *expect* Winkfield girls to be keen.

Sloane girls can be very keen—but nothing kinky, no sado-masochism or being tied up to a bed for hours. Prolonged inaction is *not* Sloane. Sloane women love their bosoms being fondled (childhood near a farm). Henry may like being spanked (beaten at school) but Caroline is no good at it, it makes her giggle. She loves that thing though—it reminds her of a lamb's muzzle.

Caroline will chomp away with a will, and she's not totally averse to buggery. Any perversion that doesn't go against the grain she could adopt without knowing it was odd. Caroline might mention some quirk to a friend, and both shriek with laughter, but sex is not a subject she wants to discuss at length.

Sloanes do approach sex with qualms; Henry because he likes to do his best and is often drunk, Caroline because she likes to do her best and is often tired. Caroline will turn her back after her efforts, and recover herself *by* herself. Henry is more affectionate, likes to go to sleep hugging.

But they approach the serious subject of issue with great seriousness. Sloanes who aren't producing will go to their sweet gynae, who will tell them to stand on their heads afterwards. 'It's because you're a bit broad in the beam, dear girl, and the only problem is he can't get it far enough *in*.' They follow instructions with gusto.

SHALL WE USE THE BRIDAL SUITE?

NO DARLING, I'LL JUST HANG ONTO YOUR EARS

Sloanes should be seduced politely, after dinner. If they have men back to their bedroom it's pretty and tidy (she tidied it in readiness) with a clean sprigged nightie. They like to be taken to *nice* hotels in Paris or the Fenice in Venice, and titled foreigners have more success with them than misters, of course.

They do like flowers, or at least a telephone call, next morning.

The modesty of the Sloane rules out any sort of 'acting', 'look at me' lovemaking, but for fun they photograph each other with no clothes on, doing sexy things, when they are first married. Then they don't know where to have them developed, and Henry takes them to a quick place in the City and gives a false name, which he forgets, and by the time he finally succeeds in collecting his pictures he and his name are indelibly engraved on the assistant's mind.

Sloanes are embarrassed by tell-tale sheets—what will the daily think, and the laundryman? Sex *is* a bit messy. They have two separate duvets (they hate duvets but hate bedmaking more) to avoid bedclothes fights. Caroline puts a lot of Nivea on her dry skin at night.

Gradually they sink into not doing it any more, and may even have separate rooms. 'He moved into his dressing-room.' But they go on joking about sex in front of friends and pretending they're ready to do it, right this minute.

YOUR LOVER

Caroline is normally prevented from having a lover by two facts. One, Henry might find out and divorce her from the *children and the house*. (She never got a proper training, and Labby would hate living in a town.) Two, she is terrified of showing her stretch marks and duck bottom to anyone new.

Henry may be unfaithful with (one or all three) his secretary, the nanny and his best friend's wife but most Henrys are much more talk than action.

Sloane Home Truths

Basic married quarters

One can't actually use the word 'home' except with an 'at' in front. A Sloane lives in a *house*, a *flat*, a *villa* or, very occasionally, a *cottage*.

Principles of decoration

Sloanes feel they Know A Bit about how things should look. They may do it professionally for a few years 'for friends'. Certain decorating firms are Sloane businesses.

The principle of Sloane decoration is *don't* do it like the architects, serious designers and aesthetes do it. You know they've got it wrong, and though your taste is considered awful by 'all those poncy decorators', you know they don't understand the key points. *You* know that the point of doing up a house is a) so that one can invite one's friends in and b) so that one can live comfortably in the manner to which one is accustomed. *They* agonise over colour, proportion and historical correctness, things that frankly don't matter a damn. In fact, too much Taste is a bad sign. A Sloane interior is governed by a set of well-defined rules:

1) *A room should have one's history in it.* This includes reminders of one's family, both living and dead. It's instructive for one's visitors to see the faces of one's pretty children, fine animals and distinguished forebears—together with their plasticine, medals and rosettes.

2) *A house should be a manor house.* What if you do live in a Victorian workman's cottage in Clapham or a cramped 1970s flat in Manchester? You call upon voluminous velvet curtains (Jonelle Dupion —fake raw silk—is also highly favoured), rows of riding macs, a zoo of silver game birds and animals, bowls of potpourri, a large shiny dining table and enough other Sloane signals so that your dwelling says Eighteenth Century Gentleperson At Home in an unmistakable accent.

Actually, your rooms reveal a nineteenth-century view of the eighteenth century: a lot of what Sloanes *think* is correct is not what eighteenth-century squires had. They lack the robustness of a real Fielding setting. But it doesn't matter. Your style is composed of tokens of gentrydom. You are squiresque. Carry on, Squire Henry.

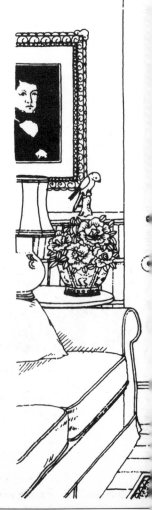

THE RIGHT ADDRESS

You should be careful where you live: a good address still means what it says. But the districts have shifted slightly. In London, Sloanes have been driven out of Mayfair and Belgravia by the rich and the Mayfair Mercenaries, Americans and international merchant wankers. Saki's dreaded 'north of the Park' has expanded to a (smarty) Sloane zone centred on Holland Park and environs, while gentrification has cleansed Clapham ('Clahm'), Kennington, Stockwell, Wandsworth and Camberwell. SW11 and Battersea ('Bahsea', 'Bahterzayah' or 'Swone one), Barnes, Putney, Hurlingham and Earl's Court have all been Sloane zones for ages. Pimlico has claimed many of those pushed out of nearby Belgravia.

However broad-minded the Sloane is though, when the bridge cards are down, the London heartland for the married Sloane is still the rose-red canyons of Knightsbridge, South Kensington, Fulham and Chelsea (SW3, SW1, SW7, SW10, SW6 and SW5 in that order). How many miles-from-the-centre you are is, of course, measured from Sloane Square.

All British cities have their Sloane zone. It is a state of mind—not simply a place. In Manchester it is Didsbury; in Edinburgh, Morningside and Stockbridge; outside Cardiff, the Vale of Glamorgan.

If you like the country, your aim is to inhabit The Old Vicarage or The Old Rectory or The Mill House. It's amazing that there are enough of these to go round.

You take out a mortgage on your chosen building (probably redbrick Victorian, though in theory Sloanes despise 'redbrick'. And they always say 'I'm afraid it's only Victorian', as they know Things Should Be Georgian). You slap the white paint all over it and wait for the wisteria to grow.

You cultivate the other Big Houses (see p 148).

3) *A house must be suitable for animals.* Dog bowls and leads litter the hall, and walking sticks cluster in a tall ceramic vase—or in an umbrella stand, if you're an older Sloane. A special part of your country-pine kitchen is set aside for the all-important dog basket.

4) *Every room displays your tokens of membership.* These range from eighteenth-century prints of soldiers of your regiment, a painting of your ship, or a photograph of yourself (passing out) at Sandhurst to

(for non-military Sloanes) a shield of your school, a print of your college, a photo of Caroline on her first (Thelwell-type) pony —complete with Pony Club tie; crossed oars, an olde map of your countye, your golf cups or your Goodwood member's badge.

5) *The downstairs rooms must say warrior and landowner.* This is accomplished with at least six martial or hunting tokens, eg oils of Scottish moors with stags, antlers mounted on shields, horse paintings, a horse's hoof made into a cigarette box, hunting prints, fox masks, real shields, real swords in scabbards on walls, swords not in scabbards on walls, Indian daggers in scabbards on chests, flintlocks (but not all at once). If you haven't enough of these, you can retrieve the situation by having shooting or hunting scenes on your red or green table-mats.

6) *Furniture must look old.* Georgian or Victorian. But it doesn't have to *be* old— there just weren't enough squires in the eighteenth century to have commissioned all the Hepplewhite and Chippendale chairs and sideboards needed by the Henrys of today. Sloanes adore repro— especially those little nests of gilt-tooled green-leather-topped tables—and repro ideas (taking off friends' better inspirations) are also very acceptable.

The Sloane wood (and all furniture must be wood, aside from granny's papier mâché occasional table) is mahogany, followed at some distance by yew—even if it has to be repro. Oak is a worry—it is too rustic and not symmetrical.

7) *A room should have objects from one's travels and colonial service.* Benares brass, Eskimo soapstone, walruses, carved wooden impalas, ebony African women, Egyptian patchwork, Chinese bowls, Beleek, carved tusks, Indian wood tables, and a polo helmet or topi all give a room that worldly look.

8) *Show silver—the Sloane metal.* The drawing-room and dining-room should have a display (pewter and brass can be scattered about too, but these metals are optional). You must have silver candlesticks, those silver grouse and dogs, etc.; engraved christening mugs, silver pill boxes, silver show cups and a presentation salver, silver porringers, silver baskets.

9) *Observe the visible floorboard rule*. Floorboards should be visible somewhere in a room. Sloanes see completely fitted carpets as the mark of the beast (though paradoxically they adore fitted bookcases, wardrobes and kitchen units).

10) *There should be a china cache-pot or two*. Pour cacher les plastic flowerpots holding the azaleas (Sloanes *know* they should be earthenware). There is more unwieldy porcelain in the china cupboard. Sloanes always have one. If the china cache-pots run out, you always have plaited straw baskets.

Extending the idea of a Sloane manor house, there may be a secret corner—under the stairs or in the pantry—that acts as a substitute flower room. There reside scraps of Oasis and wire, pinholders, Mummie's lesser crystal vases and plastic mist-sprayers.

11) *Upholstery and fabric are timeless*. They should be a) comfortable and b) the same as your mother's. This means *chintz*: either 'Persanes' (birds in squares) or 'Indian Tree' (birds in branches). Breakaway Sloanes discovered William Morris in the Sixties (branches but no birds). You can't go wrong with a chintz in the small patterns of the Laura Ashley variety, though some more chic, disciplined Sloanes have recently opted for G. P. & J. Baker's treillage.

12) *Colours should be Sloane*. One quite likes a dash of mauve or orange sometimes—after all, one is adventurous—but the top Sloane colour is green, followed by turquoise, silver-grey, and blues of a vividness startling to anyone used to middle-class beige subtlety and sludgery. Sloanes like clear, bright colours. On the warmer side of the spectrum, they go for bright pink, coral and crimson.

On chintzes, providing the foreground is colourful, the clear beige of a petit-point canvas is acceptable as a background. The busy, cluttered overprint camouflages cat-hairs, dog puddles and spilt whiskys better than anything else known to Sloane.

For picture frames, they like old gold, black and gold or (for photographs) silver or the sage green of Fortnum's velvet ones.

A Sloane household has a dilemma with bottle green and crimson. Which one should it be for the table-mats and dining-room curtains? And the same—or the other—for the Hermès ashtrays?

13) *A dining-room should have appurtenances for the Great Rituals of Life*: claret- and port-drinking and nut-cracking. The confines of the room should include several decanters with silver labels round their necks. Regency wine coasters, fancy stemmed glasses ('My grandfather's rummers'), and nutcrackers perched on piles of dusty-looking nuts in the nut-bowl.

14) *There should be embroidery about*. This can be the work of yourself or a relation. At least one chair seat or cushion needs to be petit-point. Heirloom embroidery is sometimes framed and hung, while American-influenced Sloanes adore those *cute* square cushions with one's name worked in bent stitch—Diana, Sarah.

15) *Cane and bamboo furniture lightens things up*. (Not too much bamboo though —that's for hairdressers.) Sloanes see bamboo as thoroughly Empire (see rule 7), and they also like bamboo patterns or other trellis-work ('treillage') on wallpaper or carpeting.

16) *Walls should look soft, not 'architectural'* Sloanes feel uneasy encased in glossy, dark, decoratory walls. They like them dragged, stippled, wallpapered, covered in fabric. Many have learned to sponge and drag for themselves. Jocasta Innes's book, *Paint Magic*, was a Sloane best-seller and has started a minor Sloane industry. Oxfordshire and Wiltshire are full of girls called Felicity and Philippa stippling and stencilling the dining-rooms of friends-of-friends.

17) *There must be a fireplace.* Very preferably with a real fire. Besides, there's got to be somewhere to display the invitations and stand with one's hand behind one's back like Prince Philip. An Adamesque surround in classical proportions (most probably from Hallidays of Beauchamp Place) should be installed if the original has gone up in smoke.

18) *Symmetry is good discipline.* There should be a pair of Rockingham castles, Meissen pugs or Staffordshire dogs on either side of the clock on the mantelpiece. Victorian lustre glass vases will also do. There should be a built-in bookcase on either side of that with cupboards below, complimented by a matching pair of table lamps, etc. Sloanes love pairs.

19) *Ding-dong doorbells or chimes never peal in a Sloane home.* Only the traditional nerve-rattling zing. If it breaks, the guests use the doorknocker—a brass lion, dolphin or a wreath only.

20) So far, a bit TOO good. *There should be jolly or lovable novelties you have fallen for.* You are well aware (and proud) that your decor is now exactly the same as in any upper-middle-class house. *Now* is the time to add your own Terrible Touches. What about your collection of Czech glass animals? Or your Gonks or other furry toys with big heads and woolly hair and protuberant eyes? You have amusing ceramics (the Casa Pupo frog toothbrush holder), a pair of pebbles painted as ladybirds, a Snoopy dog bowl and many other things with cartoons on them or associated with private jokes. There are also pictures in the same modern vein—little boys doing rude things; bright, splashy flowers on a white ground. You are not an old fogy.

A questionnaire for householders

Q. How do I know if I am a Sloane Ranger or not?

A. Test your dwelling against the foregoing rules. If it conforms to any five, you are living in solid-state Sloanehood.

Where you go to buy

You might browse round all sorts of famous or cheap shops, but you will probably buy your Sloaniture and Sloanishings from one of the following:

— Rather fun

London Sloanehome shops

AND SO TO BED, 7 New King's Road, SW6 (731 3593)
Victorian and Edwardian brass and four-poster beds—but stay away from the extravagant camp numbers.

LAURA ASHLEY, 183 Sloane Street, SW1 (235 9728)
Arch-SR shop, *tremendous* (SR adjective) for tiles, wallpaper, fabrics, borders for wallpaper and matching lampshades that fold up like concertinas. SR do-it-yourselfers go to Laura Ashley and Peter Jones on Saturday morning, grab a bottle of vino from the Bouzy Rouge on the way back for a quick lunch of quiche and salad before starting a painting party which lasts all afternoon.

J. D. BEARDMORE, 3 Percy Street, W1 (637 7041)
Brass doorknobs, knockers and locks.

THE BEDCHAMBER, 3 Cadogan Street, SW3 (589 1860)
Owned by Sloane Hugh Blackett, run by Sloane Liz Williams. Rangery four-poster beds with v Sloane decor. Whole bedrooms done—curtains, chairs, cushions etc.

CASA PUPO, 56 Pimlico Road, SW1 (730 7111)
Every SR house had a Casa Pupo rug (circa late Sixties/early Seventies), with its enormous fringe and stunning colours. Occasionally used on beds or hung on walls by older Sloanes. Also Casa Pupo table centrepieces of piles of Spanish lemons, giant green cabbage-leaf plates and white bamboo shelves.

CLARE HOUSE, 35 Elizabeth Street, SW1 (730 8480)
Beautiful silk lampshades—by royal appointment. Also bases. Make to order, convert vases and candlesticks, etc.

Coles, 18 Mortimer Street, W1 (580 1066)
Superb wallpapers, often copied from originals in stately homes. Coles' dragged papers on base colours of bottle green, royal blue or terracotta very popular for dining-rooms and halls, especially with male SRs.

Elizabeth David, 46 Bourne Street, SW1 (730 3123)
One of the two kitchen equipment shops in the central Sloane zone—essential for Sloane cooks.

Designers Guild, 271 King's Road, SW3 (370 5001)
Fabrics, etc.

401½ Workshops, 401½ Wandsworth Road, SW8 (622 7261)

General Trading Co, 144 Sloane Street, SW1 (730 0411)
Along with Peter Jones, this is the kingpin of the central Sloane zone. It's owned and staffed and customered by Sloanes. Sloanes have their wedding lists here (the Princess of Wales was no exception). Waste-paper baskets, trays, salt and pepper mills, dinner services, Hovis toast racks, ice buckets, le Creuset casseroles in strong bright colours, etc.

Harrods, Knightsbridge, SW1 (730 1234)
The house departments.

Harvey Nichols, Knightsbridge, SW1 (235 5000)
Sloane forays into high chic.

Hermès, 155 New Bond Street, W1 (499 8856)
Rectangular porcelain ashtrays with red or green border.

Hippo Hall, 65 Pimlico Road, SW1 (730 7710)
Children's furniture, fabrics, murals etc. by Vanessa Headley and Annie Sloane (by name and nature!).

Home Decorating, 83 Walton Street, SW3 (584 6111)
Sloanes (including the Queen) buy their wallpaper here. They love trustable Sloane owner Anna Garnett.

L. M. Kingcome, 304 Fulham Road, SW10 (351 3998)
Super Sloane soft furnishings.

Locks and Handles, 8 Exhibition Road, SW7 (584 6800)
Run by senior Sloane. Door decor galore.

London Bedding Centre, 26 Sloane Street, SW1 (235 7542)

David Mellor, 4 Sloane Square, SW1 (730 4259)
Kitchen equipment in the best square in the world. Sloane wedding lists.

Merchant Chandler, 72 New King's Road, SW6 (736 6141)
A Sloane local, for bits and pieces for the kitchen and garden, also cane furniture.

W. H. Newson, 61 Pimlico Road, SW1 (730 6262), 481/491 Battersea Park Road, SW11 (223 4411)
DIY-ers, especially SR men—part of the Saturday morning syndrome after Peter Jones et al. Front doors, mouldings to brighten up dreary whitewood fitted cupboards.

John Oliver, 33 Pembridge Road, W11 (221 6466)
Wallpapers, and own paints in original colours. Marvellous shades. Very one-up to have this and not Dulux, Sanderson, etc.

Osborne & Little, 304 King's Road, SW3 (352 1456)
Hyper-Chelsea papers and fabrics, especially the trellis range.

Peter Jones, Sloane Square, SW1 (730 3434)
Mecca to all Sloanes. Watch the Major (Mummie) up from the country, and the 2nd Lieutenant (daughter) on weekday manoeuvres. Saturday morning visit is a must for couples choosing sheets or lights or carpeting or curtain rods. *The Wedding List* was here too, of course. PJ is basic, key, fundamental, *right*. Other shops in the John Lewis group are also seen as Sloanes' own, they are just so dependable, consistent. etc.

The Pine Mine, 100 Wandsworth Bridge Road, SW6 (736 5312)
SR pine paradise of Victorian stripped things, run by David Crewe-Read and Charlie Rolandi. Doors, cupboards, tables etc.

Rain, 20 Battersea Rise, SW11 (228 2235)
Specialists in new and second-hand bamboo. Furniture and accessories.

Real Flame Log Fires, 80 New King's Road, SW6 (731 2704)
Anything's better for a Sloane than no fire at all and if you can't have real logs then this is the best alternative (run by a Sloane, of course).

Treasure Island, 81 Pimlico Road, SW1 (730 3630)
Nice shop for cache-pots, ashtrays, fabric samples etc, owned by Lady Charles (Jane) Spencer-Churchill. With full decorating service.

Tryon Gallery, 41 Dover Street, W1 (493 5161)
Sporting and natural history pictures. One needs several of those.

Tulley's, 289 Fulham Road, SW10 (352 1078)
The sofas specialist. See below.

Christopher Wray's Lighting Emporium, 600 King's Road, SW6 (736 8008)
Pretty reproduction oil lamps, coloured glass shades, brass fittings, all Victoriana.

Curtains suitable for Sloanes

One must have one's curtains and festoons looking right: lots of pretty pelmets and a few swags, variations on the theme of stage curtains—not like those dreadful draped net affairs one sees from the bypass.

Sloanes who are not doing it themselves or using their interior decorator go to Enriqueta Lindesay-Bethune (*Enriqueta*) or Fiona Campbell (*Fiona Campbell*). Enriqueta's workshops are at Barley Mow Passage, Chiswick, W4 (995 6659) and she runs a mail order service —marvellous for Sloanes in the shires. Fiona is at 259 New King's Road, SW6 (731 3681). She's a really super trouper.

Sloane sofas and armchairs

So important to have big comfortable sofas and chairs. Anything stiff and Louis, or that big black leather designer sofa that sticks to the backs of one's legs, is *not* Sloane.

The Sloane's first sofa is usually one of Mummie's cast-offs with a change of loose-cover, probably re-covered by Peter Jones from their Warners or G. P. & J. Baker collections. Or it might be bought from Tulley's in Fulham Road and re-covered. Some Sloanes do the Inner London Education Authority's course on upholstery so that they can do these things themselves.

Rich and about to-be-married Sloanes go to L. M. Kingcome in Fulham Road, who make sumptuous sofas, chairs and so on to fit your space (often made-to-measure, as Sloanes do have longer legs than the proletariat or foreigners) and covered as you choose. (Sensible Sloanes then have them Scotchguarded so they're not immediately ruined by visiting Labradors and little Jeremy's Ribena.) Full interior design service available.

London decorators you go to

Some richer Sloanes get a decorator to interpret their taste. The following know it by heart.

David Ashton-Bostock, 21 Charlwood Street, SW1 (828 3656)
A very delightful Sloane.

Nina Campbell, 48 Walton Street, SW1 (584 9401)
Sloanehome shop owner and decorator. Did Mark's Club, Annabel's.

Colefax & Fowler, 39 Brooke Street, W1 (493 2231). 149 Ebury Street, SW1 (730 2173)
Top trad decorators who did half the stately homes Sloanes are so keen on. (But *David Mlinaric*, who is not particularly Sloane, does most of the big National Trust work since John Fowler's death.)

Danielle, 148 Walton Street, SW3 (584 4242)

Mrs Danielle Doran is a Frenchwoman (aided and abetted by Sloanes) who can extend beyond Sloane taste.

ELIZABETH EATON, 25a Basil Street, SW3 (589 0118)

'Elizabeth Eaton' (Mrs King) loves French rural and French Sloane taste (if you can't imagine what that could be, think Mme Giscard d'Estaing). Lovely shop too.

CHARLES HAMMOND, 165 Sloane Street, SW1 (235 2151)

Large old trad decorators whose shop is also super for fabrics etc. Sloane decorator training ground.

KEEBLE, 13 Walton Street, SW3 (581 3676)

Traditional Sloane decor.

LENYGON & MORANT, 21 Warwick Street, W1 (734 4454)

Distinguished old Mayfair firm.

JENNY MACLEAN, 3 Old Barrack Yard, SW1 (235 9971)

Trained at Charles Hammond. To see her work, look around you when next in the Savoy.

MURIEL MICHALOS, 57 Elizabeth Street, SW1 (730 7666)

Decorates with her own fabrics, prints, etc. Sells pretty antiques too.

MRS MONRO, 11 Montpelier Street, SW7 (589 5052)

It's daughter Miss Jean Monro now, but Sloanes still love the firm. Shop also has own chintzes, antiques etc.

DUDLEY POPLAK, 13b Stratford Road, W8 (937 0835)

The Prince and Princess of Wales' decorator. Need one say more?

JOHN SIDDELEY, 4 Harriet Street, SW1 (235 8757)

Randle Siddeley is John's son, now Lord Kenilworth. Decorating, garden design.

SLOANE DECORATORS, 43 Pimlico Road, SW1 (730 2388)

What better recommendation than its name?

GEORGE SPENCER, 36 Sloane Street, SW1 (235 1501)

'George Spencer' directors are Mrs (Peggy) Laurie, Miss Georgina Cooke and Miss Cecilia Hay. Their furniture, fabrics and colours are pretty and rather dashing. Very popular in Royal Gloucestershire.

TREASURE ISLAND, 81 Pimlico Road, SW1 (730 3630)

Lady Charles Spencer-Churchill decorates as well as shopkeeps for Sloanes.

ELIZABETH WINN, 15 Onslow Gardens, SW7 (589 4189)

Sloane houses, no commercial work.

Learning to decorate the Sloane way
Certain Sloanes feel that their own judge-ment is not enough, and so 'train' in decor-ating. Apart from apprenticeships with firms like Charles Hammond, there is really only one place to go:

THE INCHBALD SCHOOL OF DESIGN, 7 Eaton Gate, SW1 (730 5508)

By, with and for Sloanes. Jacqueline Inchbald who started and runs it has remarried and is now Mrs Brigadier Thwaites.

Streaking—The clothed Sloane way
For those Sloanes with a practical bent toward handiwork:

IAN CAIRNIE, 59 Upper Tollington Park, Stroud Green, N4 (272 5367)

Freelance *trompe l'oeil* artist, gives twice-yearly week long courses in dragging, stippling, ragging, marbling and all the other techniques plied by Felicity, Philippa and their small army of competitors.

JAMES SMART RESTORATIONS, 2 Monro Terrace, Cheyne Walk, SW3 (352 7236)

Smart is probably the kingpin of the stipple and drag brigade. Besides working himself, he regularly takes on trainees after they have left art school. Their reputation after leaving him is assured.

Other practitioners include:

NEMMIE BURGESS, 9 Montpelier Square, SW7 (589 0309)

GRAHAM CARR, 54 Lavender Gardens, SW11 (223 3954)

JONATHAN COLCHESTER, 156 Elgin Avenue, W9 (289 9103)

ALAN DODD, 295 Caledonian Road, N1 (607 8737)

MICHAEL HOWELLS, 113 Coleherne Court, Old Brompton Road, SW5 (373 2286)

QUENTIN LOWE and MARK EDWARDS, 14 Belsize Park, NW3 (435 1063)

Country Sloanehome shops and decorators
You can assemble a Sloanehome without setting foot in Sloane Street. These are some of the non-met Sloane shops and interior dec-orators. Colour Counsellors are all Sloane and all over the country: their HQ is 187 New King's Road, London SW6 (736 8326).

Aberdeen
DESIGN STUDIO, Bridge Street, Bath Street (Aberdeen 546 84)

Bath
COEXISTENCE, 10 Argyle Street (Bath 61507)

Blackpool
LIVOCKS FURNITURE HOUSE, 121 Red Bank Road, Bispham (Blackpool 54072)

Brighton
CASA PUPO, 8 Brighton Place (Brighton 26895)

Cambridge
JOSHUA TAYLOR, 59 Sidney Street (Cambridge 314151)

Cardiff
RICHARD BEERE, 111 Woodville Road (Cardiff 20144)

HONE & JONES, 7-8 Mill Lane, The Hayes (Cardiff 29071)

Chester
JAMANDIC, 22 Bridge Street Row (Chester 312822)

Interior decorator (Mrs McParland) as well as fabrics etc.

Chipping Campden
GREEN DRAGON, High Street (Evesham 840 379)

Good swatch-books and accessories.

Cobham
TARRYSTONE, 40 High Street (Cobham 7494)

Interior designer Mrs Hanbury.

Darlington
ARCH INTERIORS, Coniscliffe House, Northumberland Street (Darlington 53168)

Pine kitchens etc.

Glasgow
TOWN HOUSE–COUNTRY HOUSE, 458 Crow Road (Glasgow 357 2250)

Fabrics, wallpapers, rattan.

Harrogate
WOODS, 65 Station Parade (Harrogate 64112)

Old-established builders and decorators.

Manchester
SIMON GREEN, 47 King Street, West Deansgate (Manchester 834 8903)

Norwich
THE GRANARY, 5 Bedford Street (Norwich 23220)

Poole
CIRCLE GALLERY and STUDIO, Unit 2, 133 Commercial Road, Lower Parkstone (Parkstone 722556)

Reading
HOLMES, 115 Chatham Street (Reading 586 421)

Salisbury
PEMBERTON SOMERVILLE, 16 West Street, Wilton (Wilton 3249)

Stockport
PETER CARLSON INTERIORS, Great Underbank (Manchester 480 8164)

Totnes
HATCHETTS INTERIORS, 51 High Street (Totnes 862 154)

The British Decorators' Association (Director K. A. C. Blease), 6 Haywra Street, Harrogate, Yorks HG1 5BL have a full list of firms, on application.

The Sloane Lavatory

Nous in the loo

Being alone is no fun for a Sloane. Lavatories, which give such pleasure to intellectuals and homosexuals, merely offer the possibility of loneliness and boredom. So you make your lavatory (loo, bog) as amusing and peopled as a flat full of silly friends.

Unlike non-Sloanes—who either pretend it doesn't exist (witness the furry abattoir look) or pretty it up, pink-and-blue with embarrassment—you treat the loo as a *real* room; a personal joke-room plus a history-of-me room. Up go cartoons by Marc, Osbert Lancaster, Calman, Giles. (Rich Sloanes buy the original. Rich and famous Sloanes might be *in* the original.) You hang funny pictures, particularly if you have Spy or Ape cartoons of your grandfather, and clusters of anatomically explicit postcards sent by holidaying friends from Kenya, Bali and the deeper reaches of Athens Museum. Kipling's 'If' could be on the back of the door. There is Henry, on every wall in every team from prep school days, short hair and grinning. Caroline's school photos and Henry's army caricatures also manage to find space, while over the loo, like a directive, is the Mannikin Pis of Brussels. Somewhere near to hand is a shelf of suitable reading matter.

You do not have a flowered lavatory-paper holder or Blue Flush. You *do* have a huge, hairy lavatory brush, an amusing object to the Sloane mind. They are always saying that a friend's hair or dog looks like a bog brush.

One reason you fill your lavatory with jokes is the knowledge that the entire function has something naughty and forbidden about it. The realisation began early on with potty training, an initiation which has left you wanting to laugh about it for the rest of your life. The monthly nurse had Rupert on a pot on her lap at three weeks: 'Tinkle, tinkle'. Foreigners love British nannies because they know that potty training will be strict. There has been a smattering (*sic*) of laissez-faire even in Ranger nurseries over the last few years, but the neurosis is still implanted for life.

Sloanes are famous for their lavatorial sense of humour. Even their babies have 'dirty laughs', and they soon learn expressions like 'laugh like a drain'. Through prep school and public school the shower

Giving Presents To Your Lavatory

London Sloanes patronise all those shops like Parrots and Presents in the Fulham Road, and buy jokes like loo paper with crossword puzzles on it; the Mrs Thatcher loo-paper holder; dirty parts soap (bottoms, penises and bosoms); cheeky mugs (more bottoms and bosoms); toothbrushes and razors in the female form. (No Sloane Christmas is complete without plastic dog messes and spilt ink.)

Anything brass, blue tiles—all the proper old things (except mahogany loo seats—see p 25)—are also very sought-after. So are baskets lined with chintz for lavatory paper and anything pretty for soap—shells, hands, flower dishes. Bathroom luxury fascinates Sloanes. They like his and her basins, sunken baths, marble. They don't *dare* dip more than a toe in A Bigger Splash, 119 Fulham Road, SW3 (584 7454), which is slightly too exotic to take the calmer waters of a Sloane household, but they love to *look* at the showers, saunas, glittering circular baths. It is Sloane Babylon with bubbles.

of lavatory jokes continues. This prep-school humour is the staple of their comic heroes—John Cleese, Rowan Atkinson, John Wells and the rest of *Private Eye*, and Barry Humphries.

The bugbear of the Sloane is constipation. Your medicine chest has Syrup of Figs and Milk of Magnesia at the ready—and just in case the old innards do an about turn, Kaolin too. You find the French and their suppositories horrifyingly hilarious. Trained to go after breakfast, if you can't you worry. (The Sloane household pulls the plug again and again

A Sloane Work of Art

The gents' cloaks at the Rectory is the biggest room in the house, and its High Landowner *day core* definitely a Sloane contribution to style. There is pleasure for every sense, particularly the Sloanes' favourite. You recognise the smell at once: a subtle well-aged mixture of green wellies, old Guccis and Gucci look-alikes; the trug and trowel, gardening gloves; green macs, riding macs, Huskys and riding hats, cloth caps, hunting boots; a wooden boot jack; lino; antlers, fish and fox masks hung on the wall or in cases; walking and shooting sticks, grandfather's spyglass; Pear's clear soap; old black picture frames, bone handles on whips, and the dog's drinking bowl.

at half-past eight—ten on Sundays: no guest can sleep through it.) But needing to go too often is worse—it's frightfully infra dig. Remember what the Duke of Wellington said on the subject. One has to have good mpg.

You find common expressions and American euphemisms quaint and delightful. It's allowed to talk in quotes about 'using the *toy lits*', 'going to the bathroom', 'powdering your nose' or 'going to the little girl's room'. However, when things are serious, a Sloane 'wants to have a pee'. Men *and* women used to say 'spend a penny', but that was in the early Sixties—before decimalisation and

before the franker words were all right. Children still spend a penny. They also wrestle with biggies. Numbers one and two are no longer generally understood.

Sloanes see bidets as menacing symbols of the sinful from the land where the suppositories grow. They make their children pee in it in foreign hotels and wash their own feet in it. Sometimes they try to bring a bidet to heel by soaking socks in it.

Sloanes also have a thing about smell (see p 22), and lavatories occasionally contain not their own prized smells but other people's (*sum* I am a gentleman, *es* thou art a fool, *est* he is a stinky bomb that's stinking up the school). They don't like what scented aerosols do to the air either. A bit of a PONG here. Tart's boodwah.

And, ranging at night, they still have so much of the dog in them that they must pee in the open air (leave their spoor). When drunk in London, Sloanes pee between the railings on to the front doorstep of the basement flat. Some get arrested for exposing themselves. They are safer doing it through the French windows and into the roses after dinner.

They pee in swimming-pools, rivers, lakes and the sea. There is a lot of truth in the old joke about a prep school sending the pool water to be analysed and being told 'Your horse has diabetes'.

BOOKS IN SHARED-FLAT LOOS

Not the Royal Wedding
Beryl Cook's *Private View*
Pooh's Pot of Honey—and other little gifty-books abridged from *Winnie-the-Pooh*
Monty Python's Big Red Book
Books of collected seaside postcards (male SRs only)
This book

BOOKS IN MARRIED SLOANE LOOS

A crossword puzzle book
Osbert Lancaster's *From Pillar to Post* or another
The English Gentleman—Debrett's first little red book (but *not* the others)
Very old *Punches, Playboys* and *Private Eyes*
P. G. Wodehouse's *Carry on Jeeves* or another
Books of Trog, Giles or Charles Addams' cartoons
This book
The Specialist by Charles Sale

Baby Sloane

Having the rat

Henry and Caroline intend to have children, of course. Sloane Ranger culture, which is based on a happy childhood and parties is bound to want a) children b) glasses. For a married couple to refuse to have children is unSloane—unconventional and selfish. Some Sloane girls become unmarried mothers and IF—a big if—they can 'carry it off' socially, it's all right with younger Sloanes.

Other types of person don't believe in posterity any more and look horizontally, to their own generation, for their friends and enemies. Sloanes believe in posterity (posterity will have to keep the hedge clipped) and that what you are given by your parents, you give to your children, even if it's only a rigorous upbringing. The whole Sloane ethos is based on handing things down. As in the Arab world, where even a man who has not yet married is seen as a potential patriarch and is called affectionately 'father of X', so a Sloane baby is already a grandfather in the Sloane scheme.

So, you're pregnant, Caroline. Finding out that Jamie or Sophie is in there is a thrill. After all, one knows one can cope with a physical ordeal—and mopping up after puppies and training them is rather fun. You leave work immediately—what a relief to get away from the Office Crone. (Some SRs stop work *in order* to get pregnant. They pack in their jobs in May. Then they get pregnant one night on holiday, after lots of vino. SRs try not to be preggy during the summer—the heat.) That doesn't mean you are now idle: you are still Doing the House, and there's your charity, going to see your gynae, taking your Rest, buying things for the baby (It, the Lump, the Bloody Nuisance —or a name like Bert). You also spend a lot more time in the country with Mummie, to whom you have suddenly become very close.

The first baby is private. 'Next time Henry says we'll do it on the Health'— Henry having gone *white to the lips* at the £800 bill. Once a week, you go to Betty Parsons' classes. Fellow classmates all wear princess-line pinafores, sometimes in corduroy with pussy-cat bows— unquestionably most unflattering. But Mummie has given them the dresses from Sloane Street, 'Because you must look pretty for your husband, darling.'

A very few, the nonconformists, go to classes run by the National Childbirth Trust. The two or three SRs sit together,

MATERNITY CLOTHES SLOANES WEAR

Dresses Mummie buys them at Just Jane, Young Motherhood, Elegance Maternelle, Maternally Yours in Sloane Street, Harrods, Balloon, and Peter Jones. Laura Ashley smocks and Monsoon cover-all dresses (size 16 on an otherwise sized-12 Caroline) also do well. Evening dresses come from David Neil and Julia Fortescue and Great Expectations. 'Pass on' pregnancy clothes from good friends. Their country clothes, Henry's baggy cords and large navy guernseys and fisherman's smocks.

an island of differentness in a sea of pregnant women in dungarees or wrinkly tights that fall off. Sloane Rangers wear real pregnancy tights, which cost a fortune but fit.

At Betty Parsons', there are lots of awfully nice people in the same class as Caroline, waving their legs about too. It's quite a giggle. Suddenly you need these chums to talk to about all the dreaded details. Breast-feeding, Gerbers or Ostermilk? Real nappies and all that washing, or disposable? Sloanes know it ought to be terry squares—like real hankies—but you usually settle for Snugglers or Cosifits —horrendously expensive but marvellous when you're out to tea.

Thank goodness for Betty Parsons and her gym-mistress briskness. The ones who have 'produced' tell the whales 'She's fantastic. You might not like her sense of humour but you have to admit she really *gets you through it.*'

HOSPITALS SLOANES BOOK INTO

St Teresa's, Wimbledon ('they really treat you as a person, and the nuns are specially kind to fathers too'); the Lindo Wing at St Mary's, Paddington (the royal family's choice of where to go); Queen Charlotte's (though 'Queen Harlot's a dreadful conveyor belt'); the Royal Berks (which Sheila Kitzinger gave a horrific write-up to, but country Sloanes know is OK); Mount Alvernia in Guildford for Surrey affiliates; the John Radcliffe in Oxford; the Claremont Nursing Home, Sheffield (nuns again); the Westminster in London—popular with those with medical histories, as they can be under the experienced hand of de Vere; the West London. Richer Rangers go to Welbeck Street Nursing Home. They don't go to St Thomas's or Guy's unless pa-in-law is a consultant obstetrician there.

Betty Parsons, in a black leotard, lies on the floor groaning, trying to explain to you about gestation, childbirth, and post-natal depression. Husbands go for a lesson too, 'Father Class'. The lift down is full of thoughtful Sloane men who have just realised life is about to change.

Many Sloanes do have the tests, ultrasound ('greasy tum') and amniocentesis: this is to detect Down's Syndrome. It also detects sex but most Sloane mothers prefer not to be told—it's like opening a Christmas present before Christmas. Caroline doesn't want the baby induced —this is her feat. She doesn't want it timed by someone else. And as she is the heroic type, the dash in the middle of the night, or better still middle of the party, is more her.

At last

Caroline races off to the hospital with her suitcase, containing her own feather pillow, a real sponge, a lemon to suck

when in labour, her Stephanotis bath essence and an aerosol spray of Evian water to refresh the country complexion. Also open-fronted night-dresses from Fenwick's and Laura Ashley, a Night Owls dressing-gown and two sturdy nursing bras from Contour.

Henry is with her. The older generation (ten years older) usually wasn't, but Prince Charles showed what correct form now is.

Henry sits holding Caroline's hand. As it gets worse, he wants her to have an epidural. Betty Parsons said it was all

right: 'I am determined that my girls should never feel failures because they had to resort to anaesthetics.' If they don't get an epidural, Sloanes like pethidine, which releases inhibitions rather than kills pain ('So you can "relax"!')

Sloanes rarely relax, so pethidine, plus the 'orrible rigours of birth, make them very loose-tongued and naughty. They compare notes afterwards about what they actually said.

If it's a first they want a boy. Sloane husbands are very keen to propagate and pass on their names. But Henry's very chuffed with whatever lies there; 'It's *incredibly* red and wrinkly'. He has already planned to change the sports car for a four-door hatchback blue Rover 3500 or a Volvo estate.

Meanwhile, the Ranger bush telegraph has been humming, and Caroline's room

---

CONGRATULATIONS PRESENTS CAROLINE GETS FROM HENRY AND PRESENTS FOR THE RATLET

Ring or something else from Jones, Hooper Bolton. 'Thin again' clothes. A holiday—the rat is left with nanny or grandparents and Henry and Caroline go to old favourites (his, mostly) like Scotland, South of France, Kenya.

The ratlet receives lots of knobbly cardigans, shawls, leggings, mitts and bootees knitted by old nannies and fond relations. Also bunnies, teddies, toys from Harrods; Kiddicraft from bazaars, battery-free Fisher-Price and music boxes, balls; Tiger trikes and trolleys; rattles; spoon and fork sets; ducks for bathtime; faded cots of suspect date; Beatrix Potter bowl and mug; embroidered pillowcases.

LAYETTE FOR THE RATLET

The labels Caroline loves are Cherub, Viyella, Petit Bateau, Chilprufe, Absorba. Babygros are a Sloane joke—they call them Grobags. Harrods and Peter Jones get batches of Sloanes buying baby vests, nappies (Harrington squares), prams and Moses baskets which Caroline lines herself with Designers Guild fabric. Sometimes Sloanes have hand-me-down Marmet prams and Silver Cross pushchairs (baby faces you not the traffic). Caroline only goes to Mothercare for plastic pants, and to Marks & Spencer for other basics. For best, she buys from the White House, and Fortnum's baby department (now open again after being closed for seven years).

Everything is in white, of course, except for pale blue cardigans. Other mothers complain there aren't good *modern* baby shops in London, but Sloanes don't mind because the Sloane baby's wardrobe is intended to show he or she's a miniature Sloane. The training's already begun.

---

receives a flurry of greetings telegrams ('DEVASTATING NEWS NEVER KNEW YOU HAD IT IN YOU TONS OF LOVE TO YOU AND BERT, TIM AND CHARLOTTE'), pots of cyclamen which instantly droop, bunches of chrysanths. The hospital staff dread Sloanes. Sloane friends know one is knackered after having a baby, but they feel they can pop in for a quick gawp and a screech of congratulations, disregarding visiting hours and bearing bottles. Those who don't go, telephone. 'Just a tiny tinkle, lovey—how's the little rat?' Caroline spends hours on the telephone.

Breast-feeding: the fashion is swinging back towards it with Sloane Ranger mums, though they lose interest after six weeks ('Duty done, I think'). Circumcision: fifty-fifty. It costs so much.

A week or ten days later, Caroline is delighted to get back to her little house, because she has been rather worried about Henry and *very* worried about the Labrador.

The Sloane abroad

Sloane Ranging is done best in Britain, but it's a worldwide network. Some people think that Sloane Rangers *must* be British: that Americans can hardly be Sloanes and Arabs certainly can't. Actually, Rangers appear in most countries and all races. They are the brisk upper-middles, the ones who run things, the ones who get up in the morning and make appointments, attend meetings and don't believe in 'leisure' or pleasure or philosophy or anything else that involves thought and inaction. This they call *serving* the community. Anti-Sloanes call it *bossing* the community and maintaining the status quo. Such detractors always feel it would be better if the government ran things and looked after the disadvantaged. But the government doesn't, does it?

Sloanes are therefore *rushed off their feet* all over the world: Kuwait Rangers, Westmount Rangers, Vienna Rangers (the 'Schubertring Gräfin'), Munich Rangers (lots), Öslo Rangers, Fiji Rangers, Taiwan Rangers, Cairo Rangers ('Groppi's Horse'), Jaipur Rangers, São Paulo Rangers, Melbourne Rangers (in broderie anglaise to show off their tan), Lusaka Rangers, Tokyo Rangers, Rome Rangers. Indian and Japanese Rangers, for two, don't always wear western dress, though a short skirt is good for leaping in and out of cars—something all Rangers spend part of each day doing.

Next time you go abroad, try saying you want to do something useful while you are here. You will be told, 'You should talk to Mrs So-and-so—she will know what you could do', and you will be introduced to . . . a Sloane.

But the British Sloane is an undeniably important minority. Henry and Caroline love seeing the world—either when 'posted' abroad, or for a holiday.

The holidaying Sloane

In the mid-1950s, after the last war, the Sloane Ranger's beat extended only as far east as Florence and as far south as the Côte d'Azur. SR girls were sent to Florence to learn Italian with a respectable Italian contessa and were recalled for their season minutes before discovering sex on a Fiesole picnic with the contessa's nephew.

Now, the same SR has been to as many as three continents (courtesy of cheap flights), though probably to outlying islands rather than to the mainland: the West Indies, Manila, Hong Kong, Singapore, Corfu, Corsica, Ibiza, Tenerife.

Caroline used to take one annual holiday, plus a week's skiing at Easter. Now she takes two holidays, one of which is probably attached to Henry's business trip to America or the Far East. Much of the year is spent looking forward to holidays, which are booked up far in advance. New clothes and sun creams and Blue Guides and maps ('can't trust the frog road-signs') are bought, but not dictionaries. Although SRs periodically go on safari (which they see as an extension of stalking holidays in Scotland), they really do not have more than a passing interest in foreign countries. They don't want to become like French peasants. A holiday is meant to be a *rest*.

True tiredness is for Sloanes with children at boarding-school. Childless or have-nanny-will-travel Sloanes find *business brainwaves* (cheap labour) in places like Morocco, India and Thailand: people who can make up your clothes designs, or copy famous European makes of bag, etc. The Sloane sets up a little business selling to friends, and might expand into a shop. Female Sloanes are a nation of undercutting shopkeepers in the 1980s.

There are four main ports of call, however, which characterise the Ranger experience of growing up and experiencing The World.

Italy

Italy is the land of Gucci, Pucci and Smoochi. Sloanes never lose their affinity

Trust the Frogs . . .

for this country where marbled blotters are half the price of the same thing at the GTC.

Italy, of course, achieved its early Sixties SR fame as the land where the Guccis ('Guckies') grew and, until duty was removed when GB joined the EEC, SRs always slunk guiltily through customs with a new pair of smart brown Guccis on their feet.

France

Twenty years ago the Brittany coast became, for a time, the up-market SR Frinton, and nannies took their charges for gym classes on the beach. France, and the S of F in particular, remains the most wholesome SR holiday destination, though Sloane Rangers have always been a shade concerned by the presence of big money in St Tropez and Cannes.

Sloane Rangers do, however, take villas around Le Lavandou and Grasse, where they expend a great deal of energy complaining to the local agent that the house is insufficiently equipped. Where, for instance, are the *blankets* for the beds and where is the kettle? (They do, however, know what the bidet is meant for these days: wet swimsuits.)

America

Caroline has become increasingly familiar with the Americans, and they, in turn, have become increasingly familiar with her. Among the many worrying things about America is the 'Have a nice day' chit-chat with waitresses and such like— too chummy by half. Disneyland (and Disneyworld in Florida) are, however, essential tourist sites on the SR itinerary, and the sight of a group of slightly embarrassed-looking prep-school boys emerging from the Haunted House wearing Mickey Mouse ears is now a standard feature.

India

Sloane Rangers do go on Serenissima and other tours of India, especially of the Punjab palaces, but touring holidays are not really suited to the under-45 SR mentality. There is too much packing and unpacking, and never time to hang anything up properly, and tours do not fulfil the SR mother's need for a good rest.

LIVING ABROAD: OUTPOSTS OF SLOANE SQUARE

British Sloanes living abroad enjoy their tour of duty, and get their visitors to bring them the little symbolic things they can't live without: Bath Olivers, digestive biscuits, Earl Grey tea. *The Times* still arrives, thank God, and since 1973, Sloanes have had the vital *Good Book Guide*, a Sloane mail-order service (PO Box 400, Havelock Terrace, London SW8), through which they keep in touch with country-house incest and new ways of nobbling favourites in Lambourn. *The Good Book Guide* people speak Sloane and know what's needed.

Kenya

Sloane Rangerism (African chapter) is found most easily in the hotels and bars of Nairobi. Young SR singles congregate in the Thorn Tree Café of the New Stanley Hotel, where they order White Cap and Premium beers one at a time to keep the waiters powerless to throw them out. Married SRs take innumerable candid photos of the rough loveplay of the game park lions, and come back pregnant themselves.

Hong Kong

Sloane Rangers returning to England after a long posting in Hong Kong often discover that they have become more Ranger than the Rangers, particularly SRMs working for Jardine's, Swire's and the Hong Kong and Shanghai Bank. Hong Kong—capitalism's last remaining frontier town—has become an extraordinary SR haven where Sloane Rangers (who all live on the Peak) are pickled for eternity in sweet-and-sour sauce.

The catchment area for recruiting remains almost entirely Oxbridge, or hereditary HK Johnnies from Dumfriesshire. These are reckoned to have the greatest resistance against going barmy in the heat. They eat roast beef, whitebait, ploughman's lunches and shepherd's pie and buy drinks for the famous Hong Kong 'fishing fleet', girls from Britain trawling for husbands.

New York

A lot of Sloane men go there for a start, usually to work in a Wall Street bank or money broker's. They make friends with their American cousins the Preppies and get themselves invited to the Hamptons, Kentucky and New England to sail in the summer. They buy blue-and-white seersucker jackets, and even the Preppies have never seen such freeloading . . .

Canada

Just north of the water where the New York Sloane freeloaders have been invited to sail, the Montreal Sloane freeloaders have been invited to sail, at Chester. Sloanes used to like to spend a year or two in Montreal but as the English-speaking businesses moved out of Montreal to Toronto, so did the Sloanes. They also go to Calgary (skiing, oil) and Vancouver (skiing, sailing, anglicised culture).

The family (flower) plot

The Sloane couple's first real gardening comes with the move to the country house. The tubs on the patio did not prepare you for the three acres which now stare you in the face. However, per ardua ad backache, as Henry says. The Chelsea Flower Show Members' Day now becomes as important to you as Ascot.

Principles of Sloane gardening

1) *Your garden is a Gentleman's Garden.* It's the *grounds* of your house, a miniature estate. You would adore to have a park, but we can't all. If your house is only a borderline gent's res, the garden must clear up the doubt. Seven ways are to:

● *Build walls.* A low brick wall round the swimming-pool or rose garden, or a wall between garden and road, or just two bits of wall running wing-like up to the gate-posts. Always brick—never fancy stone-work.

● *Add urns, old stone sinks, finials or staddle-stones.* Ball or lion finials on the gateposts; staddle-stones to keep guests' cars off your lawn.

● *Have lawns.* (See 3.)

● *Build a terrace at the back.* You could combine this with a low wall and urns to be even more like a stately home.

● *Build a conservatory extension.* This is the modern Sloane's obsession. Every Henry is either Before, During or After conservatory.

● *Paint all your fences* bright white or fierce black (creosote). Bright white is the Sloane's favourite colour. You use it for the window frames and wooden bits of your house.

● *Add 'deer' to your 'park'.* Get one or two Jacob's sheep or a pony or peacocks or Chinese geese or at the very least a teth-ered tortoise.

2) *Your garden is a setting for social life.* It has more facilities than Hurlingham.

● *A drinks lawn.* Guests must be able to stroll on to the lawn from the house, G and T in hand. When you looked over the house you assessed whether the garden would do for the summer party and where the marquee might be for the coming-out dance and later, the wedding. You would not have bought the house if it hadn't had French windows.

● *Swimming-pool.* This must be built if there isn't one, so you can invite friends. It doesn't mean a £30,000 Hollywood job—just a suitable splashing-hole.

● *Tennis-court.* Another necessity. You must have both swimming and tennis, if possible. So what if you can barely squeeze both into your garden? It will shorten the walk to the drinks lawn and Pimm's (borage from the border).

● *Croquet.* This can share the drinks lawn —Henrys *love* vicious games of 'poison'.

● *Garden furniture.* Weathered teak benches. You *might* have iron chairs and table, but they're a bit nouveau and arty. Sloanes also like the discipline of getting out a batch of deck-chairs and setting them up and taking them down again afterwards.

● *Drive and parking.* Must be impressive. Sloanes *love* a drive a mile long even when it's not theirs.

3) *The grass is paramount.* Here Henry, who does nothing in the garden except mow, prune and clip, takes precedence (again) over Caroline, who digs, plants, weeds, mulches, rakes, hoes, thins, beds out, stakes, orders seed, writes labels, picks and deadheads. (Neither of the Sloanes does much spraying. It kills wild life.) While Caroline is o/c flowers, which are decoration, Henry is o/c grass, which is the outdoor drawing-room. To the Sloane mind, it's obvious that:

A box of tennis balls beats an apple tree,
A croquet hoop beats a pergola.

'Spend the money on machines' has been Henry's motto since his eighth birth-day. Henry is quite unpatriotic when he shops for machines. He owns garden

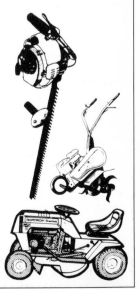

weapons made by most of the warlike nations: Japan, Germany, America, South Africa, Britain. Henry buys like a soldier. His ideal armoury would consist of: an American Mountfield Commando tractor, from £1,600, or the newer British Westwood, from £650. He likes to sit on it and do 'a bit of tractoring'. A Suffolk Colt or Ransome Twenty-Four cylinder mower (the Rover of cylinder mowers). Henry gets the one with a seat, £850. (You have to have a cylinder mower to have stripes and *you have to have stripes*.) A big Flymo, from £110, to do the bumps and edges and behead the enemy. A Spintrim, from £100, to mop up stragglers along the edges. A Paice-setter (Japanese), a whirring blade on a pole, from £85, with a harness like a parachute. Henry suspends it from his shoulders and goes out killing weeds and any grass that's trying to hide beside walls. He thinks the khaki jersey with the shoulder patches makes him look dangerous.

Henry could well end up with about £3,000 or £4,000 tied up in his garden machines—more than he intended, but you have to pay for your fun. And current property prices support his garden pride instead of branding him a bloody fool.

Henry has a compost heap, testimony to the size of his estate. He piles the dead and dying into a huge memorial mound, which is used to grow marrows on (a favourite veg) and rhubarb next spring (another favourite, for sound purgative reasons).

4) *Your garden is a testimony to the travels of earlier Sloanes.* Sloane gardens are museums of Chinese and South American and Himalayan plants and trees. The Victorian rectories Sloanes live in are planted with the rhododendrons, hydrangeas, pampas grass, bamboos, monkey-puzzle trees, Wellingtonias brought back by Victorian Sloane plant-hunters. Fashion has turned against these bold exotics and back to native British,

but the Sloanes keep the monkey-puzzles flying. (Caroline could never murder a bush or tree and certainly not on grounds of *taste*.)

5) *Your garden is a tribute to your heroes:*
● *Christopher Lloyd.* You like his articles in *Country Life* and you grow his speciality, clematis.

THINGS THAT BRAND A GARDEN UNSLOANE

Crazy paving. It's Surrey. Caroline shudders at the Gertrude Jekyll school of gardening and also at the gin-and-Jag belt she did it in.

The cottage-garden look. Sloanes want to build their cottage up to look like a manor-house, not draw attention to its plebian origins.

Fifties conifers. Victorian conifers are all OK but the blue and gold and monstrous dwarfs are definitely not.

Heathers. They should stick to moors.

A wrought-iron front gate. Surrey again. Sloanes go for wood or cattle-grids. They're manly and show it's cattle country.

New fancy topiary. The only acceptable shapes are balls, birds, crenellations or elephants (elephants as at Rockingham Castle).

A lily pond under 200 square feet. An ornamental sheet of water must be big, preferably a lake.

Gardens
Open to the Public
in England and Wales

76

THE ROYAL HORTICULTURAL SOCIET

VINCENT SQUARE, LONDON, SW1P 2PE
TEL. 01-834 4333

Patrons, Council
and Officers 197

● *Vita Sackville-West.* You admire her (both as a gardener and in life: what a goer). You think your garden is a bit like Sissinghurst: grey plants, white flowers. (All the scarlets and bright blues and yellows with them ruin the effect, but you don't know that.)

● *The Statelies.* You have plants 'from Cranborne', 'from Powis Castle', and so on, bought when the gardens were open to the public.

You like the flowers shown in the *Temple of Flora* and Redouté's *Roses*, which you have, either as prints on the walls or as table-mats.

6) *Your garden puts on a good show.* You don't aim to have to walk round pointing out rarities nobody would otherwise have noticed. Plants must be bright and beautiful and visible from the house.

7) *You have a rose garden.* It's traditional. And you have earth in between the rose-bushes. All this fear of earth and fuss about groundcover is poncy.

8) *The garden must look spontaneous.* But the laissez-faire leads to a situation which Caroline does not like at all: the Sloane garden is *garish.* Why? Because Caroline is too soft. She insists on having rosemary, lavender, honeysuckle and wallflowers. She never prunes hard enough or scraps unhappy plants. She wavers between wanting a wild garden and fretting because the edges aren't cut—and ends up with an unhappy mixture. The garden is overrun by blackspot, rabbits, pigeons and moles and she earnestly discusses methods of extermination at parties—which she doesn't put into practice.

9) *Vegetables.* Now that there's pick-your-own (and freezers) Caroline doesn't need such time-consuming (and space-consuming) acreage devoted to things like raspberries and peas. She grows decorative veg these days, scarlet runners and globe artichokes and butter lettuces nestling at the marguerites' feet.

Country nurseries Sloanes like

ALLWOOD BROTHERS, Clayton Nurseries, Hassocks, Sussex (Hassocks 2115): pansies.

DAVID AUSTIN, Bowling Green Lane, Albrighton, Wolverhampton (Albrighton 2142): roses.

PETER BEALES, Intwood Nurseries, Swardeston, Norwich (Mulbarton 70 631): roses.

BEES, Sealand, Chester (Chester 501): everything.

BRESSINGHAM GARDENS, Diss, Norfolk (Diss 464): herbaceous plants.

BETH CHATTO, UNUSUAL PLANTS, White Barn House, Elmstead Market, Colchester (Wivenhoe 2007).

JACK DRAKE, Alpine Plant Nursery, Aviemore, Inverness-shire (Kincraig 287).

HILLIER NURSERIES, Ampfield, Romsey, Hampshire (Braishfield 68733): everything.

CHRISTOPHER LLOYD, Great Dixter, Northiam, Sussex (Northiam 3107): clematis.

JOHN MATTOCK, Nuneham Courtenay, Oxford (Courtenay 265): roses.

R. C. NOTCUTT, Woodbridge, Suffolk (Woodbridge 3344): shrubs and trees.

RATHOWEN DAFFODILS, Knowehead, Dergmoney, Omagh, Co Tyrone (Omagh 2931).

SHERRARDS, Snelsmore Road, Donnington, Newbury, Berkshire (Newbury 47845): shrubs and trees.

IAN SMITH, 127 Leaves Green Road, Keston, Kent (Biggin Hill 72531): new species from expeditions, rock-garden plants.

JAMES SMITH & SON, Scotland Nurseries, Matlock, Derbyshire (Matlock 3036): yews for hedges and other plants, very hardy, as nursery is high.

THE SUNNINGDALE NURSERY, Windlesham, Surrey (Ascot 20496): shrubs and trees.

J. WATERER, SONS & CRISP, The Nurseries, Bagshot, Surrey (Bagshot 72288): everything.

Any country house when the garden's open. The unusual plants are sold out by 3.

Not garden centres—those are for the conifer brigade.

Note to Sloane supergardeners

If you're really keen, you can do a course in garden design, planning and skills:

The Garden School Godspiece Leaze, Norton St Philip, nr Bath (Limpley Stoke 2540) runs four-day fully residential courses from May to September, one on Flowers and Music coinciding with the Bath Festival in May. Separate courses on planning, history and skills, each £150 plus VAT. Non-residential, £75 plus VAT.

The Inchbald School of Design 7 Eaton Gate, SW1 (730 5508). Ten-week Garden Design course including landscape design, draughtmanship, plant-care and instruction on greenhouses, water and lighting, £1,076; or three-week Garden Design Drawing course, £445.

The Middle Years

Henry and Caroline after 25

When they have a toddler, Henry and Caroline move to the country. 'You can't bring up children in a town.' They will be back with a pied à terre in about twelve years, when the daughters need a flat. Caroline is having to find new devices and Henry wants to say goodbye to old vices.

London Sloanes like moving to the west (more Sloanes, warmer gardens). They love sliding away from Paddington on the 125 or beetling along the M4, M5 or M40 (exit 14 to Newbury; the West Country; Monmouth, now Gwent; Royal Gloucestershire). But this may not suit Henry's work ('I commute, for my sins,' he says; but that doesn't of course, make him a *commuter*). It doesn't really matter where you go, as long as it's to a gentleman's house. You can even live in Surrey, though Sloanes jeer 'very Surrey', 'gin and Jag belt', 'mock Tudor', 'stockbroker belt' (as though 90 per cent of stockbrokers weren't Sloane). What Sloanes don't like about Surrey is that *all* the houses are big houses. This is obviously wrong. There must be *a* leader's house in any district for the Person Who Runs Things (the Sloane).

You do up your new house exactly like your town house or flat, but you are appalled by the number of windows. Sloane windows need curtains with a capital C: with pelmets, twiddly bits, bands, tassels, tie-backs, edging. They cost a bomb. You spend months sewing and then give up, leaving the last hems pinned.

As soon as you're in the leader's house, the Old Rectory, you are approached by the other local chiefs, all wanting to 'rope you in'. Be careful, Caroline! The Sloane country whirligig is relentless. You will never sit down, unless you count the Renault. You'll be dashing in and out in your jeans, banging stable/shed/car/barn/deep freeze/house/horse-box doors. You may become 'incredible' (hard as nails)—subtlety, wit, tolerance and humility having been thrown out so you can go faster.

You try to start gradually, perhaps putting a new pregnancy between yourself and agreeing to everything. But you get Jamie a pony for you to love, which does throw you into the thick of it.

Hunting

Riding to hounds is on the increase by reason of the increased horse population: finding work for idle hooves to do. Hunting suits Sloanes who can afford it (the subscription can be over £1,000, plus the day's cap): it's dangerous, noisy, and the vocabulary, dress and things one does and doesn't do are a secret between Sloanes.

You love to say at London parties 'We hunt with the Pytchley or Cottesmore (Cotsmore), Quorn, Fernie, Belvoir (Beaver)'—in other words, in the Shires. Or you might be in 'the Leicestershire of the west'—in Blackmore or Sparkford Vale country in Dorset. You call what people do on the edge of London 'hunting over dustbins'. If you're in the Cotswolds, you have the Beaufort (Princess Anne), Cotswold, Heythrop, Vale of the White Horse and Bicester to royal name-drop about: 'Prince Charles was out with us the other day...'. It's sporting of him to distribute his favours among several different hunts. But if you're in west Gloucestershire—with the Berkeley—or in Ireland, where you *really* have to jump, you call the east Cotswolds 'a funker's paradise, full of stockbrokers who never leave the ground'.

Henry and Caroline own a Baily's—the hunting reference book—and dress utterly correctly, in 'ratcatcher' clothes for cubbing (bowler hat, hacking jacket, brown or black boots) on an unclipped horse. But there is a Cinderella transformation on 1 November into top hat and red coat for Henry (only pedants say 'pink' coat—called after Mr Pink, not the

Sloane vs. Saboteur.

A rare breed: Caroline gets her gun.

on one of the Aussie or Kiwi (male) polo groupies to help with the ponies for the season. For the first two months, Henry thinks it's jolly sporting of Caroline not to complain...but then there's a big argy-bargy. (Polo isn't really Sloane—it's too *liberated.*)

Shooting

The one thing all Sloanes are good at. They are charming good shots, or charming bad shots, but they all know the form. Yorkshire breeds the real dead-eyes. New-comer Henry is invited either by the local landowner or by a member of a syndicate (one guest each). Seven out of nine of the guns are Sloane. There may be a few millionaires and foreigners, but in a sense all shooters are Sloane, because the clothes are standard (green Husky, Barbour, tweeds), the rules are rigid, the ritual perfected for the defence of men against birds.

Henry started on rooks with a .22, got a .410 at twelve, and by seventeen was shooting with a 12-bore. A Spanish AYA (Ayala y Aguirre) is perfectly acceptable —especially as it's under £300 and a Purdey is £9,500. Smart Sloanes do have grandfather's guns—long out of proof. But a Sloane is Safe. Not like the French, who form circles and shoot towards each other.

Caroline does not shoot, but in middle age becomes a picker-up, with the help of her Labrador. Now, while in her prime, Caroline victuals the army for the war against birds. She is glad to get all those pheasant, duck, partridge and grouse for the deep freeze, but a pheasant costs £10 in keepering, feeding, beating, shooting, so it's not really *cheap.*

Meanwhile, Caroline has made a large picnic with much alcohol (thermos half sherry/half consommé; hip-flask half cherry brandy/half whisky; port mid-morning) or even had all those wet muddy bottoms to lunch (she longs to ask them to sit on newspapers). After shooting they

colour) and black coat, black boots, Persil-white tie round her neck for Caroline. Everyone boasts shiny horses. Caroline is thinking of getting a side-saddle; so many women ride side-saddle now. There are jokes about it being the riding astride that makes all hunting women mad for the Master, but it may only be his iron rule over his obedient field.

Point-to-pointing

All Sloanes go, even those who don't ride. You have to go, to parade your girlfriend/daughter/Labrador, pass the hip flask, and get deep-frozen, despite the sheep-skin, while eating the picnic.

Polo

Depends where you live, unless you're very rich. If you have a polo ground near enough and you play, you probably take

need tea, fruit cakes, scones; after tea they need whisky. If you want to see money literally fly, join a shoot.

Scotland

Sloanes go north every August, travelling second class with dogs, guns, rods, tweeds and paraphernalia, mostly green. You have taken/are staying at a shooting lodge (large Victorian house). You are surprised to find that the hills are alive with Robin Hoods in feathered caps—the foreigners. You yourselves are baggy and tatty in guernseys, Viyella checks and murky old tweeds, whereas the estate keepers have their own estate tweed with deerstalker in identical sett (made up by Burton's), one of the last pleasures of feudalism.

You are too poor to have done much stalking, so you deserve what happens on your one day on the hill. You crawl for hours through wet bogs. Then the stalker rejects the stag as too good—keep for the Germans—and makes you crawl on round another mountain. When you do kill (you feel awful) it is gralloched instantly and up whizzes a Unimog or Snocat and takes it away in order to qualify for EEC meat rules: 24 hours kill to chill.

Your deep freeze

Caroline is fixated on the non-ecology of this sort of frozen compost heap: you keep making things for it, and remembering things you can't eat because they have been in there too long. Once every two months you take the Land-Rover and drive miles with your best friend to the nearest Cash and Carry. There you produce a farmer's or caterer's card you have illegitimately obtained, and stock up with more things to lose in it.

Your best friend

As mentioned earlier, Sloane marriages usually break up over 'MY BEST FRIEND!'. A couple starts seeing another couple, and after they've played bridge together ('We want our revenge!') and tennis together ('Your service—have some China-

man's balls') and been skiing together to St Moritz ('They call that Friday train the gnomes come on "le train coqu"') and been to Cor F U together, they split apart to form one new combination, leaving a hurt and bewildered Sloane man and a furious vengeful Sloane woman, who buys a sports car (Gramps having just died, helpful to the end), enrols in NADFAS (the National Association of Decorative and Fine Art Societies) and books a Serenissima trip. A woman scorned becomes a culture vulture.

The Party

The Sloane Ranger always works for the Conservative Party. You may flirt with the idea of voting Social Democrat, but you will work for the Conservatives. A few years ago, Caroline might have voted Labour once or twice, but things are no longer what they were. You do the fête, and the ball, but you are busiest on Election Day, when you drive Conservative voters to the polls ('proles to the polls', your London friends call it, but it doesn't sound right in the country). Sometimes you are unable to winkle out poor old True Blue Dad who lives with his obstructive Red children. 'It's CRIMINAL,' you tell your friends, not realising that it

We do admire her but she does go on.

really is. But with the Sloanes working as one giant votes-harvester, the Conservative machine sweeps the candidate in.

Politics are also a door-opener socially. The member or young Tory with political ambitions will be married to a Sloane or, if not yet, looking for one. It is political suicide to go before a selection committee for a seat without being married, but a nice Sloane wife carries the day. A girl-friend rather than a wife will do, but some committees are suspicious: bach-

the Sloanes appear with their boxes and containers. They are ready with their opinions of Sloane lateness and idea of a good meal. You meet the young at Riding for the Disabled, personally walking them round the local riding school three times a week on a scruffy pony on a leash.

Oh dear, real life! Thank goodness for such bulwarks against meeting it as Guide Dogs for the Blind, the Injured Jockeys' Fund, the wire fund for the hunt, the British Field Sports Society, the World

The Sloane Dog

The faithful Labrador

Sloane children have all the usual pets—hamsters, gerbils, guinea-pigs, tortoises, cats, white mice— but the mark of a Sloane is a Labrador. The noble yellow fellow (or big black beautiful blackamoor) is Caroline's secret love, the one she can give all her thwarted affection to, the one whose smell she dotes on, the one she knows naps on the beds and hopes Henry won't catch.

It is a myth that Sloane Labradors are well-trained shooting dogs. Three-quarters of them are the indulged squire of the woman of the house, dangerous on even a country road, won't come to heel, and roam (males) when there's a bitch on heat, or just because they feel like it.

A *few* even steal, making off with the first course while the guests are having cocktails. ('The slob-berador has eaten the game terrine!'). Sloanes are amused by their own and their friends' dogs' naughtiness, as long as it's a hound—even only a miniature dachshund with a deep voice. (They can't stand what they call 'kick dogs'—nervous yappers.) They say 'He'll eat their poodle!', 'He'll pee against the sofa', 'Blagdon is simply the most terrible dog in the world.'

Other dogs, after labs, are Jack Russells, Sealyhams, boxers, Yorkshires, King Charleses, dachshunds. Dachsies are *highly* favoured. Sloanes don't like poodles or pointers—there's the docked tail and 'They've got such rude bums.' Ideally, a dog should have a pedigree.

Sloanes can't bear the fact that dogs don't live as long as they do. When a Sloane bachelor commits suicide, he shoots his Labrador, then himself. (If you don't believe this, look in the papers.) United in death as in life.

elors have been known to borrow an obliging Sloane for the interview.

Your good works

Henry is a church warden (job goes with the house), but Caroline is the charity worker. Sloanes give hundreds of pounds to charity, but they're not allowed to just give it. There have to be Ideas, gimmicks, tombola, coffee mornings, committees, lunches, stalls, balls, 'chains'. It can take weeks of your time to give Mental Health £50.

Mind you, those weeks are spent with other Sloanes. You hardly ever get money from non-Sloanes, or meet the beneficiaries of your work. Meals on Wheels is an exception. The old people love seeing

Wildlife Fund, SSAFA, the Lifeboats, the Nurses, your Diseases, Save the Children, and of course the British Legion and poppy day. Lots of cocktail parties for these and other charities, invited by friends (no one can remember *which* charity, but dinner was excellent).

Your balls

The best thing about charity work is the bollocks. You go to other bollocks too. A conscientious married couple should manage about six a year. You call your friends' dances bollocks too—to their faces. 'Your bollock'. You go in a group of ten or so, throw bread rolls, drink too much, whizz about and fall down. Hunt balls are wonderful for falling down at the end of the Gallop. But Highland Balls are the best, because they are the most traditional and formal: white tie. The Caledonian at the Hyde Park Hotel in London even needs red trim on the collar —if Henry is not knickerless in kilted glory. Very keen Scots Sloanes wear total Victorian combination of kilt and jacket. The Campbell clan affect nasty triangular silver buttons which scratch. Women wear white or something else simple to set off the tartan sash—and there are whoops and shrieks and bagpipes and barbaric dances (Sloanes who have forgotten them brush up either at a dancing class or with Roderick Martine's book *The Swinging Sporran*).

Your drinks parties

Still stand-up-and-shouts. No change from your young days. You talk all the time, loudly. One non-Sloane reproved a Sloane: 'To be silent is not to be dull', but you know that's not true. You 'sing for your supper', and for your alcohol.

Your dinner parties

Dins parties. The 'boys' now stay behind with the port after dinner to give Caroline a chance to be boring about the rat. Numbers always even, guests punctual, leave about midnight *slightly* châteaued, with Rupert in his carrycot. There is a bond feeling about dinner parties: Sloane, Sloane together. The great thing is to be 'on good form'. *Never* thirteen at table— either a teddy or an obedient pet saves the day. Sloanes help the ball hostess by giving dinner parties before it.

Your house parties

You were guests, you become hosts. You know that when you offer to put up people coming for a local dance or wedding that you will be given two nice couples and one awful one—the latter have to be spread around. The easiest house parties are for a sport—racing, three-day event, shooting. You have to have a dinner party on Saturday, where

FOOD & FUN FOR WRINKLIES

Eating out in London

You like good value, but most of all you like to see other Sloanes. You want to eat your avocado, chicken casserole à la Froggy and crème brulée in the civilised world. So you go to the Ark, the Bistro Vino, Charco's, Dan's, Drakes, Drones, the Hungry Horse, Julie's, Khan's, Mark's Club, Meridiana, Nineteen Mossop Street, Monkeys, the Pizza on the Park, the Poissonerie de l'Avenue, the Pontevecchio, the Poule au Pot, the Sailing Junk, the Brasserie St Quentin, San Frediano (San Fred's), San Lorenzo, San Quintino, San Ruffillo, Shezan, Tai-Pan. For once-a-year big events (birthdays, anniversaries) you save up for the Connaught or one of the top Good Food Guide places. You *do* know they exist.

Henry's clubs

Terribly expensive, but Henry hangs on in case he has to impress an American client, and then there will be Sophie's wedding in a few years.... Henry doesn't spend much time in the Club—Sloane wives want to know the reason why. But he belongs to *one* of the following: Army and Navy (the 'Rag'); Athenaeum; Caledonian (Scottish Sloanes); Cavalry and Guards; East India, Devonshire, Sports and Public Schools; Garrick (almost too 'achiever' to be Sloane); Gresham; National Liberal (dark and threadbare, but amazing billiards room); Naval and Military ('In and Out'); Oriental; Royal Automobile; Royal Thames Yacht; Savile; Travellers'; Turf; or United Oxford and Cambridge University, the English Speaking Union (for Americanophiles). The really grand clubs are now only for getters and spenders. They are not Sloane.

Caroline's clubs

Hurlingham (a godsend before you moved to the country), the Sloane Club (a godsend since), the Lansdowne (*the* family club).

Your night clubs

You prefer the ones done up like Sloane country houses: Annabel's, Raffles. A night at Tokyo Joe's allows one to see one's friends' children bopping.

the awful couple demonstrate their awfulness.

All your house party propitiate you with chocolates (Charbonnel & Walker, Fortnum's or Bendick's), or Floris and Culpeper soaps. But most forget to propitiate your helpful Mrs Snooks, and you go round on Monday morning early leaving the magic greenies.

Being a horse parent

'A Sloanie has a pony' is so ingrained in the Sloane mind, and 'If you want to get ahead get a horse' in the mind of social climbers, that Britain in the 1980s has the largest horse population since Victorian times. And these thousands of animals have to be kept busy. Boxing one's child and its pony to and from hunter trials or meet or gymkhana takes up at least one day a week for two grown-ups. (If Henry doesn't help at the weekend he feels cuckolded by this four-legged male Caroline and Sophie are so mad about. Also a heel, because Alfie always resists walking the plank.)

Letting Jamie and Sophie ride is expensive (pony £300; second-hand Rice trailer, £600; Pony Club sub, £6; saddle, £290, let alone the rest of the tack for child and horse, and the feeding). But it's a wonderful way of keeping in touch. Sloanes get so hooked on the horse calendar that one

adulterous couple turned up at the local hunter trials the week after moving in with their best friends' husband and wife. There they were, all four, in their *sheepskin* coats and Johnnie in *brothel* creepers —frightfully embarrassing, but how could one not have gone?

Sloane children belong to the Pony Club, and they go on to eventing, *not* show-jumping. At Pony Club camp in the summer, Henry and a fellow Sloane father have to stay up all night when it's their turn to patrol the tents to see no harm comes to Sophie (from randy young Rupert in the next tent, but they pretend it's because motorbike boys sometimes roar round the field terrorising the Sloanes). It's a charming piece of medievalism—especially as at teenage parties, Jamie and Sophie and all the enterprising Sloanes and Sloanettes sneak up to the bedrooms, lock the door and fumble, until they hear Henry knocking and admonishing in a furious low voice.

A CEREAL LOVE AFFAIR

Our correspondent with the Tickham reports

Sophie's first love is Sammy. He is a 12 hh Thelwellian grey with hairy heels and thick eyelashes fringeing his innocent blue eyes. With hoots of laughter his parents enter him for classes filled with glossy show ponies ridden by children in washable coats, rubber riding boots and new blue hats. Sophie has jodhpur boots and a tweed coat recently shaken out of moth-balls, belonging to her mother. She and Sammy have to be dragged into the ring and once there he refuses to do anything he is told. If he catches sight of Caroline he makes a dash for her, diving under the ropes and throwing Sophie on to her back in the mud. Sammy is wilful, wicked, stubborn, stupid, lazy and lovable. 'Sammy is a Pig.' Sophie adores him and dreams of bending-races and rosettes.

Sophie's feet are nearly touching the ground, dear old Sammy doesn't go fast enough, he gets laminitis every summer and besides Daddy is fed up with carting that little turnip around every weekend in his brand-new (second-hand) Rice trailer.

Sophie's new love is Hannah, a 13.2 hh palomino beauty with a blond tail nearly sweeping the ground. She and Sophie go to Pony Club camp for the first time. Caroline has to make two trips to carry all their belongings up to the circle of tents: the wheelbarrow, tack and suitcase take up one load, the hay and Sophie's bedding another. Caroline will be there nearly every day, making tea, taking children home for bath night, returning the jods which she washes and dries overnight. Sophie pretends not to notice when her mother arrives, but after Caroline inspects the mark sheet pinned to Hannah's stable door they meet by chance behind the tent. Hannah frets in the stable and is mareish. She tries to kick when Sophie picks her feet out. 'Hannah is a Cow.' But Sophie will never let her down. She swears she broke her own collar-bone vaulting on to the concrete, and that it is really stones which leave horseshoe-shaped bruises. She dreams of Chase-me-Charlies and putting Hannah in foal.

Red is a 14.2 hh chestnut with a good pop in him. Sophie can just hold him in a grackel and a running martingale, but she wouldn't be seen dead in a pelham. She is doing quite well in the local jumping and working pony classes and her bedroom is festooned with rosettes. Two years, three cups and out-of-juniors later she is into eventing and insists on attending the Boxing Day meet. She weighs nine stone and Red suddenly starts to refuse. 'Red is a Bugger.' But Sophie understands him. She dreams of Hickstead, and getting thinner.

Alfie is a gentleman, a 16 hh bay gelding with a sweet nature, brave and loyal, whose performance brings tears to the eyes. Let the others have showjumpers, the Sloanes stick to their hunters. Sophie and her friends see each other at the meet, at the hunter trials, at the one-day events, at point-to-points. With Alfie between her legs, Sophie laughs at the dramas related by her contemporaries who are 'into boys'. She has a black cloth coat from Harrods, leather boots and Daddy's Swaine, Adeney whip, her hair tucked away in a net, leather gloves and her cap, and club biscuits stuffed in her pocket. 'Alfie is a Gentleman.' She loves him. She dreams of Burghley, Badminton and the handsome joint-Master who has recently had a divorce.

Long live the Sloane

The worst thing about the death of someone close to you is that it calls attention to yourself. You don't want your red eyes to give some awful person the chance to ask you if you're 'all right'. You put extra pairs of sun-specs into your bag, and pop them on as soon as the organ hits a minor key. You pass a pair along the pew to a glistening friend. Sloane funerals look like the Miami scene in *Midnight Cowboy*.

You're not a cry-baby. It doesn't matter if *you* are all right. What matters is that your Sloane relation gets recognition for a lifetime's service to the Army, County Council, Girl Guides, National Farmers Union, Conservative party, Meals on Wheels and at wherever else he or she was steadfast...

There is so much to *arrange*. You put the announcement in the Deaths column of *The Times* and the *Daily Telegraph*: '...Private funeral, no flowers, donations if desired to...(a medical charity—animals or the local hunt seem rather frivolous). Thanksgiving service to be announced later.'

But you have already started your campaign to move your Sloane up from dusty Deaths on to the Court and Social page—into the Obituaries, the Memorial Service and the Latest Wills. The obit is the most pressing, and can't be bought. If you're not convinced the paper has planned one of their own, you urge a colleague of your Sloane to send in one of those 'A.R.V. writes:' or 'A correspondent writes:'. Its publication is, of course, at the discretion of the Obits Editor, so the colleague contacts Mr Tilley (*Telegraph*) or Mr Colin Watson (*Times*) first to see if he's interested (the two papers of record won't print the same personal obit).

For your Sloane's body, as opposed to his fame, you do less than the lower orders. You have a cheaper coffin, fewer flowers, no 'lying in state' in the funeral parlour, no angels on the gravestone (but

Latest Wills

			Net	
Lillias E. L., ...ssex			131,472	...oritz, of Whit-...... £275,626
...sie A., West ...Vest Sussex			157,762	...rjorie Laird, of ...ssex... £223,584
...H., Selly Oak,			305,767	

it has his honours: the CBE, the Lieut-Colonelcy...). As an undertaker remarked in *The Guardian*: 'Among the middle classes it's a matter of keeping down with the Joneses...our biggest funerals almost always come from people living in council houses.'

You put your Sloane in the hands of Harrods or Kenyon's (same thing) or the local firm or the Co-op. Their gluey professional sympathy gets you on the raw: 'What kind of coffin do you want for *Father?*' The answer is a plain 'burying' one. Sloanes believe in burial not cremation (on the compost principle), and rarely donate their bodies or parts of them to medicine or science (a pity, because many Sloanes are interesting specimens. Having neglected minor aches, they become increasingly rheumaticky and acquire artificial joints in elbows, knees and hip joints. Good teaching material.)

With country Sloanes, Daddy has sensibly paid for a slice of the local churchyard. 'We chose the shady side specially; the flowers keep longer.' But in London you are often forced to cremate, when you find that your church overflowed its cemetery years ago and parishioners have to go to Gunnersbury. 'I'd rather scatter his ashes over Verbier than have him dumped in some ghastly modern grave in NW29.' Some Sloanes always wanted to be scattered in a favourite spot anyway. One was to be sprinkled over the South Downs, but at the crucial moment the wind got up, and the ashes flew in the widow's face.

It's more fun at sea. The RNLI agreed to take one family out in a rubber dinghy to scatter Daddy's ashes. It was wet and blustery, the sea was rough, they lost the ashes and a son nearly fell overboard; they all ended up laughing helplessly. At times like this, you say 'Well—Daddy would have hated us to be mopy and tearful'.

You don't feel you have to wear a hat, or black. Navy blue is the Sloane black. But you expect the men to wear a black tie.

Even at a private funeral there's always someone with no manners, snuffling and dabbing as soon as 'The Lord's My Shepherd' soars up into the vaulting. Like Churchill, weeping as he met the Queen on the tarmac when she arrived back from Africa on her father's death. She did not break, and neither will you. A Sloane only weeps when alone (except at television). If anyone proffers the dreaded empathy, you bowl straight back at them in a cheery voice: 'Well, he had a pretty good run', '. . . innings', 'He was living on injury time . . .', etc. To a close friend you might say in a low voice, 'I suppose we all have to turn our toes up some time.'

The lower the tone, the more moved the Sloane. The Edwardian Sloane writer Saki noted the phenomenon in *The Unbearable Bassington*: ' "I am waiting for very bad news," said Francesca, and Lady Caroline knew what had happened. "I wish I could say something; I can't." Lady Caroline spoke in a harsh, grunting voice that few people had ever heard her use.'

Flowers will arrive, whatever you say. Some of the more expensive, ornate and cellophaned bunches and wreaths have a stilted message from the office or the cleaning lady. You have arranged to send the flowers to the local hospital or old folk's home—some (non-Sloane) guests actually hover around hoping to get some.

It's all too sordid and *like other people*. Sloanes have therefore developed their own form of send-off, the memorial service or thanksgiving-for-the-life-of, a cocktail party for the dead which is now

almost de rigueur. As it's a month or so after the real funeral (a sedate wake without the silent host), everyone can make plans to be there. You can also plan a special service sheet—something Sloanes like to keep to mark their principal church appearances.

For three times the price of the Personal Columns, you can announce the memorial service on the Court and Social page. You would like a report of it there too, with the smart names in 'among others present...' If you are grand, the Social Editor will want to go herself, or send a stringer. If you are not, you can ask to pay to have it in—companies often do when their chairman dies.

You devote the weeks before the service to packing up clothes for Oxfam, and answering your letters of sympathy. After the first ten letters, you give up and write the same reply to everyone. It makes you feel rather guilty and undermined and you get snappy with anyone who suggests tranquillisers.

The great day provides a family get-together and a pageant of your Sloane's life—members of his regiment, pals in the wine trade, representatives from the old firm and the grateful organisations. You have ushers and a pew-plan, of course. You have a reading from the classics and an address by a distinguished old chum of your Sloane's. You do not have 'Sheep may safely graze' (though one Eton butcher did)—you don't want jokes like 'old Tom never did manage to train a dog properly.'

Afterwards, the cocktail party. Eyes leer that watered an hour before. 'Tom should have been here—he probably is.' 'Tom was very fond of this wine—still he'll be drinking something better now.'

The party may be a substitute wake, but most rituals to do with death have quietly slipped away from English Sloanes, who in most other things are a living museum of old modes of behaviour. Gone are pulling down the blinds, covering the looking-glass, black-bordered mourning paper, black or white mourning for a year for a widow; though older Sloane widowers wear a black tie for a year. Gone (or almost) are the visit to the dead bedside with a kiss and a prayer, and the handful of earth thrown on to the coffin. Gone is the memorial lock of hair: Sloanes, whose jewel box always contains a Victorian locket with hair, shrink from cutting one themselves. Victorian Sloanes knew about mourning. Present-day Sloanes know more about evening.

The Scots and the French are still traditional. In Scotland, Sloane funerals are for men—even the relict may not attend. Oatmeal and whisky at the graveside. Respects for the widow afterwards (sometimes). Sherry, and the lawyer then reads the will. The French are strict about mourning and half-mourning (grey and lavender—*très élégant*) and paying one's respects to the body.

You want your Sloane to have done well enough to shine in Latest Wills, but you can't influence that. Smee & Ford, the press agency, collect all the figures from Somerset House and send them to the papers. If you're titled or well known you'll be in, particularly if you left peanuts. If you're nobody, you have to have left around £200,000 (since it includes the house, it's hard to leave less these days). Sloanes gnash their teeth to see their fathers deliberately failing to use loopholes in the inheritance laws so they will make a good showing in the Wills.

Your parents leave you a last dowry. You get some money, a gold watch, a tweed suit or fur coat, perhaps a house. And grief—certainly. Sloanes love their family and are accustomed to being *useful* to them. The Sloane widow is pitiable until she finds other causes. But Sloane parents have trained their children so hard it's almost as though Mummie or Daddy were still there, instructing you, urging you to kick on; even death cannot break the links in the Sloane chain.

Remembering dead Sloanes: The Cavalry Memorial Parade in Hyde Park (St George was a Sloane too).

Sloane Dictionary

A1 *adj.* Very good, reliable.

actually *adv.* Means nothing, but used at beginning or end of a sentence to give rhythm. 'Actually it's very good.' 'It's very good, actually.' Key Sloane word.

anon *adv.* Archaism used by Sloanes, as in 'I'll see you anon.'

Bang *v. t. & n.* Sexual intercourse (male Sloanes say it).

banging his bishop *v.* Masturbate (males).

bate *n.* Rage. Schoolboy word—'He was in an awful bate.' Sloanes have lots of words for anger and its consequence, some of them doggy. 'Saw red', 'Tore him off a strip', 'Gave him a ticking off', 'Gave him stick' ('I got stick'), 'In the doghouse'.

beetle *v.* Go. Sloanes don't like the word go—too boring—and usually find a synonym. See 'whizz'.

Bells, The *n.* Annabel's in Berkeley Square, the smartest Sloane night-club in London.

bin *n.* Mental hospital.

bit of a giggle *n.* Fun. 'It was a bit of a giggle.'

bog *n.* Lavatory.

bollock *n.* Ball, as in hunt bollock, charity bollock (even Caroline says this).

bread rolls *n pl.* What Sloanes throw at each other at big dinners. They eat, order and talk about 'rolls' but throw 'bread rolls'.

Howzat!

brill *adj.* Brilliant. 1980s expression.

bun-fight *n.* Crowded party where you have to fight to get something to eat. (The Oxford Dictionary errs in supposing bun-fight means tea-party.)

bumph *n.* Paper. As 'Why does the Ministry send out all this bumph?' or 'Have you any writing bumph?'

Call for Hughie *v.* Vomit.

charlie *adj.* Cheap attempt at style, flashy, non-U, as in 'a bit charlie'.

châteaued *adj.* Sloshed on wine.

chuffed *adj.* Pleased. 'I was really chuffed.'

clutch *n.* Dance, as in 'Come and have a clutch, Caroline'.

completely mad *ad.* Slightly unconventional.

cosy *n.* A cosy—sexual intercourse (female Sloanes say it).

cottage in the country, my *n.* Four-or-more-bedroom detached house, in the Green Belt out of London. Rich City Sloanes say it.

creep *n.* Two-faced climber, or otherwise disliked person.

cross *adj.* Angry, but older Sloanes pronounce it crawss. 'Mummie's crawss with you, she says your behaviour's a bit orf and is it because you've got a corf or are you going sawft in the head?'

crumbly *n.* Sloanes aged 50–70, beyond *wrinkly (qv)*.

cushy *adj.* Easy. 'I've got a cushy job.'

Defug *v.* Open the windows. Sloanes are very conscious of there being 'a bit of a fug in here'.

dinky *n.* A big car.

disaster *n.* 'A complete and utter disaster' means a mild mistake.

do *v.* Word much used by Sloane girls. 'Shall I pop in and see you?' 'Oh yes, *do*.' '*Do* come to dinner...' 'Do tell us *everything* (but they won't listen for long).'

DOM *n.* Dirty old man.

dripping *adj.* Gutless, totally wet.

drag, *n.* 'A bit of a bore'.

drain *n.* What older Sloanes think they laugh like. 'I laughed like a drain.'

duly *adv.* 'which I duly did'. Victorianism kept alive by Sloanes.

dusty *n.* Really old Sloanes, aged 70 to The Finish. See *crumbly* and *wrinkly*.

Eff orf *v.* 'Why don't you eff orf?' Used by both genders to send someone away.

elbow *n.* 'She gave me the big E'. Used by young Sloanes to mean she told me to go away. 1967 term has worked its way to the Sloanes.

Fast black *n.* London taxi cab.

fix *v.* Solve a problem. 'Can you fix it?' 'Please fix it.'

fodder *n.* Nicely cooked food.

four-letter man *n.* A terrible fellow. (S**T? C**T?)

frank and fearless, a *n.* A discussion.

Fred's *n.* Fortnum & Mason.

fuck-up *n. & v.* An organisational disaster.

GMFU *n.* Major organisational disaster: grand military fuck-up.

go *g.* Verb Sloanes find boring, perhaps because they are always g***g somewhere. See 'whizz'.

God *n.* Used a lot but they don't see it as blasphemous. 'Oh God...' 'God that's awful...'

good doer *n.* Probably doesn't do good, but has a good appetite and is healthy.

grockle *n.* An outsider, an oik, a weed.

grotty *adj.* Unpleasant, disorganised. Younger Sloanes' word.

gucky *adj.* Makes you feel sick.

Gucky *n.* Gucci (makes you feel the opposite of sick).

gunge *n.* Sauce or gravy or mud.

Hand *n.* Each four inches of one's horse's height. Abbreviation hh.

Horlicks *n.* Mess. As in 'make a Horlicks of it.'

Interior decorating *n.* Sex in the daytime.

Jew's canoe *n.* Jaguar. Mild anti-semitism has also produced:

Jewy Louis *adj.* The kind of interior decoration Sloanes don't like.

jodhpurs *n.* All Sloanes have a pair, but old Indian Army families pronounce it Joe Pores, others jodpurrs.

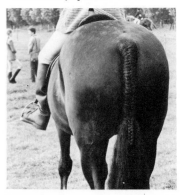

jungly *adj.* Disorganised, unsmart. 'Went to a jungly hunter trial last weekend.'

Kick on *v.* Riding term for 'press on' (another Sloane expression).

killing *adj.* Funny (older Sloanes). 'We killed ourselves.'

Leg it *v*. To get away (from a boring party, conversation, situation).
livid *adj*. Angry. 'I was livid.'

MTF *adj*. Must touch flesh. Female description of an octopus Sloane.
major *adj*. Big. 'There's been a major row.'
making noises *v*. Lobbying.
motoring racer *n*. Small car.
Mummie *n*. My mother, married to Daddy (the fact that she ends in -ie and he in -y is one of those tiny secrets that distinguish Sloanes from the rest. Mummie's mother is either Grannie or Granny. Sloanes over 20 call their parents 'My M'ma and P'pa' to other Sloanes).

Naff *adj*. What old SRs call 'poll'. They don't know what naff means exactly but they use it of clothes etc that look wrong, unfashionable, drear.

OTT *adj*. Over the top—outrageous. Usually 'absolutely' or 'totally OTT'.
OT and E *adj*. Used of children, means overtired and emotional.
one *pron*. 'I' in Sloane.

Park a custard *v*. Vomit.
peasant *n*. Anyone living in the country who isn't an aristocrat or a Sloane. So 'peasant shooting'.
pimpsy *adj*. Far too easy. 'The course was pimpsy.'
pissed *adj*. Drunk. 'To get pissed up' implies more aggressive drunkenness.
pissed it *v*. 'It pissed it' equals won the horse-race easily. 'Trotted up' is synonymous with it won. These expressions are never used by racehorse trainers, jockeys, or anyone else in the game, but always by owners and other non-participants.
play-away *n*. A weekend staying with somebody in the country.
plucky *adj*. Sloane word for brave until the Sixties, but dying out.
poncy *adj*. Sloane word for anyone more aesthetic or effeminate than them, or *anything* aesthetic and overdecorated. 'It's poncy.' 'He's a bit of a ponce.'
pong *n*. Unpleasant smell. Used of loos, socks, cigars.
pop *n*. A horse's jumping ability. Must have a good pop in him to pop over the fences.
pushed *adj*. Poor. 'I'm a bit pushed at the moment.'

Quids in *adj*. At an advantage.

Riveting *adj*. So interesting you sat still and shut up for a few minutes. 'I was riveted to hear about Julian's divorce.' 'The procession was riveting.' (*Not* a modern engineering metaphor—Middle English, as usual with Sloanes, from 'river' meaning clench.)

ringburner *n*. The results of a heavy curry the morning after.
Rods *n*. Harrods.
Roller *n*. As in Rolls-Royce.
rolling *adj*. Rich. Short for 'rolling in money' —another horse metaphor.
rude *adj*. Sexual.
rude parts *n*. Private parts.

SOHF *adj*. Sense of humour failure. Someone is not amused by Sloane antics.
said *v*. What it says. In contrast to all the substitutes for 'go', Sloanes do not like any euphemisms for 'said'. They consider 'interjected', 'questioned', 'opined', 'whined', 'murmured', 'breathed' or any other substitute dreadfully vulgar.
saucy *adj*. Sexy.
serious, seriously *adj & adv*. The Sloane way of exaggeration. 'He's seriously rich', 'serious eating', 'serious drinking'. Serious overuse has made it meaningless.
shoot a cat *v*. Vomit.
show the flag *v*. Go to an official do, eg 'I suppose we'll have to show the flag at the fête worse than death' (actually, they love it). 'We should put in an appearance' is another way Sloanes pretend the party is an arduous duty.
sit ye down or **doun** *v*. Old Sloane's invitation to use the Windsor chair or the Knoll sofa. Sloanes' vocabulary, like Sloanes' furniture, preserves many old touches (such as always offering a toast before starting drinking) which the international rich have long left behind them.

soggies *n*. Breakfast cereal.
spag bog or **bol** *n*. Your favourite pasta.
spastic *adj*. Temporarily unintelligent. Sloanes don't consider lack of intelligence should be insulted: one, they are basically kind; two, they are unintellectual themselves.
stiffy *n*. Engraved invitation card.
Swone one *n*. Battersea, home of many a Sloane (London postal district SW11).

Tatty *adj*. Shabby.
Thelwell *n*. The illustrator who knows more than anyone about Sloane Ranger child riders and their hairy little mounts.
thick *adj*. Temporarily unintelligent. See 'spastic'.
thunder bowl *n*. Lavatory.
tie one on *v*. Get drunk.
twit *n*. Silly person. Usually with silly; 'silly twit'.

v.g. *adj*. Very good—like school mark. Sloanes use v. with anything. 'This is v. delicious, Caroline.'

Wasted *adj*. Killed (Army).
weedy *adj*. Small and pathetic. Schoolboy term affected by Sloanes. 'I was weedy and decided I couldn't face it.'
wet *adj*. Synonym for weedy, but usually used to describe other, non-Sloane, weeds.
whizz *v*. Go. Sloanes do not like to say 'go' —it doesn't describe the way they ... well, whizz. They will say rush, toddle, beetle, tear, almost anything in preference.
wizard *adj*. Fifties word for wonderful still used, though almost in inverted commas.
Woler *n*. Rolls-Royce.

wrinkly *n*. Middle-aged Sloane—between 40 and 50. See *crumbly* and *dusty*.

XXX *n*. Three kisses, put beside her name by Caroline when she signs a personal letter.

Yonks *n*. A long time, as in 'I haven't seen him for yonks.'

Zoom *v*. One of the many Sloane euphemisms for go.

Acknowledgements

The authors and the publishers are grateful to the following for permission to reproduce their photographs: *pages 6* Graham Portlock; *7* Kit Houghton; *11* Kit Houghton; *17* Langton Gallery; *18* Popperfoto; *20* Tim Graham, Photographers International; *21* Tim Graham, Syndication International; *22* Christian Dior; *23* Hermès; *26* Michael Yardley; *30* John Timbers; *31* John Timbers, Michael Yardley; *32* Jennifer Beeston, Graham Portlock; *34* Sue Carpenter; *35* Graham Portlock, Michael Yardley; *37* Graham Portlock; *38* Graham Portlock; *43* John Timbers; *44* Harry Green, Sue Carpenter; *45* Graham Portlock; *46* Graham Portlock; *47* John Timbers; *48* Arabella Campbell McNair-Wilson; *49* Barnaby's Picture Library; *50* Graham Portlock; *51* Graham Portlock; *53* Graham Portlock; *54* Graham Portlock; *56* Chris Moyse; *58* Graham Portlock; *61* Graham Portlock; *63* Benyon Poole; *64* Desmond O'Neill; *65* Suzanne Martin; *67* Gamma; *70* Jocelyn Bain Hogg; *72* Kit Zweigbergk/Colour Form Associates; *77* Desmond O'Neill; *81* Lucie Clayton College; *82* Jocelyn Bain Hogg; *83* Stephen Julius; *85* Graham Portlock; *86* Michael Yardley; *88* Michael Yardley; *89* Michael Yardley; *90* Popperfoto; *91* John Timbers; *92* Gamma; *93* Sue Carpenter; *94* Dick Evans, Simon Taylor; *95* Dick Evans; *96* Harry Green, Dick Evans; *99* Dick Evans; *100* Henrietta Donald; *101* Michael Yardley; *103* Clare Reilly, Michael Yardley; *105* Sue Pritchard; *106* Michael Yardley; *107* Michael Yardley; *108* Sue Carpenter; *109* Peter Dazeley; *112* Tim Graham; *113* Michael Yardley; *114* Evening Standard/Freddie Mott; *116* Michael Yardley; *118* Michael Yardley; *119* Sue Carpenter; *120* Harry Green; *121* John Timbers; *122, 123* John Morgan Travel; *125* Benyon Poole; *126* Tom Hustler; *129* Dawson Strange; *138* Graham Portlock; *139* Graham Portlock; *140* Tim Graham; *143* Tim Carpenter; *148* Dick Evans; *149* Claire Wickham; *150* Barry Swaebe; *153* Harry Green; *154* Graham Portlock; *156* John Timbers; *157* John Timbers; *158* Harry Green; *159* John Timbers.

The verse of 'Lines and Squares' from *When We Were Very Young* by A. A. Milne is reproduced by kind permission of Methuen Children's Books. The illustration by E. H. Shephard from the same volume is reproduced by kind permission of Curtis Brown Ltd.

Cover: Photographs by John Timbers and Tim Graham: frames courtesy of Atkinson: fabric 'Blue Thistle' courtesy of Colefax & Fowler Ltd.